WORSHIP LEADER
Types

Exploring Musical and Non-musical Bible Characters

Dr. John & Martha Johnson

Worship Leader Types by Dr. John & Martha Johnson
published by Watersprings Publishing,
P.O. Box 1284 Olive Branch, MS 38654
www.waterspringspublishing.com
Contact publisher for bulk orders and permission requests.

Copyright © 2025 Dr. John & Martha Johnson. All rights reserved.

No part of this publication may be reproduced, distributed, or transmitted in any form or by any means, including photocopying, recording, or other electronic or mechanical methods, without the prior written permission of the publisher, except in the case of brief quotations embodied in critical reviews and certain other noncommercial uses permitted by copyright law.

Scripture quotations are taken from the Holy Bible, New International Version®. NIV® Copyright 1973, 1978, 1984 by International Bible Society. Used by permission of Zondervan. All rights reserved.

Scripture quotations marked (NLT) are taken from the Holy Bible, New Living Translation, copyright © 1996. Used by permission of Tyndale House Publishers, Inc., Wheaton, IL 60189 USA. All rights reserved.

All credit for cited quotations go to the rightful owners, as indicated in the end notes. We do not own that content. The inclusion of these brief passages is to promote the readers' application of the instructional content in the Worship Leader Types. Copyright infringement is not intended.

Printed in the United States of America.

ISBN-13: 978-1-948877-48-0

Contents

Acknowledgments v
Introduction vii
Chapter 1: Abraham 1
Chapter 2: Moses 13
Chapter 3: Miriam 29
Chapter 4: Aaron 35
Chapter 5: Hannah 45
Chapter 6: Samuel 51
Chapter 7: Gideon 61
Chapter 8: David 69
Chapter 9: Elijah 89
Chapter 10: Asa 99
Chapter 11: Jehoshaphat 107
Chapter 12: Joash/Jehoash 117
Chapter 13: Hezekiah 123
Chapter 14: Josiah 131
Chapter 15: Ezra 139
Chapter 16: Nehemiah 147
Chapter 17: Job 155
Chapter 18: Ezekiel 167
Chapter 19: Daniel 179

Chapter 20: Shadrach, Meshach and Abednego 193

Chapter 21: Hosea 203

Chapter 22: Habakkuk 211

Chapter 23: Zephaniah 217

Chapter 24: The Wise Men 225

Chapter 25: Peter 233

Chapter 26: John-Disciple of Jesus 247

Chapter 27: John the Baptist 261

Chapter 28: Martha 271

Chapter 29: Mary of Bethany 277

Chapter 30: Paul 283

Chapter 31: Jesus 297

Answers 311

Sources 327

About the Authors 329

More from Dr. John H. Johnson 331

Acknowledgments

It has taken seven years to complete this book. I could not have done this alone! I want to take the opportunity to acknowledge those who, in one way or another, have contributed to its completion.

First, I thank the Lord, who gave me the idea of taking a close look at leaders in the Bible who faithfully loved Him and led His people to do the same. These characters were more lifestyle oriented in worship than just performing a worship meeting.

Next, I thank Genesis Stackhouse Burns, my student worker, who faithfully labored and researched with me on this project.

Additionally, I appreciate Pastor Gus Johnson of We Care Ministries, Natchitoches, Louisiana, for his financial contribution that made publishing this book possible.

Finally, I express my love and gratitude to my lovely wife Martha, who has written each character's biographies and typed, edited, and researched this book with me.

"I am a companion of all those who fear, revere and worship you, and those who observe and give heed to your precepts."
—Psalm 119:63

Introduction

This book was born out of examining significant Bible characters, both from the Old and New Testaments, which exemplified character traits that modern worship leaders would do well to emulate. There is no reference to the term "worship leader" in the Bible. However, as I researched the lives of the characters chosen for this book, one of the things that stood out is that they were leaders and remained faithful in their worship devotion to God and their service to God and His people. I wanted to know whether their personalities helped or hindered them from accomplishing their tasks. It has been said that "As the leader goes, so go the people." This signified that we all have some measure and sphere of influence, and we have a responsibility to God and our brothers and sisters as to how we live and speak. Below are the standard criteria used with all the characters chosen for this book.

In examining the background in which they lived and led God's people, I wanted to see how the time's political, social, and religious atmosphere influenced them and the people they led. Concerning their personal lives, I wanted to see the factors that equipped them for the task they were given. I also wanted to know what their personalities helped or hindered them from accomplishing their tasks. What kind of relationship did they have with God? This was a vital criterion for all the characters because we can only give or lead from our intimate relationship with the Lord. What revelations did they receive and were then able to convey to the people? The importance of this is that to the degree of our revelation of the Lord and His will and purpose will be our responsiveness to Him. I also note at least three lessons that we could glean from the character that could be of help in our lives today. For example, what do we know of their worship relationship with the Lord? What can we discover from their prayer life and obedience to the Word?

Writing a book that explores how worship was expressed from Abraham to the book of Revelation might seem daunting. In many ways, it was, but seeing how worship was expressed and experienced throughout the Bible has always intrigued me. I realized that the way we experience worship, as often a thirty-minute song service on Sunday morning, is much different from Abraham offering up Isaac, his long-awaited son, as a burnt sacrifice and Moses and the Israelites dancing with joy at their escape and victory against their Egyptian taskmasters. King David composing worship songs as he protected his flock of sheep and dancing before the Lord with such exaltation that his clothes fell off when the Ark of the Covenant was returned is so much more demonstrative and dramatic than our sometimes-lackluster song services in the church. Today's worship leaders lead a church service, but those of old led an entire nation.

However, we are in a different time, at least in Western churches, where we sing original songs and old hymns to express our love and devotion to the God of Abraham, Isaac, and Jacob. Some of us have even been caught dancing before the Lord. Some have felt the deep stirrings of the presence of God as we sing His praises. And all of us seek to know what God has called us to do in the world in which we live. It is still a challenge to obey His will today as it was then.

As we study the characters in the Bible, let us appreciate their courage and strength in leadership under adverse circumstances so we might be inspired to worship with a greater depth of understanding and passion ourselves.

1
Abraham

Over three billion people in the modern world cite Abraham as the "father" of their religion. The three largest religions, Islam, Jewish, and Christianity, found their beginnings in him. In the Koran, Abraham is revered as a great prophet of the Muslim faith. In the Torah, Abraham's story is found in the Lekh Lekha, (meaning "Go" and "Leave!"), which is similar to the book of Genesis in the Bible, in which Abraham is introduced in chapter 11.[1]

The stories of the Bible are fairly terse, and we must often surmise motivations, reasoning, and true feelings in their re-telling. It is said that a person's character is formed by his family, (his DNA and inherited characteristics) and his environment. This being true, we don't have much to go on in the story of Abraham's family, but we do have a rich storehouse in terms of environment (historical clues).[2] We know about where Abraham lived and the place from which he and his clan departed, Ur of the Chaldeans, in Mesopotamia. "Ur was then a capital city of more than 100,000 inhabitants, a place of beauty, graced with towers, palaces, temples, law courts, market squares, statues, shrines, gardens, mosaics, friezes, reliefs and monuments."[3]

"We know some personal details about Abraham. He belonged to a race of Semites who traced their ancestry back to the dawn of human existence, and who had settled at Ur some 1,000 years before his time, a race the local Sumerians called Chaldeans. His was probably a family of merchant traders, buying and selling in Ur's rich markets. All his long life, Abraham loved one woman, Sarah. He spoke four or five of the main languages of his time. He was a skilled rider, hunter, and fighter. Fiercely independent and an inveterate haggler (he even bargained with God); he had one central quality: faithfulness. And, if even one quarter of the words ascribed to him are authentic, he must have had as large a mind as any man ever born."[4]

---

1 https://biography.yourdictionary.com/abraham
2 Blaiklock, E.M., Today's Handbook of Bible Characters, Bethany House Publishers, Minneapolis, MN.,1979
3 "Footsteps of Abraham", Martin, Malachi, New York Times, March 13, 1983
4 NYtimes.com/1983/03/13/travel/footsteps-of-abraham-by-malachi-martin.html

Living in this polytheistic, rather lawless culture, Abraham must have felt something stirring in his heart that caused him to take his entire clan and depart from Ur. According to *Today's Handbook of Bible Characters,* "The world was lost in degrading views of God... it was one wide story of burdensome corruption." (p. 18) *Seeing* and knowing all this, Abraham felt compelled to depart from the depravity around him with his entire clan and, instructed by God Himself, as shown from this excerpt from the Old Testament, Abraham and his family began their journey.

> *"I will make you into a great nation, and I will bless you;*
> *I will make your name great, and you will be a blessing.*
> *I will bless those who bless you, and whoever curses you I will curse;*
> *and all peoples on earth will be blessed through you."*
> Genesis 12: 1-3

Abraham's father, the patriarch of the clan, agreed to take all his family and follow God's call to migrate into the wilderness and to find a more suitable place than the pagan port city of Ur.

In the book of Joshua, the clan of Abraham was called "worshipers of alien gods." So, it was interesting to note that Terah, the father, would agree to this revelation his son received. Yet they did depart and travelled to Haran, where they stayed until the death of Terah, and for a time, the old indignation Abraham felt for the corruption of such a populated city was put on the back burner.

Next came the journey into Egypt, again a place of a great civilization and a fertile land where Abraham and his clan could prosper. But every choice has its drawbacks, and in choosing Egypt, Abraham found a land as corrupt as that which he had left behind. The comfort of civilization was a strong lure for a clan that had only experienced the hustle and bustle of Ur. Living in the wilderness was rough. Finally, Abraham and his clan settled in Canaan, the place the Lord had intended.

Abraham was a man who knew God, and who heard Him speaking to him. He was also a man who obeyed even when he didn't know what the future would bring. However, he did know that trusting in God's providence and provision was the best course of action. Many times, in the tales of the life of Abraham and Lot, we see the hand of God protecting, rescuing, and assisting the members of his growing clan. Even after settling in Canaan, new problems arose.

> "Now Lot, who was traveling with Abram, also had flocks and herds and tents. But the land was unable to support both of them while they stayed together, for they had so many possessions that they were unable to coexist. And there was discord between the herdsmen of Abram and the herdsmen of Lot. At that time the Canaanites and

the Perizzites were also living in the land. So, Abram said to Lot, "Please let there be no contention between you and me, or between your herdsmen and my herdsmen. After all, we are brothers. Is not the whole land before you? Now separate yourself from me. If you go to the left, I will go to the right; if you go to the right, I will go to the left." *Genesis 13:5-9*

Faced with this dilemma, Abraham decided they must split up. Lot and his tribe must go one way, while Abraham and his group would go the other. He gave Lot the first choice, and Lot chose the fertile and choice land "towards Zoar." Abraham, in deferring to his nephew, was showing his trust in God. He had learned a deep lesson of faith in Egypt after the debacle with the Pharaoh and nearly losing Sarai into the Pharoah's harem, possibly to be seen no longer. God Himself intervened in that situation, and the Pharaoh was told in a dream that Sarai was Abraham's wife, not his sister, as Abraham had told him.[5] So this time, he left the whole matter in the hands of God.

Many events happened in the life of Abraham, but the most pivotal is the birth of Isaac to Sarai when she was, according to the Bible, 90 years old, way past her childbearing years. Abraham himself was 100. God prophesied this to Abraham, at which he scoffed. *(Who wouldn't?)* Then, two "strangers" came to visit Abraham and Sarai's tent, for whom Abraham provided the usual customary hospitality, calling for food and drink. These strangers (possibly angels) told Abraham that Sarai would bear a son, which caused Sarai, who was eavesdropping, to laugh. After all her years of barrenness, disappointment, and humiliation over her childlessness, this was too much for Sarai to believe! After years of expectantly waiting to become pregnant, then doubting, and finally accepting her barren fate with great pain and disillusionment, this would have been pretty unbelievable to her.[6]

But Isaac was born, and his name commemorates Sarai's disbelief, meaning laughter. Also, Isaac probably brought about much laughter as he toddled about the tent being cared for by two very old people! But undoubtedly, they were thrilled for the unexpected turn of events and the fulfillment of God's promises to them.

The culmination of all these stories of the miraculous interventions of God, and of a man who learns to trust in God's leading and obedience was the birth of Isaac, the son of promise. Equally momentous was the birth of Abraham's son Ishmael, leading to the formation of the great Muslim religion. In fulfillment of the prophecy, Abraham's offspring were indeed as numerous as the stars. His life story holds many key truths from which we can draw in our own lives of faith and belief.

---

5 Genesis 12:10-20 NIV
6 Genesis 17:17, 21:6 NIV

WORSHIP LEADER TYPE PROFILE
ABRAHAM

BACKGROUND

- **Political Conditions:** Abraham and his family left a prosperous city because of immoral conditions and followed God's command.
- **Social Conditions:** The conditions were difficult living as a refugee, but they were hoping to establish their own identities and lives.
- **Religious Conditions:** They left a pagan culture based on God calling them out to establish their relationship and worship of one God.

Called of God. Abraham was simply called by God, by the name Abram at that time, to go forth; Genesis 12:1-4

> The Lord had said to Abram, "Go from your country, your people and your father's household to the land I will show you."
> *Genesis 12:1, NIV*

Blessed by God. God blessed Abraham abundantly, and his children; Genesis 12:2-3, 24:34-35, Nehemiah 9:7-8 Romans 6:13-14

> I will make you into a great nation, and I will bless you; I will make your name great, and you will be a blessing.[a]
> *Genesis 12:2, NIV*

ABRAHAM'S PERSONALITY

Obedient. Abraham faithfully obeyed God in everything He told him to do; Genesis 12:4, 17:23-27, 21:4, 22:1-10, Hebrews 11:8

> So, Abram went, as the Lord had told him; and Lot went with him. Abram was seventy-five years old when he set out from Harran.
> *Genesis 12:4*

ABRAHAM'S RELATIONSHIP WITH GOD

Very intimate. Abraham loved God, and God dearly loved Abraham. God kept Abraham close to Him and confided in him; Genesis 12:1-4, 18:1-5, 17-33

> Then the Lord said, "Shall I hide from Abraham what I am about to do?
> Abraham will surely become a great and powerful nation, and
> all nations on earth will be blessed through him.
> *Genesis 18:17-18, NIV*

He feared God. Abraham's willingness to sacrifice Isaac showed his righteous fear of the Lord; Genesis 22:12.

> "Do not lay a hand on the boy," he said. "Do not do anything to him.
> Now I know that you fear God, because you have not withheld
> from me your son, your only son."
> *Genesis 22:12, NIV*

THE REVELATION OF GOD THAT ABRAHAM CARRIED TO THE PEOPLE

God's promises are faithful, true, and sure. God showed Abraham time and time again that His promises were true and that he could hope and trust in them; Genesis 12:2-3,7, 13:14-17, 15:4-5,18-21, 17:2-8,16-19, 21:1,11-13, 22:17-18, Hebrews 6:13-15, 11:17-19

> "Then I will make my covenant between me and you and
> will greatly increase your numbers."
> *Genesis 17:2, NIV*

This was fulfilled when a vast number of people were delivered from Egypt.

God is the Mighty Warrior. God fought for Abraham when rescuing Lot; Genesis 14:14-20

> "Blessed be Abram by God Most High, Creator of heaven and earth.
> And praise be to God Most High, who delivered your enemies into your hand."
> *Genesis 14:18*

God is our Protector. God promised to protect Abraham.

> After this, the word of the Lord came to Abram in a vision: "Do not be afraid, Abram.
> I am your shield, your very great reward."
> *Genesis 15:1, NIV*

El-Shaddai-God Almighty. God reveals Himself to Abraham as Almighty God and calls him to a holy life.

> "When Abram was ninety-nine years old, the Lord appeared to him and said,
> "I am God Almighty; walk before me faithfully and be blameless. Then I will make my
> covenant between me and you and will greatly increase your numbers."
> *Genesis 17:1-2, NIV*

God answers prayer. God answered Abraham's prayer concerning sparing Lot; Genesis 19:15-16, 22

> "With the coming of dawn, the angels urged Lot, saying, "Hurry! Take your wife and your
> two daughters who are here, or you will be swept away when the city is punished." When
> he hesitated, the men grasped his hand and the hands of his wife and of his two daughters
> and led them safely out of the city, for the Lord was merciful to them."
> *Genesis 19:15-16*

> "That is why the town was called Zoar."
> *Genesis 19:22*

God is righteous. God is merciful, but He does not tolerate sin, especially among those He calls His; Genesis 12:17, 20:3-7,17-18.

> "Now return the man's wife, for he is a prophet, and he will pray for you, and you will live.
> But if you do not return her, you may be sure that you and all who belong to you will die."
> *Genesis 20:10, NIV*

> "But the LORD inflicted serious diseases on Pharaoh and his household because of
> Abram's wife Sarai."
> *Genesis 12:17, NIV*

God is the God of the impossible. God can do all of the things we, as humans, consider impossible; it was considered impossible for Abraham and Sarah to have children together, but God did it; Genesis 21:1-7, Romans 4:17, Hebrews 11:19

Then Sarah said, "God has made me laugh, and everyone who hears of this will laugh with me." She added, "Who would have told Abraham that Sarah would nurse children? Yet I have borne him a son in his old age."
Genesis 21:6-7, NIV

Yahweh Yireh - God will provide. God revealed Himself as Provider when He gave Abraham a ram to sacrifice instead of his son; Genesis 22:14, NIV

"And Abraham called that place The LORD will provide. So to this day it is said, "On the mountain of the LORD it will be provided."
Genesis 22:14, NIV

LESSONS LEARNED FROM THIS WORSHIP LEADER TYPE

Our sins not only affect us, but everyone around us. When Abraham and Sarah lied to the two different kings, God judged the kings and their people: Genesis 12:15-20, 20: 17, 18.

"Then Abraham prayed to God, and God healed Abimelech, his wife, and his female servants, so they could have children. For the Lord had caused all the women to be infertile because of what happened with Abraham's wife, Sarah."
Genesis 20:17-18, NIV

When God is with us, no one can stand against us. Abraham defeated an entire king's army with about 300 men. Genesis 14:14-16

"When Abram heard that his relative had been taken captive, he called out the 318 trained men born in his household and went in pursuit as far as Dan."
Genesis 14:14, NIV

Wait on the Lord and trust Him. Impatience met with doubt leads to sin. It is imperative to just wait on the Lord and trust His Word and promises; Genesis 16:2-4, 21:1-7, Hebrews 6:13-15

"So she said to Abram, "The LORD has kept me from having children. Go, sleep with my slave; perhaps I can build a family through her." Abram agreed to what Sarai said."
Genesis 16:2, NIV

Here is one example of people not trusting God's promises but relying on their own ingenuity.

God's promises are conditional. Abraham and his children had a responsibility to keep the promise of God, just as we do; God's promises are based on our obedience.

> "Then God said to Abraham, "As for you, you must keep my covenant, you and your descendants after you for the generations to come."
> *Genesis 17:9, NIV*

God blesses obedience. God blesses us when we choose to obey Him; Genesis 22:16-18

> …"By Myself I have sworn, declares the LORD, because you have done this thing and have not withheld your son, your only son, indeed I will greatly bless you, and I will greatly multiply your seed as the stars of the heavens and as the sand which is on the seashore; and your seed shall possess the gate of their enemies. "In your seed all the nations of the earth shall be blessed, because you have obeyed My voice.
> *Genesis 22:16-17, NIV*

Love for the Lord
Obedient. Abraham showed his love for the Lord by being obedient; Genesis 12:4, 17:23-27, 21:4, 22:1-3, Hebrews 11:8

> When his son Isaac was eight days old, Abraham circumcised him, as God commanded him.
> *Genesis 21:4, NIV*

Love for His people
Intercessor. Abraham interceded for the righteous - his family- in the land of Sodom and Gomorrah to be spared; Genesis 18:23-33

> "Far be it from you to do such a thing—to kill the righteous with the wicked, treating the righteous and the wicked alike. Far be it from you! Will not the Judge of all the earth do right?"
> *Genesis 18:25, NIV*

Zeal for the Lord
Followed where the Lord led Him. Abraham was faithful and went where the Lord told him to go; Genesis 12:1-5, Hebrews 11:8-10

> "So, Abram departed as the Lord had instructed, and Lot went with him. Abram was seventy-five years old when he left Haran."
> *Genesis 12:4, NIV*

FACTORS IN EQUIPPING FOR THE TASK

Worshipper
Altars. Abraham built altars and worshiped everywhere he settled; Genesis 12:7-8, 13:4,18, 21:33

> "This was the same place where Abram had built the altar,
> and there he worshiped the Lord again."
> *Genesis 13:4, NIV*

Prayer Life
Transparent about his concerns. Abraham was very honest and open in his prayer life, even with his worries and doubts; Genesis 15:2-3,8, NIV

> "But Abram replied, 'O Sovereign Lord, how can I be sure that I will actually possess it?'"
> *Genesis 15:8, NIV*

Intercessor. Abraham prayed for the righteous, his family, in the land of Sodom and Gomorrah, and pleaded that they be spared; Genesis 18:23-33, NIV

> "Surely You wouldn't do such a thing, destroying the righteous along with the wicked.
> Why, you would be treating the righteous and the wicked exactly the same! Surely you
> wouldn't do that! Should not the Judge of all the earth do what is right?"
> *Genesis 18:25, NIV*

Ability to hear and respond to the Lord. He heard clearly and responded immediately with obedience - When Abraham heard from the Lord, he always responded with obedience; Genesis 12:1-4, 17:23-27, 22:1-3, NIV

> "On that very day Abraham took his son, Ishmael, and every male in his household,
> including those born there and those he had bought. Then he circumcised them,
> cutting off their foreskins, just as God had told him."
> *Genesis 17:23, NIV*

Prayer dialogue
Abraham practiced conversational prayer, recognizing true prayer is a dialogue and not a monologue. Genesis 18:23-33, NIV

> "Then Abraham spoke again. 'Since I have begun, let me speak further to my Lord,
> even though I am but dust and ashes. Suppose there are only forty-five righteous
> people rather than fifty? Will You destroy the whole city for lack of five?'
> And the Lord said, 'I will not destroy it if I find forty-five righteous people there'."
> *Genesis 18:27-28, NIV*

Presenter/representative of the Lord. Abraham was willing to sacrifice his one and only son, just as God our Father was willing to sacrifice His one and only Son. The difference is that Abraham was spared the sacrificing of his own son, whereas it was necessary for God to sacrifice His only Son to atone for the sins of the world. Genesis 22:3-10, Hebrews 11:17-18

> "And Abraham picked up the knife to kill his son as a sacrifice."
> *Genesis 22:10, NIV*

ABRAHAM'S FAITH/TRUST IN THE LORD

Unswerving obedience. Abraham practiced unswerving obedience that showed no hesitation; Genesis 12:4, 17:23-27, 21:4, 22:3-10.

> "The next morning Abraham got up early. He saddled his donkey and took two of his servants with him, along with his son, Isaac. Then he chopped wood for a fire for a burnt offering and set out for the place God had told him about."
> *Genesis 22:3, NIV*

Believed God. Abraham took God at His Word and believed in His promises. Genesis 15:6, 22:7-8, 24:5-7, Romans 4:3, 20-22.

> "And Abram believed the Lord, and the Lord counted him as righteous because of his faith."
> *Genesis 15:6, NIV*

Willing to sacrifice his only son. Abraham trusted God's promise that He would give him a son and that He would have countless descendants through him, and so he was not afraid; Genesis 22:3-10, Hebrews 11:17-19

> "[9] When they reached the place God had told him about, Abraham built an altar there and arranged the wood on it. He bound his son Isaac and laid him on the altar, on top of the wood. [10] Then he reached out his hand and took the knife to slay his son.
> *Genesis 22:9-10, NIV*

CHAPTER 1
REVIEW QUESTIONS
Abraham/Abram

1. Which country was Abram a part of when God called him out?

2. When God told Abram to sacrifice his only son, Isaac, and since he had two sons at the time, why did God say, "Your only son Isaac?"

3. Name at least three revelations the Lord revealed of Himself to Abraham. Why are such revelations necessary for worship?

4. What were some of the indicators that Abraham was an obedient worshipper?

5. What is the meaning of Isaac's name, and how did he receive this name? Tell of the account.

6. What important aspects of Abraham's life make him a worship leader type whom we can follow as we lead in worship?

7. What are some mistakes that Abraham made which, surprisingly, did not disqualify him from God using him?

Revelation is an act of revealing or communicating divine truth; an enlightening or astonishing disclosure.

2
Moses

Moses' life began in extraordinary circumstances, and his survival as a newborn among the Hebrew slaves was nothing short of miraculous. The exceedingly cruel command of the Egyptian monarch, simply called Pharaoh in this story, was to kill every male child, a sort of ancient population control.[7] This diabolical command harmed everyone involved. Imagine being a midwife who was ordered to kill the child whose birth you have just assisted. This is where I say, "Thank God for women. They have ways of keeping men from their worst impulses."

Moses' survival was also a testament to the ingenious plan of his mother to save him from being put to death as Pharaoh commanded. In a new twist on the ancient practice of "exposing" a newborn, leaving him to the elements, or throwing the baby in the river, the desperate mother, Jochebed, put the baby in a basket and set him adrift on the river Nile.[8] Jochabed was following the cruel edict from the Pharaoh, yet God intervened on her behalf. Miraculously, the Pharaoh's daughter was 'bathing' in the river, and her heart and attention were caught by the tiny child in his ingenious ark of safety. The Egyptian woman's heart was softened towards the tiny baby, and she took him in. Then, Miriam, Moses' sister who was hiding among the bulrushes, offered to find 'a Hebrew woman' to nurse the baby, and ran to tell her mother that her plan succeeded beyond the wildest of dreams. Jochebed was able to nurse her own child in the palace of the Egyptians.[9]

What a story! With a beginning as dramatic and heart-wrenching as this, one would expect a great life for Moses, and his story does not leave us disappointed. Raised in the palace, Moses must have become aware of his own unique ancestry and the difference between him and the Egyptian royalty surrounding him. Moses was a man, who became self-aware, and then became aware of others and of the injustice and inequality in the world around him. His growing awareness of his identity as a Hebrew must have caused him to look with anger and indignation at the way the Egyptian overlords were treating

---

7   Exodus 1:16
8   Exodus 1:22
9   Exodus 2:1-10

the Hebrew slaves. He felt compelled to protect his people and to wreak vengeance on their oppressors. After killing a man who was beating a Hebrew slave, Moses became a fugitive, running into the wilderness to avoid being executed by the Egyptians.

So, Moses fled to the wilderness, and while sitting beside a well, he became embroiled in a dramatic rescue of the seven daughters of a priest, whose flock they were tending and who were being harassed by shepherds of another flock. This 'Priest of Midian,' named Reuel, was told by his daughters that Moses fought for them, and then He even drew water for their sheep. Moses was taken in by the patriarch of this small tribe, and then he was given one of the daughters as his wife.[10] So, Act 2, scene one finds Moses making a new life for himself far from the luxuries of the Egyptian court. Scene 2, God enters.

THE CALL

While tramping about in the wilderness, tending the sheep, Moses has an encounter with God - a burning bush, a voice from within, and instructions for the next phase of his life. God said, "You thought you were just going to camp out here in the wilderness and raise a family? Think again!"

So, off goes Moses, after arguing with God a bit about the insanity of this endeavor, to fulfill his destiny. It took quite a bit of arguing with God, but hey, this looked like a fool's errand. After much reassurance from God that he would be with Moses, and after giving him a "rod" which had seeming supernatural qualities, Moses struck off to do God's will. The rod, by the way, does not give the Israelites permission to use magic. As the following writer asserts, this rod did not have any power apart from God Himself.

"The staff is purely a tool of the Almighty activated through human agency. Miracles result, but not by virtue of magic. The insignificance of the staff is underscored by the fact that Moses on occasion triggers or terminates a miracle without using it at all, simply by waving his hand (Exodus 10:22) or offering a heartfelt prayer (Exodus 10:18). God needs no staff to alter the course of nature nor does the staff possess any power independent of God. It never becomes a relic." [11]

Accompanied and encouraged by his brother, Aaron, Moses takes the Israelites into the wilderness so they can "worship their God." At first Pharaoh refused, since most of his workforce would be going. But the arrival of Moses to free the slaves just happened to coincide with the period of greatest oppression. The departing Israelites were nearly returned by force by a group of charioteers, but a series of miracles assisted them in their flight to freedom. We shall end with this quote, describing the purpose for the Israelite's journey from Egypt to the wilderness:

---

10   Exodus 2: 21

11   Schosch, Ismar, "The Staff of Moses", Jewish Theological Seminary, Torah Online, January 24, 2004

"The revelation Moses received culminated in an event that was of supreme significance for the Israelites. A solemn agreement or covenant was contracted between God and Moses, which in effect constituted the nomadic Israelites as the chosen people of God. Henceforward they were to be a united group with an awareness of national status, implemented by Divine protection."[12]

Worship Leader Type Profile
MOSES

BACKGROUND

- **Political Conditions:**
  - Moses was the leader, following God's prompts as the entire tribe of Israelites migrated from place to place. His word was law. This could be called a theocracy.
- **Social Conditions:**
  - After being enslaved in Egypt, the Israelites found themselves living as refugees, always on the go, as they searched for their own land and identity as free people.
- **Religious Conditions:**
  - Abruptly leaving a pagan culture when God called them out, they sought to establish their relationship with and worship of the one God, Yahweh.

FACTORS IN EQUIPPING FOR THE TASK

The Person

Adopted into Pharaoh's family. Pharaoh's daughter found Moses in the river and took him into her home to raise; Exodus 2:10

> "Later, when the boy was older, his mother brought him back to Pharaoh's daughter, who adopted him as her own son. The princess named him Moses, for she explained, 'I lifted him out of the water.'"
> *Exodus 2:10, NLT*

Called by God. God's calling alone qualified Moses for the task for which he was being called; Exodus 3:4

> "When the LORD saw Moses coming to take a closer look, God called to him from the middle of the bush, "Moses! Moses!" "Here I am!" Moses replied."
> *Exodus 3:4, NLT*

---
12 Harrison, R.K., <u>Old Testament Times</u>, Hendrickson Publishers, 1970, p. 140

Signs and miracles. God gave Moses the ability to perform His signs and miracles before the Egyptians; Exodus 4:2-9

> "The LORD said to Moses, "If they do not believe you and are not convinced by the first miraculous sign, they will be convinced by the second sign."
> *Exodus 4:8, NLT*

Sent with a companion. Because Moses was afraid, God sent his brother Aaron alongside him to complete the mission God had for the Israelites; Exodus 4:13-16,27-29, 7:1-2.

> "Talk to him, and put the words in his mouth. I will be with both of you as you speak, and I will instruct you both in what to do."
> *Exodus 14:15, NLT*

MOSES' PERSONALITY

Humble. Moses was known as the most humble man on earth. Moses never boasted in himself or his abilities; Exodus 3:11, Numbers 12:3

> "Now Moses was very humble - more humble than any other person on earth."
> *Numbers 12:3, NLT*

Obedient. Moses, for the most part, lived a life of obedience to God; Exodus 4:18-20, 7:6,10,20, 9:22-26, 10:1-3, 12:28, Leviticus 8:4-5, 16:34.

> "So, Moses and Aaron did just as the Lord had commanded them."
> *Exodus 7:6, NLT*

MOSES' RELATIONSHIP WITH GOD

Close, intimate. Moses' relationship with God was more intimate than the people who followed him was. Moses spoke directly to God, and he was the only one to whom God showed Himself. Exodus 33:11-23.

> The Lord would speak to Moses face to face, as one speaks to a friend.
> *Exodus 33:11*

Exodus 33 describes Moses' unique relationship with Yahweh, of whom the rest of the people were afraid to approach, let alone speak to. To them, God was fearsome, yet to Moses, God was a friend.

> "The Lord replied to Moses, 'I will indeed do what you have asked,
> for I look favorably on you, and I know you by name.'"
> *Exodus 33:17, NLT*

God Himself rebuked Miriam and Aaron for speaking out against Moses;

> "Then He said, Hear now My words: If there is a prophet among you, I, the Lord, make
> Myself known to him in a vision. I speak to him in a dream. Not so with My servant Moses;
> He is faithful in all My house. I speak plainly and not in dark sayings; And he sees the form
> of the Lord. Why, then were you not afraid to speak against my servant Moses?"
> *Numbers 12:6-8*

REVELATIONS GIVEN TO MOSES FROM THE LORD

God is amazing. God is spectacular, and can do spectacular things; Exodus 3:2-3, 4:2-4,6-7.

> "There the angel of the Lord appeared to him in a blazing fire from the middle of a bush.
> Moses stared in amazement. Though the bush was engulfed in flames,
> it didn't burn up. 'This is amazing,' Moses said to himself.
> 'Why isn't that bush burning up? I must go see it.'"
> *Exodus 3:2-3, NLT*

God is holy. There is no one like God, and there is no darkness or sin in Him, He is to be feared and reverenced as such; Exodus 3:5, 19:10-22, 31:13, Leviticus 10:1-3, 11:45, 19:1, 22:31-33.

> "'Do not come any closer,' the Lord warned. 'Take off your sandals,
> for you are standing on holy ground."
> *Exodus 3:5, NLT*

God of Abraham, Isaac, and Jacob. This is one of the names God gave Moses to tell the Israelites who sent him; Exodus 3:6,15

> "I am the God of your father - the God of Abraham, the God of Isaac,
> and the God of Jacob.' When Moses heard this, he covered his
> face because he was afraid to look at God."
> *Exodus 3:6, NLT*

God sees and hears. God wanted His people to know that He saw everything that was going on and that He's heard all of their cries; Exodus 3:7-10,16.

> "Then the Lord told him, 'I have certainly seen the oppression of My people in Egypt.
> I have heard their cries of distress because of their harsh slave drivers.
> Yes, I am aware of their suffering."
> *Exodus 3:7, NLT*

Deliverer. God came to rescue His people; Exodus 3:10,17, 6:6-9, 14:21-31.

> "Therefore, say to the people of Israel: 'I am the Lord. I will free you from your oppression
> and will rescue you from your slavery in Egypt. I will redeem you with a
> powerful arm and great acts of judgment."
> *Exodus 6:6, NLT*

God is among us. God gave Moses the blueprint for building the tabernacle. Exodus 25:1-9

"I Am Who I AM" This is the name God gave Moses to tell the Israelites who sent him; Exodus 3:14

> "God replied to Moses, 'I Am Who I Am. Say this to the people of Israel:
> I Am has sent me to you.'"
> *Exodus 3:14, NLT*

Yahweh. God reveals His true name; Exodus 3:15, 6:2-3, 33:19, 34:5-7.

> "God also said to Moses, 'Say this to the people of Israel: Yahweh,
> the God of your ancestors - the God of Abraham,
> the God of Isaac, and the God of Jacob - has sent me to you.
> This is my eternal name, my name to remember for all generations."
> *Exodus 3:15, NLT*

God keeps His promises. God proved His faithfulness; Exodus 6:4-5,8, 12:42.

> "On this night the Lord kept His promise to bring His people out of the land of Egypt.
> So, this night belongs to Him, and it must be commemorated every year
> by all the Israelites, from generation to generation."
> *Exodus 12:42, NLT*

Defender. God defends and fights for His people; Exodus 14:13-14,19-20,25, 23:20.

> "He twisted their chariot wheels, making their chariots difficult to drive.
> 'Let's get out of here - away from these Israelites!' the Egyptians shouted.
> 'The Lord is fighting for them against Egypt!'"
> *Exodus 14:25, NLT*

Provider. God provided food, water, and protection for the Israelites during their time in the wilderness; Exodus 15:25,27, 16:13-15, Numbers 11:31.

> "Now the Lord sent a wind that brought quail from the sea and let them fall all around the camp. For miles in every direction there were quail flying about three feet above the ground."
> *Numbers 11:31, NLT*

> "Behold, I will stand before you there, on the rock at Horeb; and you shall strike the rock and water will come out of it, that the people may drink."
> *Exodus 13:21*

> "By day the Lord went ahead of them in the pillar of cloud to guide them on their way and by night in a pillar of fire to give them light, so that they could travel by day or night."
> *Exodus 13:21*

Healer. God calls Himself the people's Healer; Exodus 15:26.

> "He said, 'If you will listen carefully to the voice of the Lord your God and do what is right in His sight, obeying His commands and keeping all His decrees, then I will not make you suffer any of the diseases I sent on the Egyptians; for I am the Lord who heals you."
> *Exodus 15:26, NLT*

Sabbath. God emphasizes the significance of the Sabbath and demands that it be honored, as He rested after the creation of the world; Exodus 16:22-30, 20:8-11, 23:25-33, 31:12-17, 35:1-3, Leviticus 26:2.

> "Remember to observe the Sabbath day by keeping it holy."
> *Exodus 20:8, NLT*

Yahweh-Nissi. "The Lord is my banner" - God is the victory of His people; Exodus 17:15-16

> "Moses built an altar there and named it Yahweh-Nissi (which means 'the Lord is my banner.')"
> *Exodus 17:15, NLT*

God dearly treasures His people. God calls His people precious treasure to Him; Exodus 19:5-8, Deuteronomy 7:6-9.

> "For you are a holy people, who belong to the Lord your God.
> Of all the people on earth, the Lord your God has chosen you to
> be His own special treasure."
> *Deuteronomy 7:6, NLT*

Jealous. God is jealous for His people and abhors idolatry; Exodus 20:2-6, 34:14, Leviticus 19:4, Deuteronomy 4:24.

> "The Lord your God is a devouring fire; He is a jealous God."
> *Deuteronomy 4:24, NLT*

God is the Giver of Gifts. God is a creative God, who gives the gift of creativity and skills of craftsmanship; Exodus 25-28, 30:1-10, 35:31-35.

> "The Lord has filled Bezalel with the Spirit of God, giving him great wisdom, ability, and
> expertise in all kinds of crafts."
> *Exodus 35:31, NLT*

LESSONS LEARNED FROM THIS WORSHIP LEADER TYPE

God chooses the humble. God used Moses through his humility to display His glory; Exodus 3:10-12

> "But Moses protested to God, 'Who am I to appear before Pharaoh?
> Who am I to lead the people of Israel out of Egypt?' God answered, 'I will be with you.
> And this is your sign that I am the one who has sent you: When you have brought the
> people out of Egypt, you will worship God at this very mountain.'"
> *Exodus 3:11-12, NLT*

God goes with us. We are never alone when God sends us out; Exodus 3:12, 13:21-22

> "The Lord went ahead of them. He guided them during the day with a pillar of cloud,
> and He provided light at night with a pillar of fire. This allowed them to
> travel by day or by night."
> *Exodus 13:21, NLT*

> *"The Lord replied, "My presence will go with you, and I will give you rest."*
> *Exodus 33:14*

God's calling is our qualification. When God calls us, He has already given us everything we need at that time to accomplish what He is asking us to do; Exodus 4:10-12

> "Then the Lord asked Moses, 'Who makes a person's mouth? Who decides whether people speak or do not speak, hear or do not hear, see or do not see? Is it not I, the Lord? Now go! I will be with you as you speak, and I will instruct you in what to say.'"
> *Exodus 4:11-12, NLT*

The things God allows us to go through are to bring Him glory. God doesn't cause all things to happen, but everything He causes or allows is for our good and His glory; Exodus 9:15-16, 14:4,17-18.

> "But I have spared you for a purpose - to show you My power and to spread my fame throughout the earth."
> *Exodus 9:16, NLT*

Obey exactly what God says. It is especially important to do exactly what God says, or it is disobedience; Exodus 16:20, 23:21-22, Leviticus 8:4-5, 16:34, Numbers 20:8-12

> "Then Moses raised his hand and struck the rock twice with the staff, and water gushed out. So, the entire community and their livestock drank their fill. But the Lord said to Moses and Aaron, 'Because you did not trust Me enough to demonstrate My holiness to the people of Israel, you will not lead them into the land I am giving them!'"
> *Numbers 20:11-12, NLT*

All who come against the Lord will fall and fail. Everyone, including the children of Israel, who tried to stand against God failed and was destroyed; Exodus 17:14-16, Numbers 14:41-45, 16:28-35, 21:34-35, Deuteronomy 7:21-24.

> "But the people defiantly pushed ahead toward the hill country, even though neither Moses nor the Ark of the Lord's Covenant left the camp. Then the Amalekites and the Canaanites who lived in those hills came down and attacked them and chased them back as far as Hormah."
> *Numbers 14:44-45, NLT*

Share the testimonies of the things God has done. Sharing testimonies of praise encourages faith and praise; Exodus 18:8-11.

> "Jethro was delighted when he heard about all the good things the Lord had done for Israel as he rescued them from the hand of the Egyptians. 'Praise the Lord,' Jethro said, 'for he has rescued you from the Egyptians and from Pharaoh. Yes, he has rescued Israel from the powerful hand of Egypt!"
> *Exodus 18:9-10, NLT*

All offerings must be given freely with a grateful heart in order for them to be acceptable to God. God calls for those who are willing to give; Exodus 35:21-22,26,29, 36:2.

> "So, the people of Israel - every man and woman who was eager to help in the work the Lord had given them through Moses - brought their gifts and gave them freely to the Lord."
> *Exodus 35:29, NLT*

God calls us to be set apart. God is holy, and so He calls us to be holy, set apart from the world around us; Leviticus 22:31-33.

> "Do not bring shame on My holy name, for I will display My holiness among the people of Israel. I am the Lord who makes you holy."
> *Leviticus 22:32, NLT*

> "You yourselves have seen what I did to Egypt and how I carried you on eagle's wings and brought you to myself. Now, if you obey me fully and keep my covenant, then out of all nations, you will be my treasured possession. Although the whole earth is mine, you will be for me a kingdom of priests and a holy nation: these are the words you are to speak to the Israelites."
> *Exodus 19:4-6*

Unbelief is sin. We fall into sin when we choose not to believe God; Numbers 14:21-23, 28-30,36-37.

> "Not one of these people will ever enter that land. They have all seen my glorious presence and the miraculous signs I performed both in Egypt and in the wilderness, but again and again they have tested Me by refusing to listen to My voice."

Moses showed love and concern
Defended the Midianite daughters. Moses moved out of compassion to protect these women from the shepherds who were harassing them; Exodus 2:16-19

> "But some other shepherds came and chased them away. So, Moses jumped up and rescued the girls from the shepherds. Then he drew water for their flocks."
> *Exodus 2:17, NLT*

Moses was obedient. Moses showed his love for the people by being obedient to God and leading them in obedience as well; Exodus 4:18-20,29-31, 12:28,50, 13:1-16, 24:3,7, Leviticus 8:4-5, 16:34, 24:23

> "Then Moses went down to the people and repeated all the instructions and regulations the Lord had given him. All the people answered with one voice, 'We will do everything the Lord has commanded.'"
> *Exodus 24:3, NLT*

Moses interceded for the people. Moses prayed for the Israelites, especially during times where the Lord had planned to destroy them; Exodus 15:24-25, 32:9-14,31-32, 34:9, Deuteronomy 9:20

> "So, Moses returned to the Lord and said, 'Oh, what a terrible sin these people have committed. They have made gods of gold for themselves. But now, if you will only forgive their sin—but if not, erase my name from the record you have written!'"
> *Exodus 32:31-32, NLT*

Moses urged them to fully commit to God. Moses desired for the people to desire God; Deuteronomy 6:4-6

> "Listen, O Israel! The Lord is our God, the Lord alone. And you must love the Lord your God with all your heart, all your soul, and all your strength. And you must commit yourselves wholeheartedly to these commands that I am giving you today."
> *Deuteronomy 6:4-6, NLT*

Moses had a zeal for the Lord

It infuriated Moses when the people would sin against the Lord, which showed his zeal for God."Exodus 32:19-20,26-28.

> "He took the calf they had made and burned it. Then he ground it into powder, threw it into the water, and forced the people to drink it."
> *Exodus 32:20, NLT*

EXAMPLES OF BEING EQUIPPED FOR THE TASK

Praiser
Moses testified of God's greatness. Moses shared with Jethro, his father-in-law, the great things God has done for him and the people of Israel; Exodus 18:8-11

> "Moses told his father-in-law everything the Lord had done to Pharaoh and Egypt on behalf of Israel. He also told about all the hardships they had experienced along the way and how the Lord had rescued His people from all their troubles."
> *Exodus 18:8, NLT*

Celebrated Passover. Moses led the people to faithfully celebrate the Passover along with other festivals and celebrations the Lord ordained; Numbers 9:4-5

> "So, Moses told the people to celebrate the Passover in the wilderness of Sinai as twilight fell on the fourteenth day of the month. And they celebrated the festival there, just as the Lord had commanded Moses."
> *Numbers 9:4-5, NLT*

Moses was a Worshipper
Moses' obedience was worship; Exodus 12:1-27, Leviticus 8:4-5, 16:34

> "So, Moses followed the Lord's instructions, and the whole community assembled at the Tabernacle entrance."
> *Leviticus 8:4, NLT*

> "And whenever Moses went out to the tent, all the people rose and stood at the entrances to their tents, watching Moses until he entered the tent. 9 As Moses went into the tent, the pillar of cloud would come down and stay at the entrance, while the Lord spoke with Moses. 10 Whenever the people saw the pillar of cloud standing at the entrance to the tent, they all stood and worshiped, each at the entrance to their tent. 11 The Lord would speak to Moses face to face, as one speaks to a friend. Then Moses would return to the camp, but his young aide Joshua son of Nun did not leave the tent."
> *Exodus 33:8-11*

Moses was a man of Prayer
He was emotionally transparent and genuine. Moses was very honest with God concerning how he felt about what was going on or what he was asked to do. Exodus 4:10-14, 5:22-23, Numbers 11:10-15

> "I can't carry all these people by myself! The load is far too heavy!"
> *Numbers 11:14*

Moses interceded for his enemy. Moses constantly went back to God, praying for Pharaoh; Exodus 8:12-13,30-31, 9:33, 10:18-19.

> "So, Moses left Pharaoh's court and pleaded with the Lord."
> *Exodus 10:18, NLT*

Moses interceded for his people. Moses was constantly going to God for the people of Israel, pleading for grace and mercy for them; Exodus 15:24-25, 32:9-14,31-32, 34:9, Numbers 12:10-13, 14:11-20, 16:19-24,43-50, 21:6-9, Deuteronomy 9:20

> "Why let the Egyptians say, 'Their God rescued them with the evil intention of slaughtering them in the mountains and wiping them from the face of the earth'? Turn away from Your fierce anger. Change Your mind about this terrible disaster You have threatened against Your people!"
> *Exodus 32:12, NLT*

Moses ran to God for all needs. Moses was quick to run to God for every concern; Exodus 15:24-25, 17:4, Numbers 11:1-2

> "Then Moses cried out to the Lord, 'What should I do with these people?
> They are ready to stone me!'"
> *Exodus 17:4, NLT*

Conversational. Moses' prayer life was a dialogue between him and God; Exodus 3:7-15, 4:1-17, 6:28-30.

> "But Moses protested to God, 'Who am I to appear before Pharaoh? Who am I to lead the people of Israel out of Egypt?' God answered, 'I will be with you. And this is your sign that I am the one who has sent you: When you have brought the people out of Egypt, you will worship God at this very mountain.'"
> *Exodus 3:11-12, NLT*

Composer of Songs
Song of deliverance. Moses, along with the children of Israel, wrote a song of praise to the Lord for their deliverance from Pharaoh and Egypt; Exodus 15, Psalm 90, Deuteronomy 31:19

> "Then Moses and the children of Israel sang this song to the Lord: 'I will sing to the Lord, for He has triumphed gloriously; He has hurled both horse and rider into the sea."
> *Exodus 15:1, NLT*

He listened and responded to God. Moses immediately answered the Lord when He called to him from the burning bush; Exodus 3:4

> "When the Lord saw Moses coming to take a closer look, God called to him from the middle of the bush, 'Moses! Moses!' 'Here I am!' Moses replied."
> *Exodus 3:4, NLT*

Moses demonstrated his ability to hear and respond to the Lord by obeying what God said, Exodus 4:18-20, 7:6,10,20, 9:22-26, 10:1-3, 12:28, Leviticus 8:4-5, 16:34. Moses did everything just as the Lord commanded him. Exodus 40:16

> "So, Moses and Aaron did just as the Lord had commanded them."
> *Exodus 7:6, NLT*

PRESENTER/REPRESENTATIVE OF THE LORD

Moses relayed all of God's words and commands. Moses was able to go and tell others exactly what God had told him; Exodus 4:30-31, 5:1, 6:9, 39:42,43 Leviticus 16:34, 21:24, 23:44, 24:23, Numbers 29:40

Defender. Moses reflected God's heart for his people by defending others; Exodus 2:16-19, 3:19-20.

> "But some other shepherds came and chased them away. So, Moses jumped up and rescued the girls from the shepherds. Then he drew water for their flocks."
> *Exodus 2:17, NLT*

Moses and Aaron. Moses stood in the place of God to Pharaoh, and Aaron stood as his prophet; Exodus 7:1-2

> "Then the Lord said to Moses, 'Pay close attention to this. I will make you seem like God to Pharaoh, and your brother, Aaron, will be your prophet."
> *Exodus 7:1, NLT*

FAITH/TRUST IN THE LORD

Obedience. Moses had faith and trust in the Lord, even when he was afraid, to obey His instructions; Exodus 4:18-20, 7:6,10,20, 9:22-26, 10:1-3, 12:28, Leviticus 8:4-5, 16:34

Intercession. Moses interceded for the people according to the promises God made to him/them, he had faith that God would keep His word; Exodus 32:9-14

> "Remember your servants Abraham, Isaac, and Jacob. You bound Yourself with an oath to them, saying, 'I will make your descendants as numerous as the stars of heaven. And I will give them all of this land that I have promised to your descendants, and they will possess it forever.'"
> *Exodus 32:13, NLT*

CHAPTER 2
REVIEW QUESTIONS
Moses

1. Explain the political situation during Moses' time.

2. What was the social life like for the Israelites?

3. What was the religious situation?

4. What does Moses' name mean? Why?

5. How did Aaron help his brother, Moses? How did he hinder Moses?

6. Who was Moses' sister? How was she helpful to him? How did she hinder him?

7. What did Moses do that was instrumental in the development of the Hebrew nation and religion?

8. What was one of the main reasons God delivered his people from Egypt?

3

Miriam

Miriam, big sister to Aaron and Moses, was a clever little girl who helped save the life of her infant brother and insure his protection by an Egyptian princess. She helped Moses free the Israelites and form them into a great nation, complete with laws given by God Himself. We first see Miriam as the quick-witted sister of baby Moses, who saved his life by watching over him in his tiny ark, along the banks of the Nile River. She cleverly suggested to the Egyptian princess that she knew a woman who could nurse him, who just happened to be Moses' mother, Jochebed. Later on, as Moses led the people in their triumphant escape from Egypt, Miriam led the people in joyful song and dance in a great encouraging anthem for all to sing as they faced hardships and peril during their journey through the desert.

The song of Moses and Miriam is still sung in churches today. The first verse is familiar to many Christians. *"The Lord reigneth, and blessed be the Rock, And let the God of my salvation be exalted."* Miriam, the first of the singers of Israel, the first poetess, used her gift for God and for the encouragement of her people. Her song was filled with joy and exaltation, as well as reminders of what wonders God had performed.

Miriam was not portrayed as a perfect saint, but her faults were recounted as well. Miriam is mentioned in Numbers 12:1-14 when, out of jealousy sparked by Moses' second wife, a dark-skinned Cushite beauty, she and Aaron spoke against Moses, saying, *'Has the Lord spoken only to Moses?' they asked. 'Hasn't He also spoken through us?' And the Lord heard this."* This is where things get interesting. Acting like a stern but benevolent father, God calls a family meeting.

"At once, the Lord said to Aaron, Moses and Miriam, 'Come out to the tent of meeting all three of you.' So, the three went out." God came down in a pillar of cloud, and, calling Miriam and Aaron aside, He gave them a well-deserved dressing down. In defense of Moses, God said that although He usually reveals Himself to men in dreams and in riddles, with Moses, things are different. *"With him (Moses) I speak face to face, clearly and not in riddles."* When God departed, taking the cloud with Him, Miriam saw that her skin was leprous. Appalled, Aaron pleaded with Moses not to *"let her be like the stillborn infant with its flesh half eaten*

away." Moses prayed and God instructed Miriam to be confined outside the encampment for seven days, after which she was healed. There was judgment, but there was also mercy.

We first see Miriam as the quick-witted sister of baby Moses, who saved his life by watching over him in that tiny boat on the banks of the Nile, and we see her standing by Moses in all his heroic acts to free the Israelites. The final scene is set at the river, again as an important aspect of the narrative, with Miriam calling the women to dance in victory after yet another miraculous deliverance from death by drowning.

Worship Leader Type Profile

MIRIAM

BACKGROUND

- **Political Conditions:** The Israelites left the might and power of Egyptian rule to wander about in the wilderness and establish their own political and religious identity.
- **Social Conditions:** Traveling about the desert with everything you own and looking for water and food was harsh. But the people had one another, and the closeness of their tribes and clans brought them comfort.
- **Religious Conditions:** God is leading His people through the wilderness. They receive the commandments and begin to define their beliefs.

FACTORS IN EQUIPPING FOR THE TASK

MIRIAM'S PERSONALITY

Miriam was quick-witted and brave.
Enabled Jochebed to raise Moses before giving him over to Pharaoh's daughter; Exodus 2:7-8

> "Then the baby's sister approached the princess. 'Should I go and find one of the Hebrew women to nurse the baby for you?' she asked. 'Yes, do!' the princess replied.
> So, the girl went and called the baby's mother."
> *Exodus 2:7-8, NLT*

Jealous. Criticized both Moses and his wife out of jealousy of their position; Numbers 12:1-2

> "While they were at Hazeroth, Miriam and Aaron criticized
> Moses because he had married a Cushite woman."
> *Numbers 12:1, NLT*

Influential - Loved by/had a great impact on all of the Israelites; Exodus 15:20, Numbers 12:1,10,15

> "So, Miriam was kept outside the camp for seven days, and the people waited until she was brought back before they traveled again."
> *Numbers 12:15, NLT*

LESSONS LEARNED FROM THIS WORSHIP LEADER TYPE

Guard your tongue - Miriam was stricken with leprosy because she spoke out against her brother and his wife. We should keep ourselves from slander and evil speaking against one another; Numbers 12

> "As the cloud moved from above the Tabernacle, there stood Miriam, her skin as white as snow from leprosy. When Aaron saw what had happened to her, he cried out to Moses, "Oh, my master! Please don't punish us for this sin we have so foolishly committed. Don't let her be like a stillborn baby, already decayed at birth.""
> *Numbers 12:10-11, NLT*

Remain humble - Miriam's pride and jealousy reaped consequences, we must avoid comparing ourselves to others and be thankful for what God is doing in our lives and the lives of others; Numbers 12, Deuteronomy 24:9

> "They said, 'Has the Lord spoken only through Moses? Hasn't He spoken through us, too?' But the Lord heard them."
> *Numbers 12:2, NLT*

God rebukes His own - God defended Moses and his position against his own sister, as God will defend His children even against their brothers and sisters; Numbers 12

> "I speak to him face to face, clearly, and not in riddles! He sees the Lord as He is. So why were you not afraid to criticize My servant Moses?'"
> *Numbers 12:8, NLT*

EXAMPLES OF BEING EQUIPPED FOR THE TASK

Miriam was a Praiser and Worshiper
Song of deliverance - Sang and danced before the Lord after He brought them through the Red Sea and delivered them from Pharaoh; Exodus 15:20-21

WORSHIP LEADER TYPES

> "Then Miriam the prophet, Aaron's sister, took a tambourine and led all the women as they played their tambourines and danced. And Miriam sang this song: 'Sing to the Lord, for He has triumphed gloriously; He has hurled both horse and rider into the sea.'"
> *Exodus 15:20-21, NLT*

REVELATIONS GIVEN TO MIRIAM FROM THE LORD

God is the Deliverer - Exodus 15:20-21

> "And Miriam sang this song: 'Sing to the Lord, for He has triumphed gloriously; He has hurled both horse and rider into the sea.'"
> *Exodus 15:21, NLT*

God is a Righteous Judge - Numbers 12:9-15

> "As the cloud moved from above the Tabernacle, there stood Miriam, her skin as white as snow from leprosy. When Aaron saw what had happened to her, he cried out to Moses, "Oh, my master! Please don't punish us for this sin we have so foolishly committed."
> *Numbers 12:10-11, NLT*

God is our Defender - God defended Moses and his position against his own sister; Numbers 12

> "So, Moses cried out to the Lord, 'O God, I beg you, please heal her!'
> But the Lord said to Moses, "If her father had done nothing more than spit in her face, wouldn't she be defiled for seven days? So, keep her outside the camp for seven days, and after that she may be accepted back.'"
> *Numbers 12:13-14, NLT*

God's intimacy with Moses - God directly disclosed His trust of and closeness to Moses;

> "But not with My servant Moses. Of all My house, he is the one I trust.
> I speak to him face to face, clearly, and not in riddles! He sees the Lord as He is.
> So why were you not afraid to criticize My servant Moses?'"
> *Numbers 12:7-8, NLT*

God's is a healer. - Miriam's healing came as a result of her brother's prayer.

> "So, Moses cried out to the Lord, 'O God, please heal her.'"
> *Exodus 12:13, NLT*

CHAPTER 3
REVIEW QUESTIONS
Miriam

1. Who were Miriam's brothers?

2. What did Miriam do when she was young, to prove how brave and resourceful she was?

3. What were some of Miriam's personality characteristics? (Including negative ones)

4. What was the song Miriam lead the women in singing?

5. What incident prompted her to lead the people in praise?

"Worship is the highest form of acknowledging God's presence in our lives, and it is through worship that we connect with the divine."
–John Piper

4

Aaron

Aaron was called a "mouthpiece" for Moses, the loyal brother of Moses and a good friend who stood by faithfully throughout Moses' life. This man who gave Moses courage when he was lacking, gave him a voice when his confidence waned and assisted him in accomplishing all that God instructed him to do. Moses led the Israelites out of captivity, but Aaron spoke for him, held up his arms when he grew weary and walked by his side through the Exodus of the people of Israel. Moses hesitated to do God's will because he halted in speech. Exodus 4:14 tells us, *"Then the Lord's anger turned against Moses and He said, 'What about your brother Aaron, the Levite? I know he can speak well. He is already on his way to meet you, and he will be glad to see you.'"*

Aaron faithfully stood by Moses' side as he went before the Pharaoh, speaking God's words and demanding release of the Hebrew slaves. He stood by as they made the difficult trek through the wilderness and when Moses grew weary from holding up his arms, by the command of God, so that Joshua and his men would win a victory, Aaron, along with Hur, stood by him and held his arm steady until sunset. This is emblematic of Aaron's support and encouragement as Moses fulfilled his calling to lead the children of Israel out of bondage.

Of course, every man has his weaknesses, and Aaron was pressured to compromise when the Israelites insisted on making a graven image of gold. At the same time, Moses went to the mountaintop to confer with God almighty. It is quite a story in Exodus 32. Moses comes down from the mountain and sees the people dancing and cavorting around and worshiping a golden calf, which Aaron helped them make. Moses' anger burned hot. When Moses asked Aaron to explain his actions, he said, "You know these people. They are set on evil." Exodus 32:23-24. The people pressured Aaron and wondered where Moses, their leader, had gone.

"Aaron plays an important part in the inauguration and development of priestly functions, all of which are prescribed in Leviticus. Among the mature males of Israel there were three classes:
- From the tribes of Israel came the warriors.
- From the tribes of Levi came the workers
- From the family of Aaron came the worshipers.

Aaron became the first high priest of Israel...a type of Christ and His church." So, Aaron gave in to their demands and helped them to make a golden calf to worship. Many men died that day, when God sent a plague. So, they were punished for this great sin, which Aaron assisted them in doing. This was a horrible lesson to learn, and Aaron must have genuinely suffered for his part.[13]

The redeeming aspect of this story is that Aaron continued to lead alongside Moses. Even though he'd made a huge mistake, he was shown mercy and continued to assist Moses in his quest to liberate the Israelites and form them into an independent nation, slaves to no one but God.

As worship leaders, we can look to Aaron as an example of support and encouragement. He helped the Israelites to "worship God in the wilderness" as they were instructed to do. Additionally, he sets a good standard for someone who did a grievous thing against God and still was able to fulfill his calling and accomplish the task God gave him.

> "And no one takes this honor on himself,
> but he receives it when called by God, just as Aaron was."
> Hebrews 5:4

Worship Leader Type Profile

AARON

BACKGROUND

- **Political Conditions:**
  - Egypt is the most powerful kingdom in the world. The Israelites had been slaves for years. They were powerless against the might of Egypt.
- **Social Conditions:**
  - The Israelites lived in close proximity to one another. There was very little privacy, as we know it today. Travelling about in the desert presented many hardships, but they were, at last, free from enslavement. They experienced distress in their refugee status but found comfort in being together.
- **Religious Conditions:**
  - The Israelites were a group of people who worshipped Yahweh. They broke with the Egyptian gods and determined to worship in their own way.
  - Egypt is polytheistic-the Pharaoh is thought to be a god.

---

13 Lockyer, Herbert, "All the Men of the Bible" p 20, 1976, Zondervan Publishing House

> o In their transition from a polytheistic pagan culture, the Israelites had to be taught a new way, worshiping one God and remaining faithful to Him.

FACTORS IN EQUIPPING FOR THE TASK

Aaron was:
Well spoken – Aaron was skilled in speaking both privately and publicly. Exodus 4:14-16

> "Then the Lord became angry with Moses. "All right," he said,
> "What about your brother, Aaron the Levite? I know he can speak well.
> He is already on his way to meet you, and He will be glad to see you."
> *Exodus 4:14, NIV*

AARON'S PERSONALITY

Obedient: Exodus 4:27, 7:6, 10, 20, 8:17, 9:8-10, 10:1-3, 16:34, 40:31-32, Numbers 8:1-2

> "The Lord said to Aaron, 'Go into the wilderness to meet Moses.'
> So, he met Moses at the mountain of God and kissed him."
> *Exodus 4:27, NIV*

Unfaithful - When Moses was up on Mount Sinai with the Lord, Aaron allowed the people to pressure him into creating a golden calf for the people to worship:

> "Then all the people tore off the gold rings which were in their ears and
> brought them to Aaron. He took this from their hand,
> and fashioned it with a graving tool and made it into a molten calf; and they said,
> "This is your god, O Israel, who brought you up from the land of Egypt." Now when Aaron
> saw this, he built an altar before it; and Aaron made a
> proclamation and said, "Tomorrow shall be a feast to the LORD."
> So, the next day they rose early and offered burnt offerings and brought
> peace offerings; and the people sat down to eat and to drink, and rose up to play.
> *Exodus 32:3-6*

Joined in rejoicing with Moses and Jethro – Aaron joined Moses and Jethro in celebrating God's goodness and greatness.

> Then Jethro, Moses' father-in-law, brought a burnt offering and
> other sacrifices to God, and Aaron came with all the

elders of Israel to eat a meal with Moses'
father-in-law in the presence of God.
Exodus 18:12, NIV

Helpful – Aaron helped Moses in so many ways as he accomplished God's plan. Exodus 4:29-30, Exodus 5:1, Exodus 7:1, 6, 10, 19, Exodus 8:5-6

Throughout Exodus, we read that Moses and Aaron did everything together.

AARON'S RELATIONSHIP WITH GOD

Trusted by God -The LORD replied, "Go down and bring Aaron up with you. But the priests and the people must not force their way through to come up to the LORD, or he will break out against them."- Exodus 19:24, 24:1

"But the Lord said, 'Go down and bring Aaron back up with you. In the meantime,
do not let the priests or the people break through to approach the Lord,
or He will break out and destroy them.'"
Exodus 19:24, NIV

"Then the LORD said to Moses, "Come up to the LORD, you and Aaron,
Nadab and Abihu, and seventy of the elders of Israel.
You are to worship at a distance...'"
Exodus 42:1, NIV

THE REVELATION OF GOD THAT AARON HAD RECEIVED AND CARRIED TO THE PEOPLE OF GOD.

Yahweh had come to deliver His people; Exodus 3:7,16-22, 4:28-31.

The LORD said, "I have indeed seen the misery of my people in Egypt.
I have heard them crying out because of their slave drivers,
and I am concerned about their suffering."
Exodus 3:7, NIV

"Go, assemble the elders of Israel and say to them, 'The LORD,
the God of your fathers—the God of Abraham, Isaac and Jacob—
appeared to me and said: I have watched over you and have seen what

has been done to you in Egypt. And I have promised to bring you up out of your misery
in Egypt into the land of the Canaanites, Hittites, Amorites, Perizzites, Hivites and
Jebusites—a land flowing with milk and honey."
Exodus 3:16-17, NIV

"But I know that the king of Egypt will not let you go unless
a mighty hand compels him. So I will stretch out my hand and strike the Egyptians
with all the wonders that I will perform among them. After that, he will let you go.
And I will make the Egyptians favorably disposed toward this people,
so that when you leave you will not go empty-handed."
Exodus 3:19-21, NIV

God is greater than all – God is sovereign over all of heaven and earth, and nothing stands above Him; Exodus 7:10-12, 8:18,19.

"Pharaoh then summoned wise men and sorcerers, and the Egyptian magicians also did
the same things by their secret arts: Each one threw down his staff and it became a snake.
But Aaron's staff swallowed up their staffs."
Exodus 7: 11-12, NIV

God is merciful. Not only did God not destroy Aaron, but also, he let him remain in the priestly role that He appointed him. Exodus 39:1, 40:12-15

"From the blue, purple and scarlet yarn they made woven garments for
ministering in the sanctuary. They also made sacred garments for Aaron,
as the LORD commanded Moses."
Exodus 39:1, NIV

God is relentless for His people - God goes to war for His people and never stops until His blessings and promises for them have come to pass. Exodus 12:21-33

"At midnight the LORD struck down all the firstborn in Egypt, from the firstborn of Pharaoh,
who sat on the throne, to the firstborn of the prisoner, who was in the dungeon,
and the firstborn of all the livestock as well."
Exodus 12:29, NIV

God is holy and glorious – God's glory is consuming, and his holiness is incomparable. Exodus 24:9-11, Leviticus 22:31-33

> "Do not bring shame on my holy name, for I will display
> my holiness among the people of Israel.
> I am the Lord who makes you holy."
> *Leviticus 22:32, NLT*

LESSONS LEARNED FROM THIS WORSHIP LEADER TYPE

God is holy and sin must be dealt with and paid for. As high priest, Aaron was responsible for entering the Most Holy place once a year and offering atonement sacrifice for the sins of all the people of Israel.

> "Fasten a blue cord to it to attach it to the turban; it is to be on the front of the turban.
> It will be on Aaron's forehead, and he will bear the guilt involved in the
> sacred gifts the Israelites consecrate, whatever their gifts may be.
> It will be on Aaron's forehead continually so that they
> will be acceptable to the Lord.
> *Exodus 28:37-38*

Consecration - Consecration is crucial to our walk with the Lord, if we truly desire to walk with Him and worship Him. Exodus 30:29-30

> "Consecrate them to make them absolutely holy.
> After this, whatever touches them will also become holy."
> *Exodus 30:29, NIV*

Not standing up against sin is also sin – Aaron was guilty of even allowing the Israelites to get out of hand, let alone build the idol for the people. Exodus 32:25-27

> "Moses saw that Aaron had let the people
> get completely out of control,
> much to the amusement of their enemies."
> *Exodus 32:25, NIV*

Responsibility comes with the position. Aaron had large responsibilities due to the position he was in as the priest. Exodus 28:37-38; Leviticus 6:9-13, 25:30, 10:6-11, 16:2-28

> "Once a year Aaron shall make atonement on its horns.
> This annual atonement must be made with the blood of the atoning
> sin offering ᵇ for the generations to come.
> It is most holy to the Lord."
> *Exodus 30:10, NIV*

ABILITY TO HEAR AND RESPOND TO THE LORD

Answered God's initial call – Aaron immediately answered God's call to go and meet with Moses:

> "The LORD said to Aaron, 'Go into the wilderness to meet Moses.' So,
> he met Moses at the mountain of God and kissed him."
> *Exodus 4:27, NIV*

Spoke the words of the Lord to others – Aaron was able to relay God's words to His people as well as their enemies; Exodus 4:30-31, 5:1, 10:3-6, 16:4-6, 10.

> "Afterward Moses and Aaron went to Pharaoh and said, "This is what the LORD, the God of
> Israel, says: 'Let my people go, so that they may hold a festival to me in the wilderness.'"
> *Exodus 5:1, NIV*

Obedient – Aaron responded to the Lord's words with obedience; Exodus 4:27, 7:6, 10,20, 8:17, 9:8-10, 10:1-3, 16:33-34, 40:31,32, Numbers 8:1,2

> "They did this, and when Aaron stretched out his hand with the staff and struck the dust
> of the ground, gnats came on people and animals. All the dust throughout the
> land of Egypt became gnats."
> *Exodus 8:17, NIV*

PRESENTER/REPRESENTATIVE OF THE LORD

Spoke the words of the Lord to others - Aaron was a mouthpiece for the Lord to His people and their enemies; Exodus 4:30-31, 5:1, 7:2, 10:3-6, 16:4-6, 10.

> "So, Moses and Aaron went to Pharaoh and said to him, "This is what the LORD,

the God of the Hebrews, says: 'How long will you refuse to
humble yourself before me? Let my people go,
so that they may worship me.'"
Exodus 10:3, NIV

Performed the miracles of God – God used Aaron to perform the miracles and signs of God; Exodus 7:10, 20:21, 8:6,17, 9:10, 11:10

"So, Aaron stretched out his hand over the waters of Egypt,
and the frogs came up and
covered the land."
Exodus 8:6

Aaron, as a high priest, was responsible for carrying the sins of the people – Exodus 28:37-38

"Aaron must wear it on his forehead so he may take on himself
any guilt of the people of Israel when they consecrate their sacred offerings.
He must always wear it on his forehead so the
Lord will accept the people."
Exodus 28:38, NIV

AARON'S FAITH/TRUST IN THE LORD

Believed God – Aaron believed and trusted God to go and do all of the things God commanded him to do. Exodus 4:28-31

"Then Moses told Aaron everything the LORD had sent him to say, and also about all the
signs he had commanded him to perform. Moses and Aaron brought together all the
elders of the Israelites, and Aaron told them everything the LORD had said to Moses.
He also performed the signs before the people, and they believed.
And when they heard that the LORD was concerned about them and
had seen their misery, they bowed down and worshiped.
Exodus 4: 28-31, NIV

CHAPTER 4
REVIEW QUESTIONS
Aaron

1. What were the political conditions of this time?

2. What were the social conditions?

3. What were the religious conditions?

4. What were some of the factors that contributed to Aaron's accomplishing the task set before him?

5. What can we learn from Aaron's life?

6. Why do you think Aaron participated in the making of the idol?

*It is impossible to worship
God without God first giving
revelation of Himself.*

5

Hannah

Another example of a virtuous woman is Hannah, the wife of Elkanah, from 1 Samuel 1-23. Unfortunately, she was childless, and when Elkanah took on another wife, Peninnah, she had children and then taunted Hannah for being barren. The second wife, Peninnah, made life miserable for the patient and devoted Hannah, but when she complained to her husband, his only response was that she (Hannah) was his favorite and that he was indeed worth more than many sons. "But to Hannah, he gave a double portion because he loved her, and the Lord had closed her womb." (1 Samuel 1:5)

"Childlessness was a particular burden to a pious Hebrew woman. In such a fate she found herself excluded from the national destiny. "In thee and in thy seed shall all the families of the earth be blessed." (Genesis 28:14)[14] Hannah poured her heart out to her husband, but he could not assuage her distress. Reassurance of his love for her and her primary place in his affections did not lessen her feelings of loneliness and guilt over her childlessness.

It must have been an added sorrow when Hannah went to the temple, poured out her heart to God, and she was accused of drunkenness by Eli, the priest. After telling him she was not drunk, but was praying earnestly for a child, the priest finally recognized her longing and yearning for a child, and he then reassured her that she would have a child.

> "Her reply, from "Not so, my lord," Hannah replied, "I am a woman who is deeply troubled. I have not been drinking wine or beer; I was pouring out my soul to the Lord. Do not take your servant for a wicked woman; I have been praying here out of my great anguish and grief."
> *1 Samuel 1:15-16*

Then, Eli assured her that God would answer her prayers. After Samuel was born, Hannah did as she had promised and "Gave him to the Lord." She weaned him, then she turned him over to Eli to serve in the temple. In the second chapter of 1 Samuel, we read Hannah's

---

14   Blaikock, E.M. Today's Handbook of Bible Characters, Bethany House Publishers, 1979, p. 125

poem of gratitude. She received her answer to prayer, and then she gave praise to God, as we all should. The song, or poem, is a beautiful example of praise. She praises God for being the one who raises up the humble, who changes the fortunes of those who are needy and who, in her case, answers the prayers of a sorrowful woman who seemingly cannot conceive of a child. Perhaps she was thinking of the cruelty of Peninnah, who was able to bear children, and who, instead of being compassionate for Hannah's less fortunate state, she taunted her.

Hannah's prayer includes these verses:

> "She who was barren has borne seven children, but she who has had many sons pines away."
> *1 Samuel 2:5*

"The psalm of praise which Hannah sings in Eli's presence (2:1-10) reveals her understanding of divine things in an age when men had small understanding of their God. It recognized the power of God and the certainty of ultimate justice. It expresses faith in God's power to keep, and joy of answered prayer, it vibrates with gratitude."[15]

The result of Hannah's persistent prayer was the birth of Samuel. He grew up to reflect his mother's piousness. He became a man of prayer and intercession. Samuel's greatness can be traced back to his own godly mother.

WORSHIP LEADER TYPE PROFILE:

HANNAH

BACKGROUND

- **Political Conditions:** The people looked to the priest to help them navigate life. Hannah went to the temple when she was confused and frustrated with her childlessness.
- **Social Conditions:** Women were expected to have children. Motherhood was their primary function. Hannah lived in close proximity with her husband's other wives, and this produced much misery from a woman who was unkind and spoke hatefully to Hannah about a situation she had no control over.
- **Religious Conditions:** Eli is the high priest; Hophni and Phinehas (sons) are the priests of the Lord. The temple is the main place of worship and the place of prayer.

---

15 Blaiklock, E.M., <u>Today's Handbook of Bible Characters</u>, Bethany House Publishers, Minneapolis, MN. 1979, p. 125

FACTORS IN EQUIPPING FOR THE TASK

HANNAH'S PERSONALITY

Hannah was faithful.
She stayed true to her word in dedicating Samuel to the Lord; 1 Samuel 1:11,27-28

> "'I asked the Lord to give me this boy, and He has granted my request. Now I am giving
> him to the Lord, and he will belong to the Lord his whole life.'
> And they worshiped the Lord there."
> *1 Samuel 1:27-28, NLT*

HANNAH'S RELATIONSHIP WITH GOD

She leaned on the Lord and trusted Him with her sorrows and was rewarded by a son.

Hannah's revelation of God was that *He is the Giver of life*; 1 Samuel 1:19-20,26-27.

> "'Sir, do you remember me?' Hannah asked. 'I am the very woman
> who stood here several years ago praying to the Lord. I asked the Lord
> to give me this boy, and He has granted my request."
> *1 Samuel 1:26-27, NLT*

LESSONS LEARNED FROM THIS WORSHIP LEADER TYPE

Make everything a matter of prayer - Hannah was broken over her barrenness, and so she brought it to the Lord, as we should with all things; 1 Samuel 1:10-11

> "Hannah was in deep anguish, crying bitterly as she prayed to the Lord."
> *1 Samuel 1:10, NLT*

Pray until you are at peace - We should experience peace when we finish praying as Hannah did, and continue to pray until we do; 1 Samuel 1:15-18

> "'Oh, thank you, sir!' she exclaimed. Then she went
> back and began to eat again, and she was no longer sad."
> *1 Samuel 1:18, NLT*

Respond to the Lord according to the measure of His revelation or answer - We should respond with praise and obedience when the Lord answers us, as Hannah did when the Lord answered her prayer; 1 Samuel 1:28, 2:1-10.

> "Then Hannah prayed: 'My heart rejoices in the Lord!
> The Lord has made me strong. Now I have an answer for my enemies;
> I rejoice because You rescued me. No one is holy like the Lord!
> There is no one besides You; there is no Rock like our God.'"
> *1 Samuel 2:1-2, NLT*

EXAMPLE OF BEING A PRAISER AND WORSHIPPER

She offered a prayer of praise - Hannah offered to the Lord a prayer of praise for giving her a child; 1 Samuel 2:1-10

> "Then Hannah prayed: 'My heart rejoices in the Lord!
> The Lord has made me strong. Now I have an answer for my enemies;
> I rejoice because You rescued me. No one is holy like the Lord!
> There is no one besides You; there is no Rock like our God.'"
> *1 Samuel 2:1-2, NLT*

As a Worshipper, she *poured out her heart* - Hannah laid her heart out before the Lord; 1 Samuel 1:10,15-16

> "'Oh no, sir!' she replied. 'I haven't been drinking
> wine or anything stronger. But I am very discouraged,
> and I was pouring out my heart to the Lord.'"
> *1 Samuel 1:15, NLT*

She faithfully gave her son back to the Lord - Keeping her vow as well as sacrificing her firstborn son to live in the Temple was a huge act of worship for Hannah; 1 Samuel 1:28

> "'Now I am giving him to the Lord,
> and he will belong to the Lord his whole life.'
> And they worshiped the Lord there."
> *1 Samuel 1:27-28, NLT*

REVELATIONS GIVEN TO HANNAH FROM THE LORD

God is giver of life; 1 Samuel 1:19-20

> "The entire family got up early the next morning and went to worship the Lord once more. Then they returned home to Ramah. When Elkanah slept with Hannah, the Lord remembered her plea, and in due time she gave birth to a son. She named him Samuel, for she said, 'I asked the Lord for him.'"
> *1 Samuel 1:19-20, NLT*

Our response is Faith/trust in the Lord - not in mankind
Faith to pray - Hannah exercised faith in going to the Lord and asking for a child; 1 Samuel 1:10-12

> "Hannah was in deep anguish, crying bitterly as she prayed to the Lord. And she made this vow: 'O Lord of Heaven's Armies, if You will look upon my sorrow and answer my prayer and give me a son, then I will give him back to You. He will be Yours for his entire lifetime, and as a sign that he has been dedicated to the Lord, his hair will never be cut.'"
> *1 Samuel 1:10-11, NLT*

CHAPTER 5
REVIEW QUESTIONS
Hannah

1. What was Hannah's personality?

2. Why was Peninnah jealous of Hannah?

3. What did Eli do to show his preference for Hannah?

4. What was Eli, the priest's, reaction to Hannah's prayer?

5. What did Hannah promise to do when the child was born?

6. Who was the son that was promised to Hannah?

7. How did God bless Hannah?

6

Samuel

~~~~~

Samuel's life begins in an extraordinary way. His mother was Hannah, the wife of Elkanah. Hannah was barren and her life was made unendurable by the constant, cruel taunting of Elkanah's other wife, named Peninnah. Hannah went to the temple and overcome with grief, cried and prayed for a son. She was so beside herself that the priest, Eli, accused her of being drunk and rebuked her for it, God heard her prayers and Samuel was born. As an act of thankfulness, Hannah dedicated Samuel to the service of the temple at Shiloh, under the tutelage of the old priest, Eli. We can assume Samuel was 12 or older when he went to live with Eli, since he would have needed to be old enough to accomplish the tasks given to him.

According to Blaiklock's ***Today's Handbook of Bible Characters***, "It is difficult to estimate the age of Samuel in this story. He must have been old enough to serve as the immediate servant of the aged Eli, strong enough to open the temple doors, and intelligent enough to deliver a detailed message."[16]

After his unusual childhood, Samuel, the adult, filled many roles. He was a judge, a prophet, a seer, and a military leader, not to mention a kingmaker. Samuel was initially against having a king over Israel, but the people insisted, so he anointed Saul as the first king of Israel. Samuel then went away or "retired" from public service, only to reappear to announce that Saul was rejected as king by God because of his disobedience.

After renouncing Saul, Samuel secretly sought out David, the youngest son of a large family, and anointed him as the successor to the throne of Saul. Samuel served as a prophet, and later as a judge, then as a kingmaker. He served in the temple and then he rose to such prominence that he appointed kings. He remained faithful even when the sons of Eli, his old mentor, turned to corruption. He was faithful even when his own sons were corrupted by taking bribes and were notorious for the perversion of justice.

---

16   Blaiklock, E.M. Today's Handbook of Bible Characters, Bethany House Publishing, p. 127

WORSHIP LEADER TYPES

WORSHIP LEADER TYPE PROFILE

SAMUEL

BACKGROUND

- **Political Conditions:**
  - Enmity between Israel and Philistia
  - Samuel is Israel's judge, until Israel seeks out a king.
  - Saul becomes king, against the advice of Samuel, who warns the people that kings will take advantage of them, take their wealth and kidnap their daughters for their harems. Still, the people insist! So he brings Saul as king to the people.
- **Social Conditions:**
  - Families lived together in close quarters, and men often had more than one wife.
  - Women were expected to have children as their primary role.
- **Religious Conditions:**
  - Priests held power and sway among the people and had great influence with the king, the first of whom was Saul.

FACTORS IN THE EQUIPPING FOR THE TASK

The Person

Dedication before conception - His mother Hannah prayed for and consecrated Samuel before he was even born; 1 Samuel 1:11

> "And she made this vow: 'O Lord of Heaven's Armies, if you will look upon my sorrow and answer my prayer and give me a son, then I will give him back to you. He will be yours for his entire lifetime, and as a sign that he has been dedicated to the Lord, his hair will never be cut.'"
> 1 Samuel 1:11, NLT

Raised in the Temple - Lived and raised in the Temple alongside the priest of God; 1 Samuel 2:11,21

> "Then Elkanah returned home to Ramah without Samuel. And the boy served the Lord by assisting Eli the priest."
> 1 Samuel 2:11, NLT

Favored by God - Faithfully served the Lord and the Lord blessed him greatly; 1 Samuel 2:26, NLT

> "Meanwhile, the boy Samuel grew taller and grew in favor with
> the Lord and with the people."
> *1 Samuel 2:26, NLT*

SAMUEL'S PERSONALITY

Faithful - Faithfully served the Lord; 1 Samuel 2:18

> "But Samuel, though he was only a boy, served the Lord.
> He wore a linen garment like that of a priest."
> *1 Samuel 2:18, NLT*

Obedient - Did everything God told him to do; 1 Samuel 8:9-10,22, 10:1, 15:32-33, 16:4.

> "Then Samuel took a flask of olive oil and poured it over Saul's head.
> He kissed Saul and said, 'I am doing this
> because the Lord has appointed you to be the ruler over Israel,
> his special possession.'"
> *1 Samuel 10:1, NLT*

Tender-hearted - Wept over people's sins; 1 Samuel 15:10-11,35

> "Then the Lord said to Samuel, 'I am sorry that I ever made Saul king,
> for he has not been loyal to me and has refused to obey my command.'
> Samuel was so deeply moved when he heard this that he
> cried out to the Lord all night."
> *1 Samuel 15:10-11, NLT*

SAMUEL'S RELATIONSHIP WITH GOD

God was with Samuel - God walked with Samuel as Samuel faithfully walked with God; 1 Samuel 3:19, NLT

> "As Samuel grew up, the Lord was with him,
> and everything Samuel said proved to be reliable."
> *1 Samuel 3:19, NLT*

Heart fully aligned with God - Everything Samuel said and did came from the heart of God; 1 Samuel 10:3-9, 13:13-14, 15:22-23.

> "As Saul turned and started to leave, God gave him a new heart,
> and all Samuel's signs were fulfilled that day."
> *1 Samuel 10:9, NLT*

LESSONS LEARNED FROM THIS WORSHIP LEADER TYPE

Sometimes we are instructed to say scary or unpleasant things - A lot of things messages Samuel had to relay weren't necessarily good things; 1 Samuel 3:11-19, 8:7-18, 10:18-19, 15:16-19.

> "When that day comes, you will beg for relief from this king you
> are demanding, but then the Lord will not help you."
> *1 Samuel 8:18, NLT*

> "I have warned him that judgment is coming upon his family forever,
> because his sons are blaspheming God and he hasn't disciplined them."
> *1 Samuel 3:13. NLT*

Obey faithfully - Samuel remained obedient even when those around him weren't; 1 Samuel 8:9-10,22, 10:1, 15:32-33, 16:4.

> "'Do as they ask, but solemnly warn them about the way a king will reign over them.'
> So, Samuel passed on the Lord's warning to the people who
> were asking him for a king."
> *1 Samuel 8:9-10, NLT*

Trust God's selection - Samuel learned, in unknowingly looking for the next King, that God looks at the heart, not outward appearances; 1 Samuel 16:6-13

> "But the Lord said to Samuel, 'Don't judge by his appearance or height,
> for I have rejected him. The Lord doesn't see things the way you see them.
> People judge by outward appearance, but the Lord looks at the heart.'"
> *1 Samuel 16:7, NLT*

Worship is our warfare/defense - When Saul and his troops came for Samuel and David, Samuel was found worshiping the Lord and the Holy Spirit fell upon their enemies; 1 Samuel 19:18-24

> "He sent troops to capture him. But when they arrived and saw Samuel leading a group of prophets who were prophesying, the Spirit of God came upon Saul's men, and they also began to prophesy. When Saul heard what had happened, he sent other troops, but they, too, prophesied! The same thing happened a third time."
> *1 Samuel 19:20-21, NLT*

Obedient - Samuel did everything the Lord told him to do; 1 Samuel 8:9-10,22, 10:1, 15:32-33, 16:4.

> "Then Samuel said, 'Bring King Agag to me.' Agag arrived full of hope, for he thought, 'Surely the worst is over, and I have been spared!' But Samuel said, 'As your sword has killed the sons of many mothers, now your mother will be childless.' And Samuel cut Agag to pieces before the Lord at Gilgal."
> *1 Samuel 15:32-33, NLT*

Calling for repentance - Knowing that repentance restores the people to the Lord, Samuel pleaded with the people to repent; 1 Samuel 7:3

> "Then Samuel said to all the people of Israel, 'If you want to return to the Lord with all your hearts, get rid of your foreign gods and your images of Ashtoreth. Turn your hearts to the Lord and obey Him alone; then He will rescue you from the Philistines.'"
> *1 Samuel 7:3, NLT*

Led the entire nation in worship to the Lord - Samuel led the Israelites in full repentance and worship of the Lord; 1 Samuel 12

> "But be sure to fear the Lord and faithfully serve Him. Think of all the wonderful things He has done for you."
> *1 Samuel 12:24, NLT*

Faithful to intercede - Samuel consistently prayed for the people; 1 Samuel 12:23

> "As for me, I will certainly not sin against the Lord by ending my prayers for you."
> *1 Samuel 12:23, NLT*

EXAMPLE OF BEING A WORSHIPPER

Ebenezer, "The stone of help" - Samuel marked this stone as a memorial of what the Lord did for the people; 1 Samuel 7:12

> "Samuel then took a large stone and placed it between the towns of Mizpah and Jeshanah. He named it Ebenezer (which means "the stone of help"), for he said, 'Up to this point the Lord has helped us!'"
> *1 Samuel 7:12, NLT*

Altar at Ramah - Samuel built an altar in his home to worship the Lord; 1 Samuel 7:17

> "Then he would return to his home at Ramah, and he would hear cases there, too. And Samuel built an altar to the Lord at Ramah."
> *1 Samuel 7:17, NLT*

Prophesying in Ramah - When David and Samuel were running from Saul and his troops, they came to Ramah and Samuel was found prophesying there; 1 Samuel 19:18-24

> "He sent troops to capture him. But when they arrived and saw Samuel leading a group of prophets who were prophesying, the Spirit of God came upon Saul's men, and they also began to prophesy."
> *1 Samuel 19:20, NLT*

Prayer
Intercession - Consistently praying for the people; 1 Samuel 7:5-9, 12:23

> "Then Samuel told them, 'Gather all of Israel to Mizpah, and I will pray to the Lord for you.'"
> *1 Samuel 7:5*

Sought the Lord for guidance - Samuel turned to the Lord in need of guidance and direction; 1 Samuel 8:6

> "Samuel was displeased with their request and went to the Lord for guidance."
> *1 Samuel 8:6, NLT*

ABILITY TO HEAR AND RESPOND TO THE LORD

Initial call of Samuel - Samuel heard the voice of the Lord as a child and answered Him; 1 Samuel 3:4-10

> "And the Lord came and called as before, 'Samuel! Samuel!'
> And Samuel replied, 'Speak, your servant is listening.'"
> *1 Samuel 3:10, NLT*

Lord's mouthpiece - Samuel heard the Lord and would share what He was speaking; 1 Samuel 3:11-19, 8:7-18, 15:16-19.

> "'What did the Lord say to you? Tell me everything. And may God strike you and even kill you if you hide anything from me!' So, Samuel told Eli everything; he didn't hold anything back. 'It is the Lord's will,' Eli replied. '
> Let Him do what he thinks best.'"
> *1 Samuel 3:17-18, NLT*

Dialogue - The Lord spoke, Samuel would respond, Samuel spoke, the Lord would respond; 1 Samuel 16:1-4

> "But Samuel asked, 'How can I do that? If Saul hears about it, he will kill me.'
> 'Take a heifer with you,' the Lord replied, "and say that you have come to make a sacrifice to the Lord. Invite Jesse to the sacrifice, and I will show you which of his sons to anoint for Me.'"
> *1 Samuel 16:2-3, NLT*

Presenter/representative of the Lord
Samuel said what God was saying, 1 Samuel 3:11-19, 8:7-18, 10:18-19, 15:16-19

> "And he said, 'This is what the Lord, the God of Israel, has declared: I brought you from Egypt and rescued you from the Egyptians and from all of the nations that were oppressing you. But though I have rescued you from your misery and distress, you have rejected your God today and have said, "No, we want a king instead!" Now, therefore, present yourselves before the Lord by tribes and clans.'"
> *1 Samuel 10:18-19, NLT*

Faithfully interceding - As Christ and Holy Spirit intercede for God's people, Samuel interceded for the people; 1 Samuel 12:23

> "As for me, I will certainly not sin against the Lord by ending my prayers for you."
> *1 Samuel 12:23, NLT*

REVELATIONS GIVEN TO SAMUEL FROM THE LORD

Judgment on Eli's family; 1 Samuel 3:11-14

> "I am going to carry out all My threats against Eli and his family, from beginning to end."
> *1 Samuel 3:12, NLT*

Saul would not be a good king; 1 Samuel 8:7-18

> "'Do as they ask, but solemnly warn them about the way a king will reign over them.'
> So, Samuel passed on the Lord's warning to the people who were asking him for a king."
> *1 Samuel 8:9-10, NLT*

God sees the heart, not the outward appearance; 1 Samuel 16:7

> "But the Lord said to Samuel, 'Don't judge by his appearance or height,
> for I have rejected him. The Lord doesn't see things the way you see them.
> People judge by outward appearance, but the Lord looks at the heart.'"
> *1 Samuel 16:7, NLT*

FAITH/TRUST IN THE LORD

Obedient - Samuel faithfully served and obeyed the Lord; 1 Samuel 8:9-10,22, 10:1, 15:32-33, 16:4.

> "So, Samuel did as the Lord instructed. When he arrived at Bethlehem,
> the elders of the town came trembling to meet him. 'What's wrong?' they asked.
> 'Do you come in peace?'"
> *1 Samuel 16:4, NLT*

CHAPTER 6
REVIEW QUESTIONS
Samuel

1. What were the political conditions of Samuel's time?

2. What were the social conditions?

3. What were the religious conditions?

4. What were some of the characteristics of Samuel that helped him in life?

5. What can we learn from Samuel?

6. One of the major ways God equipped Samuel to lead His people was to discern and know the voice of the Lord and how to properly respond. Why do you think this is so important?

"True worship is not about singing songs or attending religious rituals; it is about surrendering our hearts and lives to God in every aspect."
–Rick Warren

7
Gideon

Even though he was described in the Bible as timid, he became a mighty leader, a strong judge and a diplomat. When we first see Gideon, he is hiding from his enemies, and threshing out wheat where he will not be seen. There is a lot made of his hiding, but my thoughts are that sometimes the wisest thing one can do is hide. During the Nazi occupation, many people were saved from death by being hidden away.

"It is not the triumphant confidence alone which is honored by God...It is clear that Gideon was a harassed and discouraged man. He bore the burdens of a long defeat. He was unaided by any strong surviving tradition. When the messenger of God had first summoned him to the task of national deliverance, it was with bitter unbelief that he first responded. (Judges 6:13) The only explanation he found to offer for the sorry state of his nation was that God, who had once been at hand with present aid, had forsaken His people."[17]

When Gideon crept up within hearing distance of the encamping enemy, he showed great courage. (Judges 7:13) He showed wisdom when he tested his soldiers by seeing which ones drank water carelessly without checking for enemy combatants and for those who looked while they satisfied their thirst. (Judges 7:5) He showed restraint when he requested a sign from God before he acted. (Judges 6:33-40) Some might think this shows a lack of faith, but it can also be wisdom to make certain of something before you act.

Reviewing the story of Gideon's life, Dr. Robert A. Watson wrote, "We find that within certain limits, he who trusts and obeys God has quite irresistible efficiency." He goes on further to say, "Gideon, when he had once laid hold of the fact that he was called by the unseen God to deliver Israel, went on step by step to the great victory which made the tribes free."[18]

---

17 Blaiklock, E.M., <u>Todays' Handbook of Bible Characters</u>, Bethany House Publishing, Minneapolis, MN., 1979, p. 106
18 Ibid, p. 109

WORSHIP LEADER TYPE PROFILE
GIDEON

BACKGROUND

- **Political Conditions:**
  - Captivity by the Midianites was a constant threat.
  - Gideon is current judge of Israel.
- **Social Conditions:**
  - Israelites constantly hiding from and on defense against the Midianites.
- **Religious Conditions:**
  - Israelites turned against God.
  - God raises Gideon to rescue His people.

FACTORS IN THE EQUIPPING FOR THE TASK

The Person

Weakest tribe - Gideon was from the smallest/weakest tribe in Israel, where God would receive the most glory; Judges 6:15-16

> "'But Lord,' Gideon replied, 'how can I rescue Israel?
> My clan is the weakest in the whole tribe of Manasseh,
> and I am the least in my entire family!'"
> *Judges 6:15*

Power of Holy Spirit - God sent the power of His Holy Spirit upon Gideon; Judges 6:34

> "Then the Spirit of the Lord clothed Gideon with power. He blew a ram's horn as a call to arms, and the men of the clan of Abiezer came to him."
> *Judges 6:34*

GIDEON'S PERSONALITY

Prudent - Gideon sought confirmation from God before jumping into what he was being called to do; Judges 6:14-21, 36-40.

> "Gideon replied, 'If you are truly going to help me,
> show me a sign to prove that it is really the Lord speaking to me."
> *Judges 6:14*

Humble - Coming from the weakest tribe, Gideon easily knew and acknowledged his inability to complete God's call on his own; Judges 6:15

> "'But Lord,' Gideon replied, 'how can I rescue Israel? My clan is the weakest in the whole
> tribe of Manasseh, and I am the least in my entire family!'"
> *Judges 6:15*

Obedient - Gideon completely obeyed the Lord; Judges 6:20, 25-27, 7:3-6.

> "The angel of God said to him, 'Place the meat and the unleavened bread on this rock,
> and pour the broth over it.' And Gideon did as he was told."
> *Judges 6:20*

Leader - Gideon led with confidence and excellence; Judges 7:16-25, 8:11-17.

> "Then he said to them, 'Keep your eyes on me.
> When I come to the edge of the camp, do just as I do.'"
> *Judges 7:17*

GIDEON'S RELATIONSHIP WITH GOD

Feared the Lord - Gideon had a fear and reverence of the Lord; Judges 6:22

> "When Gideon realized that it was the angel of the Lord, he cried out,
> 'Oh, Sovereign Lord, I'm doomed! I have seen the angel of the Lord face to face!'"
> *Judges 6:22*

Trusted the Lord - Gideon trusted the Lord in battle and leading his army; Judges 7:2-8

> "Therefore, tell the people, 'Whoever is timid or afraid may leave this mountain
> and go home.' So, 22,000 of them went home, leaving only 10,000
> who were willing to fight. But the Lord told Gideon, 'There are still too many!
> Bring them down to the spring, and I will test them to determine
> who will go with you and who will not.'"
> *Judges 7:3-4*

THE REVELATION OF GOD THAT GIDEON HAD RECEIVED AND CARRIED TO THE PEOPLE OF GOD

Only true, living God; Judges 6:25-32

> "Then build an altar to the Lord your God here on this hilltop sanctuary, laying the stones carefully. Sacrifice the bull as a burnt offering on the altar, using as fuel the wood of the Asherah pole you cut down."
> *Judges 6:26*

God is warrior and the victor of our battles; Judges 7:2

> "The Lord said to Gideon, 'You have too many warriors with you. If I let all of You fight the Midianites, the Israelites will boast to Me that they saved themselves by their own strength."
> *Judges 7:2*

> "That night the Lord said, 'Get up! Go down into the Midianite camp, for I have given you victory over them!"
> *Judges 7:9*

Ruler; Judges 8:22-23

> "But Gideon replied, 'I will not rule over you, nor will my son. The Lord will rule over you!'"
> *Judges 8:23*

LESSONS LEARNED FROM THIS WORSHIP LEADER TYPE

God uses "the least of these" - Gideon, being from the weakest tribe in Israel, was intentional in showing how God uses the smallest and weakest to display the greatness of His glory; Judges 6:14-16

> "'But Lord,' Gideon replied, 'how can I rescue Israel? My clan is the weakest in the whole tribe of Manasseh, and I am the least in my entire family!' The Lord said to him, 'I will be with you. And you will destroy the Midianites as if you were fighting against one man.'"
> *Judges 6:15-16*

Ask the Lord for confirmation - Gideon sought confirmation that only the Lord could give when He spoke to him, it is a great practice when truly desiring to obey the Lord; Judges 6:17,36-40

> "Gideon replied, 'If You are truly going to help me,
> show me a sign to prove that it is really the Lord speaking to me."
> *Judges 6:17*

The Lord fights for us - God wanted it to be known that He was the victor of Israel's battles, just as He is the victor of all of our battles; Judges 7:2,7, 22.

> "The Lord told Gideon, 'With these 300 men I will rescue you
> and give you victory over the Midianites. Send all the others home.'"
> *Judges 7:7*

Be obedient - Obeyed everything the Lord told him to do; Judges 6:20,25-27, 7:3-6.

> "So, Gideon took ten of his servants and did as the Lord had commanded.
> But he did it at night because he was afraid of the other members of his
> father's household and the people of the town."
> *Judges 6:27*

EXAMPLE OF BEING A WORSHIPPER

Yahweh-Shalom, "The Lord is peace" - Gideon built an altar the day that God revealed Himself and called him; Judges 6:24

> "And Gideon built an altar to the Lord there and named it Yahweh-Shalom
> (which means "the Lord is peace"). The altar remains in Ophrah
> in the land of the clan of Abiezer to this day."
> *Judges 6:24*

Dream of victory - God gave Gideon a response and interpretation of Israel's victory in a dream. Judges 7:13-15

> "When Gideon heard the dream and its interpretation,
> he bowed in worship before the Lord. Then he returned to the Israelite camp and shouted,
> 'Get up! For the Lord has given you victory over the Midianite hordes!'"
> *Judges 7:15*

Prayer of confirmation - Gideon asked the Lord to confirm the instructions given to him; Judges 6:36-40

> "Then Gideon said to God, 'If You are truly going to use me to rescue Israel as
> You promised, prove it to me in this way. I will put a wool fleece on the threshing floor
> tonight. If the fleece is wet with dew in the morning but the ground is dry,
> then I will know that You are going to help me rescue Israel as You promised.'
> And that is just what happened. When Gideon got up early the next morning,
> he squeezed the fleece and wrung out a whole bowlful of water."
> *Judges 6:36-38*

GIDEON'S ABILITY TO HEAR AND RESPOND TO THE LORD

Initial call - Gideon asked the Lord to confirm; Judges 6:12-13

> "The angel of the Lord appeared to him and said, 'Mighty hero, the Lord is with you!' 'Sir,'
> Gideon replied, 'if the Lord is with us, why has all this happened to us?
> And where are all the miracles our ancestors told us about?
> Didn't they say, "The Lord brought us up out of Egypt"?
> But now the Lord has abandoned us and handed us over to the Midianites.'"
> *Judges 6:12-13*

Dialogue - God speaks, Gideon responds, Gideon speaks, God responds, Judges 6:12-17

> "Then the Lord turned to him and said, 'Go with the strength you have, and rescue Israel
> from the Midianites. I am sending you!' 'But Lord,' Gideon replied, 'how can I rescue Israel?
> My clan is the weakest in the whole tribe of Manasseh, and I am the least in my entire
> family!' The Lord said to him, 'I will be with you. And you will destroy the Midianites as if
> you were fighting against one man.'"
> *Judges 6:14-16*

Obedient - Obeyed everything the Lord told him to do; Judges 6:20,25-27, 7:3-6.

> "Therefore, tell the people, 'Whoever is timid or afraid
> may leave this mountain and go home.' So, 22,000 of them went home,
> leaving only 10,000 who were willing to fight."
> *Judges 7:3*

EXPLORING MUSICAL AND NON-MUSICAL BIBLE CHARACTERS

GIDEON'S FAITH/TRUST IN THE LORD

Trusted the Lord's confirmations - Gideon had faith in the Lord and His instructions; Judges 6:17-22, 36-40.

> "Then the angel of the Lord touched the meat and bread with the tip of the staff in his hand, and fire flamed up from the rock and consumed all he had brought. And the angel of the Lord disappeared. When Gideon realized that it was the angel of the Lord, he cried out, 'Oh, Sovereign Lord, I'm doomed! I have seen the angel of the Lord face to face!'"
> *Judges 6:21-22*

Trusted the Lord in shrinking his army - Gideon had faith in the Lord in leading his army of 300; Judges 7:2-8

> "The Lord told Gideon, 'With these 300 men I will rescue you and give you victory over the Midianites. Send all the others home.' So, Gideon collected the provisions and rams' horns of the other warriors and sent them home. But he kept the 300 men with him."
> *Judges 7:7-8*

CHAPTER 7
REVIEW QUESTIONS
Gideon

1. What were the political conditions during Gideon's time?

2. What were the social conditions during Gideon's time?

3. What were the religious conditions during Gideon's time?

4. Name some of Gideon's characteristics.

5. What are at least three lessons we can learn from Gideon?

6. What were some of the instructions God gave Gideon concerning his father's altars and idols, which Gideon carried out at night?

7. Why did God have Gideon reduce the army from 32,000 to 300 men?

8
David

David was a shepherd, unlikely hero, leader of rabble rousers, king, and psalmist. We know more about David that possibly any other Bible character. His story begins when he is a young shepherd for his father's flock. Depictions show him sitting on the hillside, strumming a harp-like instrument. He was a skilled musician, and it is thought he authored many of the Psalms.

Samuel, the prophet, was looking for a successor to King Saul, when he visited the house of Jesse, father of David and seven other boys. Seven of the boys, older than David, were brought out and examined. Samuel looked at each one and said, "Nope. Not among these young men. Is there anyone else?" Seemingly as an afterthought, David was called for consideration. Perhaps Samuel recognized an intelligence, a curiosity about life, and a sort of relentless energy. Maybe he looked into David's eyes and saw a future king. Whatever he thought, he proclaimed David as the chosen one and anointed him as the next king.

David went through a lot after being anointed to be the next king since King Saul was increasingly jealous and paranoid. David's skills were called upon to sing for a depressed and anguished King Saul. At one point, Saul tried to kill the future king. The King's son, Jonathan, formed a close friendship bond with David, which is a template for male friendships to this day.

David did not give in to the temptation to hurry along the will of God by assassinating Saul when he had several chances. He honed his leadership skills by assuming responsibility over a group of men who were in debt, in trouble, and unemployed. Eventually, he became king. Even then, David is portrayed as a hero, but flawed. He took another man's wife, Bathsheba, by putting her husband, a loyal soldier, in harm's way. Taking Bathsheba as his wife, he lost their first child, and took that death as punishment for his sin.

David was a great example of manhood. He was a leader, but he was also a poet, and he was not afraid to show his great love for God. He was a worshiper. He danced so mightily with joy that he danced right out of his clothes! He was a soldier who fought the giant Goliath before everyone else cowered in fear.

Worship Leader Type Profile

DAVID

BACKGROUND

- **Political Conditions:** this was a time when the nation of Israel reached its zenith of splendor. Under David, Israel became a true kingdom. This was a time that was looked upon as the golden age.
  - "Aided by the decline of Egyptian and Mesopotamian power, David expanded Israel's land by conquest and treaty until it reached from Syria to Egypt. The city of Jerusalem was captured from the Canaanites and made the capital of Israel. David's personality and brilliant leadership made him Israel's greatest king."[19]
- **Social Conditions:** Israel became a United Kingdom with less fear of invasion under the reign of David, so social conditions improved.
  - "Israel had similarities and differences as those of societies surrounding it at the time. The main setup was patriarchal, with an emphasis on family ties. But due to its tribal customs, it naturally tended to conflict with the monarchy and their efforts to centralize the economy."[20]
- **Religious Conditions:** When Jerusalem became the place where the Israelites could come together as a nation and worship, the result was a sense of national pride.

FACTORS IN THE EQUIPPING FOR THE TASK

David was a shepherd - David kept his father's flock as a boy, this role prepared him to shepherd the people of Israel; 1 Samuel 16:11, 17:15, 2 Samuel 5:2, 7:8.

> "Then Samuel asked, 'Are these all the sons you have?'
> 'There is still the youngest', Jesse replied. 'But he's out in the fields
> watching the sheep and goats."
> *1 Samuel 16:11*

---

[19] Great People of the Bible and How They Lived, The Reader's Digest Association, Pleasantville, NY., 1974, p.22
[20] www.library.loras.edu Northern Kingdom-Religious and Theological Studies, Loras College Library.

Anointed by God - David was anointed when called by God; 1 Samuel 16:12-13

"So, as David stood there among his brothers, Samuel took the flask of olive oil he had brought and anointed David with the oil. And the Spirit of the Lord came powerfully upon David from that day on. Then Samuel returned to Ramah."
1 Samuel 16:13

Anointed by the Spirit of God - Holy Spirit was with David since the day he was chosen and anointed by God; 1 Samuel 16:13, 2 Samuel 23:2

"The Spirit of the Lord speaks through me; His words are upon my tongue."
2 Samuel 23:2

A talented musician - David was known for his special talent in music, specifically on the harp; 1 Samuel 16:8, Amos 6:5

"One of the servants said to Saul, 'One of Jesse's sons from Bethlehem is a talented harp player. Not only that but he is also a brave warrior, a man of war, and has good judgment. He is also a fine-looking young man, and the Lord is with him.'"
1 Samuel 16:18

A man of war - David was a great warrior; 1 Samuel 16:18, 17:49-51, 18:5,13,27,30, 19:8, 23:5, 27:8-11, 30:17, 2 Samuel 5:2,6-7,20, 8:1-13, 10:17-19, 12:29, 17:8, 1 Chronicles 11:5,13-14, 14:11,16, 18:1-6, 19:17-18

"Every time the commanders of the Philistines attacked; David was more successful against them than all the rest of Saul's officers. So, David's name became very famous."
1 Samuel 18:30

DAVID'S PERSONALITY

Brave - David was very bold and very confident in the Lord; 1 Samuel 16:18, 17:32-36

"'Don't worry about this Philistine,' David told Saul.
'I'll go fight him!'"
1 Samuel 17:32

Wise - David was a man of wisdom; 1 Samuel 18:14

"And David behaved himself wisely in all his ways, and the Lord was with him."
1 Samuel 18:14

Humble - David exercised great humility, especially when working under Saul after already being anointed king; 1 Samuel 16:21, 18:5,18, 24:8, 2 Samuel 7:18-19, 1 Chronicles 17:16-17

> "So, David went to Saul and began serving him.
> Saul loved David very much,
> and David became his armor bearer."
> *1 Samuel 16:21*

Diligent - David was very hardworking and was responsible with every task he was given; 1 Samuel 17:15,20, 18:5.

> "But David went back and forth so he could help his
> father with the sheep in Bethlehem."
> *1 Samuel 17:15*

Obedient - David did everything with a servant's heart, submitting to every authority, but most importantly to God; 1 Samuel 17:20, 18:5, 22:5, 23:1-5, 30:8-10, 2 Samuel 5:19-20,23-25, 1 Chronicles 14:10-11,14-16.

> "Whatever Saul asked David to do, David did it successfully.
> So, Saul made him a commander over the men of war,
> an appointment that was welcomed by the people and
> Saul's officers alike."
> *1 Samuel 18:5*

Faithful - David was unwavering in all things, in spite of others and what they did; 1 Samuel 17:15, 19:9-10, 24:11,20-22, 26:17, 2 Samuel 1:11-12, 4:8-12, 9:6-7.

> "Saul recognized David' voice and called out,
> 'Is that you, my son David?'
> And David replied, 'Yes, my lord the king.'"
> *1 Samuel 26:17*

Righteous - David did right according to the word of the Lord; Psalm 26

> "Put me on trial, Lord, and cross-examine me.
> Test my motives and my heart. For I am always aware of Your unfailing love,
> and I have lived according to Your truth."
> *Psalm 26:2-3*

Repentant - David was repentant when confronted with his wrong-doing.

Bringing in the ark of the covenant - David first consulted his leaders and
the people rather than first consulting the Lord.
1 Chronicles 13:1-4

DAVID'S RELATIONSHIP WITH GOD

God was with David - David walked with God, and God remained with David; 1 Samuel 16:18, 17:45, 18:12, 2 Samuel 5:10, 7:9, 1 Chronicles 11:9

"David replied to the Philistine, 'You come to me with sword, spear,
and javelin, but I come to you in the name of the Lord of Heaven's Armies -
the God of the armies of Israel, whom you have defied.'"
1 Samuel 17:45

Feared the Lord - David had a proper fear of the Lord, an understanding of God's holiness and righteousness; 1 Samuel 24:5-6, 26:8-11,23, 2 Samuel 24:10, 1 Chronicles 21:8

"'No!' David said. 'Don't kill him. For who can remain innocent
after attacking the Lord's anointed one?'"
1 Samuel 26:9?

Depended on the Lord - David wholeheartedly looked to the Lord for all of his strength, protection, and needs; 1 Samuel 30:6, Psalm 3, 16, 18, 22-23, 25, 27-28, 31, 35, 40, 59, 140.

"David was now in great danger because all his men were very bitter about
losing their sons and daughters, and they began to talk of stoning him.
But David found strength in the Lord his God."
1 Samuel 30:6

Man after God's heart - God dearly loved David, kept him close to His heart because of his heart for/towards the Lord; Acts 13:22

"But God removed Saul and replaced him with David, a man about whom God said,
'I have found David son of Jesse, a man after My own heart.
He will do everything I want him to do.'"
Acts 13:22

WORSHIP LEADER TYPES

Warrior; 1 Samuel 17:45-47, 2 Samuel 5:23-25, 1 Chronicles 11:9, 14:10

> "And again, David asked the Lord what to do. 'Do not attack them straight on,' the Lord replied. 'Instead, circle around behind and attack them near the poplar trees.'"
> *2 Samuel 5:23*

LESSONS LEARNED FROM THIS WORSHIP LEADER TYPE

Remain humble in waiting on the Lord - David humbly served Saul even though he had already been anointed king of Israel; 1 Samuel 16:21, 18:5.

> "So, David went to Saul and began serving him. Saul loved David very much, and David became his armor bearer."
> *1 Samuel 16:21*

We can do nothing in our own strength, but in the strength of the Lord and His alone…
1 Samuel 17:46

> "Today the Lord will conquer you, and I will kill you and cut off your head. And then I will give the dead bodies of your men to the birds and wild animals, and the whole world will know that there is a God in Israel!"
> *1 Samuel 17:46*

With God, nothing is impossible - It was most unlikely that a young teenage boy could slaughter a giant, but through the strength and might of the Lord Almighty it was made possible; 1 Samuel 17:48-51

> "So, David triumphed over the Philistine with only a sling and a stone, for he had no sword. Then David ran over and pulled Goliath's sword from its sheath. David used it to kill him and cut off his head. When the Philistines saw that their champion was dead, they turned and ran."
> *1 Samuel 17:50-51*

When we are faithful, God elevates us - David was elevated because he served God faithfully; 1 Samuel 16:21, 18:5

> "Whatever Saul asked David to do, David did it successfully. So, Saul made him a commander over the men of war, an appointment that was welcomed by the people and Saul's officers alike."
> *1 Samuel 18:5*

Walking with the Lord will turn some against us - Saul turned against David because God was with him and elevated him above Saul; 1 Samuel 18:8-11, 29, 19:9-16.

> "And he suddenly hurled it at David, intending to pin him to the wall.
> But David escaped him twice."
> *1 Samuel 18:11*

Walking with the Lord causes all of our ways to succeed - Everything David did, he did it successfully, because God was with him; 1 Samuel 18:5, 14, 30, 30:17-20, 2 Samuel 5:10

> "David continued to succeed in everything he did, for the Lord was with him."
> *1 Samuel 18:14*

Walking with the Lord overrides any evil plans plotted against us - Saul tried to kill David, but God used Saul's plan to bless David; 1 Samuel 18:23-27

> "When Saul's men reported this back to the king, he told them,
> 'Tell David that all I want for the bride price is 100 Philistine foreskins! Vengeance on my
> enemies is all I really want.' But what Saul had in mind was that
> David would be killed in the fight. David was delighted to accept the offer.
> Before the time limit expired, he and his men went out and killed 200 Philistines.
> Then David fulfilled the king's requirement by presenting all their foreskins to him.
> So, Saul gave his daughter Michal to David to be his wife."
> *1 Samuel 18:24-27*

When you are unsure, ask God - Whenever David questioned something, he inquired of the Lord; 1 Samuel 23:1-4

> "But David's men said, 'We're afraid even here in Judah.
> We certainly don't want to go to Keilah to fight the whole Philistine army!'
> So, David asked the Lord again, and again the Lord replied, 'Go down to Keilah,
> for I will help you conquer the Philistines.'"
> *1 Samuel 23:3-4*

Wait on the Lord - David learned not to take matters into his own hands, he waited on the Lord; 1 Samuel 24:3-17, 26:8-21, 2 Samuel 5:4, Psalm 37

> "Be still in the presence of the Lord and wait patiently for Him to act.
> Don't worry about evil people who prosper or fret about their wicked schemes."
> *Psalm 37:7*

Repay evil with goodness/righteousness - David didn't retaliate for Saul's actions, and his kindness was acknowledged; 1 Samuel 24:17-19

> "And he said to David, 'You are a better man than I am,
> for you have repaid me good for evil. Yes, you have been amazingly kind to me today,
> for when the Lord put me in a place where you could have killed me, you didn't do it.
> Who else would let his enemy get away when he had him in his power?
> May the Lord reward you well for the kindness you have shown me today."
> *1 Samuel 24:17-19*

Celebrate before the Lord - David was unashamed before the Lord and danced with great joy before Him.; 2 Samuel 6:5,14, 21-22.

> "David and all the people of Israel were celebrating before the Lord,
> singing songs and playing all kinds of musical instruments -
> lyres, harps, tambourines, castanets, and cymbals."
> *2 Samuel 6:5*

God sees all - God saw David's obedience as well as his sin; 2 Samuel 12:9

> "Why, then, have you despised the word of the Lord and done this horrible deed?
> For you have murdered Uriah the Hittite with the sword of the
> Ammonites and stolen his wife."
> *2 Samuel 12:9*

God does forgive; however, sin has consequences - David was forgiven, but as a result of his sin, his son died and allowed strife in his household; 2 Samuel 12:9-18, 24:10-15.

> "Then David confessed to Nathan, 'I have sinned against the Lord.'
> Nathan replied, 'Yes, but the Lord has forgiven you, and you won't die for this sin.
> Nevertheless, because you have shown utter contempt for the
> word of the Lord by doing this, your child will die.'"
> *2 Samuel 12:13-14*

Fasting - *demonstrating dire need/strong desire from the Lord through sacrifice/abstinence;* 2 Samuel 12:15-17, 22

> "After Nathan returned to his home, the Lord sent a deadly
> illness to the child of David and Uriah's wife. David begged God to spare the child.
> He went without food and lay all night on the bare ground."
> *2 Samuel 12:15-16*

Newborn children/infants who die go to be with the Lord - David knew and acknowledged that the child was in heaven and that he would join him there someday; 2 Samuel 12:23

> "But why should I fast when he is dead? Can I bring him back again?
> I will go to him one day, but he cannot return to me."
> *1 Samuel 12:23*

Pray about everything - David literally prayed about everything, from simple questions about where to live, to seeking God to save his life from his enemies; 1 Samuel 23:1-4,9-12, 30:8, 2 Samuel 2:1, 5:19,23-25,31, 7:18-29, 21:1, 24:25, 1 Chronicles 14:10,14-15, 17:1627, 29:10-18, Psalm 2-9, 11-32, 34-41, 51-65, 68-70, 86, 95, 101, 103, 108-110, 122, 124, 131, 133, 138-145

> "After this, David asked the Lord, 'Should I move back to one of the towns of Judah?' 'Yes,' the
> Lord replied. Then David asked, 'Which town should I go to?' 'To Hebron,' the Lord answered."
> *2 Samuel 2:1*

God desires transparency - David was very emotionally honest with the Lord and genuine in his prayers. He knew that He could go to God with everything; Psalm 13, 69, 139, 143.

> "Come quickly, Lord, and answer me, for my depression deepens.
> Don't turn away from me, or I will die."
> *Psalm 143:7*

Forgiveness and a pure heart before God bring joy - Joy came when David confessed his sin and experienced the unfailing and unlimited forgiveness of God; Psalm 32

> "Oh, what joy for those whose disobedience is forgiven, whose sin is put out of sight!
> Yes, what joy for those whose record the Lord has cleared of guilt,
> whose lives are lived in complete honesty!"
> *Psalm 32:1-2*

Hated the enemies of God - David was against all who were against the Lord; 1 Samuel 17:34-36, Psalm 139:19-22

> "Yes, I hate them with total hatred, for Your enemies are my enemies."
> *Psalm 139:22*

Feared the Lord - David had such a fear of the Lord that either kept him from sin or immediately convicted him of sin; 1 Samuel 24:5-6, 26:8-11, 23, 2 Samuel 24:10

> "The Lord gives His own reward for doing good and for being loyal, and I refused to kill you
> even when the Lord placed you in my power, for you are the Lord's anointed one."
> *1 Samuel 26:23*

Fought for the people - David fought against the Philistines in order to protect and save people out of their hands; 1 Samuel 17:50-52, 23:5.

> "Then David ran over and pulled Goliath's sword from its sheath. David used it to kill him and cut off his head. When the Philistines saw that their champion was dead, they turned and ran. Then the men of Israel and Judah gave a great shout of triumph and rushed after the Philistines, chasing them as far as Gath and the gates of Ekron. The bodies of the dead and wounded Philistines were strewn all along the road from Shaaraim, as far as Gath and Ekron."
> *1 Samuel 17:51-52*

Loved Saul - Despite Saul's multiple attempts to kill David, David still loved and greatly respected him, even continuing to serve him until he was forced out of the city; 1 Samuel 19:9-10, 24:11, 20-22, 26:17, 2 Samuel 1:11-12

> "Look, my father, at what I have in my hand.
> It is a piece of the hem of your robe! I cut it off, but I didn't kill you.
> This proves that I am not trying to harm you and that I have not sinned against you,
> even though you have been hunting for me to kill me."
> *1 Samuel 24:11*

Mourned for Saul and Jonathan - David mourned greatly for the deaths of Saul and his friend Jonathan, as well as the devastating defeat of Israel by the Amalekites; 2 Samuel 1:11-12

> "David and his men tore their clothes in sorrow when they heard the news.
> They mourned and wept and fasted all day Saul and his son Jonathan,
> and for the Lord's army and the nation of Israel,
> because they had died by the sword that day."
> *2 Samuel 1:11-12*

Sought healing for the land - When the Lord sent the three-day plague on Israel because of David's sin, David went before the Lord praying that He would relieve them; 2 Samuel 24:17-19, 25, 1 Chronicles 21:17-19, 26

> "When David saw the angel, he said to the Lord,
> 'I am the one who has sinned and done wrong!
> But these people are innocent as sheep - what have they done?
> Let Your anger fall against me and my family.'"
> *2 Samuel 24:17*

Ruled justly and righteously - David ruled the people in righteous and godly justice; 1 Chronicles 18:14

> "So, David reigned over all Israel and did what was
> just and right for all his people."
> *1 Chronicles 18:14*

Zeal for the Lord
In his zeal for the Lord, David had no tolerance for blasphemy or defiance against God- David had no tolerance for or patience with blasphemy against the Lord, hence the fate of Goliath; 1 Samuel 17:34-37,45-46.

> "I have done this to both lions and bears, and
> I'll do it to this pagan Philistine,
> too, for he has defied the armies of the living God!"
> *1 Samuel 17:36*

Burned pagan gods - David destroyed the gods of the Philistines; 1 Chronicles 14:12

> "The Philistines abandoned their gods there,
> so David gave orders to burn them."
> *1 Chronicles 14:12*

Openly sought to follow God's Word - David was determined to live according to the Word of God and constantly asked for better understanding; Psalm 19:7-11, 119

> "I will study Your commandments and reflect on Your ways.
> I will delight in Your decrees and not forget Your word."
> *Psalm 119:15-16*

EXAMPLE OF BEING A PRAISER AND WORSHIPPER

Magnified God for victory - David gave the glory to the Lord for his victories; 2 Samuel 5:20, 1 Chronicles 14:11

> "So, David went to Baal-perazim and defeated the Philistines there.
> 'The Lord did it!' David exclaimed. 'He burst through my enemies like a raging flood!'
> So, he named that place Baal-perazim (which means "the Lord who bursts through")."
> *2 Samuel 5:20*

Return of the Ark - David praised the Lord in bringing the Ark of the Covenant back to Jerusalem; 2 Samuel 6:3-5,12-15,21-22, 1 Chronicles 13:8

> "David and all Israel were celebrating before God with all their might,
> singing songs and playing all kinds of musical instruments -
> lyres, harps, tambourines, cymbals, and trumpets."
> *1 Chronicles 13:8*

Prayer of praise - When God blessed David and his kingdom, he praised God; 2 Samuel 7:22-24, 1 Chronicles 29:10-18

> "How great You are, O Sovereign Lord! There is no one like You.
> We have never even heard of another God like You!"
> *2 Samuel 7:22*

Songs of praise; 2 Samuel 22, 1 Chronicles 16:7-36, Psalm 9:1-12, 95, 103, 144-145

> "Let all that I am praise the Lord; with my whole heart,
> I will praise His holy name. Let all that I am praise the Lord;
> may I never forget the good things He does for me."
> *Psalm 103:1-2*

Worshipper of the Lord while returning the Ark - David worshipped the Lord while returning the Ark of the Covenant from Obed-edom's home; 2 Samuel 6:12-17

> "After the men who were carrying the Ark of the Lord had gone six steps,
> David sacrificed a bull and a fattened calf. And David danced before
> the Lord with all his might, wearing a priestly garment."
> *2 Samuel 6:13-14*

Dedicated all of his gifts from victories to the Lord - All the gifts David received from his victories, he dedicated to the Lord; 2 Samuel 8:9-12, 1 Chronicles 18:11

> "King David dedicated all these gifts to the Lord,
> along with the silver and gold he had taken from the other nations -
> from Edom, Moab, Ammon, Philistia, and Amalek."
> *1 Chronicles 18:11*

Worshiped despite his circumstances - David worshiped the Lord after his first son with Bathsheba died; 2 Samuel 12:19-20

> "Then David got up from the ground, washed himself, put on lotions, and changed his clothes. He went to the Tabernacle and worshiped the Lord. After that, he returned to the palace and was served food and ate."
> *2 Samuel 12:20*

Organized the Levites in ministry of music - He organized the musicians in the Temple, assigned "worship leaders;" 1 Chronicles 15:16-24, 16:4-6, 37-42.

> "David appointed the following Levites to lead the people in worship before the Ark of the Lord - to invoke His blessings, to give thanks, and to praise the Lord, the God of Israel."
> *1 Chronicles 16:4*

God answers prayer - David praised God for answering his prayer of sparing and relieving the people; 1 Chronicles 21:26-28

> "When David saw that the Lord had answered his prayer, he offered sacrifices there at Araunah's threshing floor."
> *1 Chronicles 21:28*

Sang songs of worship - David regularly sang songs of praise to the Lord; Psalm 8

> "O Lord, our Lord, Your majestic name fills the earth!
> Your glory is higher than the heavens."
> *Psalm 8:1, 9*

David was a man of prayer. He sought the Lord for guidance often. - David often sought the Lord for guidance and direction; 1 Samuel 23:1-4, 30:8, 2 Samuel 2:1, 5:19, 23, 1 Chronicles 14:10

> "Then David asked the Lord, 'Should I chase after this band of raiders?
> Will I catch them?' And the Lord told him, 'Yes, go after them.
> You will surely recover everything that was taken from you!'"
> *1 Samuel 30:8*

David cried out in times of trouble - David immediately turned to God when he was in trouble or needed help; 1 Samuel 23:9-12, 2 Samuel 15:31, Psalm 55, 57, 59, 70, 141.

> "But I will call on God, and the Lord will rescue me. Morning, noon,
> and night I cry out in my distress, and the Lord hears my voice."
> *Psalm 55:16-17*

David's prayers were genuine, authentic, and simple - David's prayers were very simple, not always super long or elaborate - conversational; 1 Samuel 23:10-12, 2 Samuel 2:1, 5:19,23-25, 21:1, 1 Chronicles 14:10,14-15, Psalm 69

> "Again, David asked, 'Will the leaders of Keilah betray me and my men to Saul?'
> And the Lord replied, 'Yes, they will betray you.'"
> *1 Samuel 23:12*

Offered prayers of praise and thanksgiving - David offered prayers of praise and thanksgiving to the Lord; 2 Samuel 7:18-29, 1 Chronicles 17:16-27, 29:10-18.

> "O our God, we thank You and praise Your glorious name!"
> *1 Chronicles 29:13*

Offered prayers of intercession - David prayed for the people when the Lord sent the three-day plague as a result of David's sin; 2 Samuel 24:25

> "David built an altar there to the Lord and sacrificed burnt
> offerings and peace offerings. And the Lord answered his prayer for the land,
> and the plague on Israel was stopped."
> *2 Samuel 24:25*

David was a doer of the Word
David lived according to the Word of God; Psalm 17:4, 18:21-22, 119.

> "I have followed Your commands, which keep me from following cruel and evil people."
> *Psalm 17:4*

David was a songwriter
Funeral song for Saul and Jonathan - David wrote a song for Saul and Jonathan when they died; 2 Samuel 1:17-27

> "Then David composed a funeral song for Saul and Jonathan,
> and he commanded that it be taught to the people of Judah. It is known as
> The Song of the Bow, and it is recorded in The Book of Jashar."
> *2 Samuel 1:17-18*

Funeral song for Abner - David wrote a song for Abner when he was killed; 2 Samuel 3:33-34

> "Then the king sang this funeral song for Abner:
> 'Should Abner have died as fools die?
> Your hands were not bound; your feet were not chained.
> No, you were murdered - the victim of a wicked plot.'
> All the people wept again for Abner."
> *2 Samuel 3:33-34*

Praise song - David wrote this song of praise to God for delivering him from all of his enemies; 2 Samuel 22 (Psalm 18)

> "David sang this song to the Lord on the day the Lord rescued him from all his enemies
> and from Saul. He sang: 'The Lord is my Rock, my Fortress, and my Savior;
> my God is my Rock, in whom I find protection. He is my Shield,
> the power that saves me, and my place of safety. He is my Refuge,
> my Savior, the one who saves me from violence."
> *2 Samuel 22:1-3*

David wrote man of the Psalms, songs of praise, sorrow, repentance, and need; Psalm 2-9, 11-32, 34-41, 51-65, 68-70, 86, 95, 101, 103, 108-110, 122, 124, 131, 133, 138-145

> "But you, O Lord, are a shield around me; you are my glory,
> the one who holds my head high. I cried out to the Lord,
> and He answered me from His holy mountain."
> *Psalm 3:3-4*

DAVID'S ABILITY TO HEAR AND RESPOND TO THE LORD

Sought and waited for God's voice - David went to the Lord for everything, he waited on the voice of God; 1 Samuel 23:1-4, 30:8, 2 Samuel 5:19, 23-24

> "Then David asked the Lord, 'Should I chase after this band of raiders?
> Will I catch them?' And the Lord told him, 'Yes, go after them.
> You will surely recover everything that was taken from you!'"
> *1 Samuel 30:8*

Conversational/dialogue prayer - David's prayer life was very conversational; he spoke, and he listened, God spoke, and he responded, 1 Samuel 23:10-12, 2 Samuel 2:1, 5:19, 21:1, 1 Chronicles 14:10,14-15

> "There was a famine during David's reign that lasted for three years,
> so David asked the Lord about it.
> And the Lord said, 'The famine has come because
> Saul and his family are guilty of murdering the Gibeonites.'"
> *2 Samuel 21:1*

Obedience - David obeyed when God spoke and gave him instructions; 1 Samuel 22:5, 23:4-5, 30:8-10, 2 Samuel 5:19-20,23-25, 1 Chronicles 14:10-11,14-16, 21:17-19.

> "One day the prophet Gad told David,
> 'Leave the stronghold and return to the land of Judah.'
> So, David went to the forest of Hereth."
> *1 Samuel 22:5*

PRESENTER/REPRESENTATIVE OF THE LORD

Shepherd - David was a shepherd to the people of Israel, just as Christ is a shepherd for His people; 2 Samuel 5:2, 1 Chronicles 11:2

> "In the past, when Saul was our king, you were the one who really led the forces of Israel.
> And the Lord told you, 'You will be the shepherd of My people Israel.
> You will be Israel's leader.'"
> *2 Samuel 5:2*

Loved and mourned for his enemies - David had a very compassionate heart, even toward his enemies, just as Christ loved His enemies and commands us to do as well; 2 Samuel 1:11-12, 18:5, 32-33, 19:2-4.

> "And the king gave this command to Joab, Abishai, and Ittai: 'For my sake, deal gently with young Absalom.' And all the troops heard the king give this order to his commanders."
> *2 Samuel 18:5*

REVELATIONS GIVEN TO DAVID FROM THE LORD

God is a rescuer; 1 Samuel 17:47, Psalm 20:6, 30, 54

> "I will exalt You, Lord, for You rescued me. You refused to let my enemies triumph over me."
> *Psalm 30:1*

God is a protector; 1 Samuel 18:11-12, 19:10-12, 20-24, 23:14, 26-29, 25:29

> "David now stayed in the strongholds of the wilderness and in the hill country of Ziph. Saul hunted him day after day, but God didn't let Saul find him."
> *1 Samuel 23:14*

God is an avenger; 1 Samuel 25:39, 26:9, 2 Samuel 16:12

> "When David heard that Nabal was dead, he said, 'Praise the Lord, who has avenged the insult I received from Nabal and has kept me from doing it myself. Nabal has received the punishment for his sin.' Then David sent messengers to Abigail to ask her to become his wife."
> *1 Samuel 25:39*

God is just and righteous; 2 Samuel 12:7-18, Psalm 7

> "God is my shield, saving those whose hearts are true and right.
> God is an honest judge. He is angry with the wicked every day."
> *Psalm 7:10-11*

David's kingdom would remain; 2 Samuel 7:16

> "Your house and your kingdom will continue before Me for all time,
> and your throne will be secure forever."
> *2 Samuel 7:16*

God is merciful; 2 Samuel 12:13, 24

> "Then David confessed to Nathan, 'I have sinned against the Lord.'
> Nathan replied, 'Yes, but the Lord has forgiven you, and you won't die for this sin."
> *2 Samuel 12:13*

God is powerful; Psalm 29

> "The voice of the Lord is powerful; the voice of the Lord is majestic. The voice of the Lord splits the mighty cedars; the Lord shatters the cedars of Lebanon."
> *Psalm 29:4-5*

God is faithful and true; Psalm 33

> "For the word of the Lord holds true, and we can trust everything He does. He loves whatever is just and good; the unfailing love of the Lord fills the earth."
> *Psalm 33:4-5*

Names for God

Jehovah Raah - The Lord our Shepherd, Psalm 23:1

Adonai - Adona is a Hebrew word that translates as "Lord" or "Lord maker", 1 Samuel 24:8

El Elyon - God Most High, Psalm 57:2

Tsuri V'goali - Rock and Redeemer, Psalm 19:12-14

El Sali-Gdo's - meaning "God my hiding place" Psalm 32:7, Psalm 91:1-8

Yahweh Avienu - God our Father, 1 Chronicles 29:10-20

Yahweh Oseinu - God our Maker, Psalm 95

DAVID'S FAITH/TRUST IN THE LORD

Believed God would protect him from Goliath - David had full and complete confidence that he would live; 1 Samuel 17:37

> "The Lord who rescued me from the claws of the lion and the bear will rescue me from this Philistine!' Saul finally consented. 'All right, go ahead,' he said. 'And may the Lord be with you!'"
> *1 Samuel 17:37*

Full confidence that Goliath would fall - David fully believed that Goliath would be defeated that day, regardless of his size or history of war; 1 Samuel 17:34-37,45-47.

> "I have done this to both lions and bears, and I'll do it to this pagan Philistine, too, for he has defied the armies of the living God!'"
> *1 Samuel 17:36*

Obedience - David exercised faith in God by obeying Him; 1 Samuel 17:20, 18:5, 22:5, 23:1-5, 30:8-10, 2 Samuel 5:19-20, 23-25, 1 Chronicles 14:10-11,14-16, 21:17-19, 26.

> "Then the angel of the Lord told Gad to instruct David to go up and build an altar to the Lord on the threshing floor of Araunah the Jebusite. So, David went up to do what the Lord had commanded him through Gad."
> *1 Chronicles 21:18-19*

Obedient despite fear or the circumstance - David obeyed through fear or when things looked unfavorable; 1 Samuel 22:5, 23:1-5.

> "But David's men said, 'We're afraid even here in Judah. We certainly don't want to go to Keilah to fight the whole Philistine army!' So, David asked the Lord again, and again the Lord replied, 'Go down to Keilah, for I will help you conquer the Philistines.' So, David and his men went to Keilah. They slaughtered the Philistines and took all their livestock and rescued the people of Keilah."
> *1 Samuel 23:3-5*

CHAPTER 8
REVIEW QUESTIONS
David

1. Describe David while concentrating on his roles. (Hint: shepherd, king)

2. Describe David's character traits.

3. Briefly describe three things you learned from David that you can use as a worship leader.

4. Why didn't David kill Saul when he had the chance?

5. Give three or more examples of David worshiping.

6. Which songs did David write according to references in this book?

7. Why did David send Bathsheba's husband to the front line of battle?

8. What were the consequences of this sin? Which Psalm is written as a result of this sin?

9. Which Psalm was written as a result of this sin?

10. Why did David want to build a "house for the Lord"?

11. Who was allowed to build the temple?

12. What is the main difference between the tabernacle and the temple?

9
Elijah

Elijah is one of the great figures of the Old Testament. He even appears in places in the New Testament. He appeared on the Mount of Transfiguration with Christ. Elijah "came like the lightning, ruthless, powerful; attributes the Israelites imagined appropriate in their Messiah."[21]

According to the books of Kings in the Hebrew Bible, Elijah was a prophet and a miracle worker who lived in the northern kingdom of Israel during the reign of King Ahab. Elijah performed many miracles and started a "school of the prophets." He bravely confronted Ahab for his acquiescence to the worship of Baal. Then, for fear of his life, he fled to the brook of Cherith, where ravens came and fed him for a while. After that divine provision ceased, he went to hide out with a widow in Zarephath. Because of the drought that Elijah prophesied, she had very little food, so Elijah prayed and her little store of flour and oil kept replenishing.

When Ahab confronted Elijah, he denounced him as being the "troubler of Israel," but Elijah took notice of his hypocrisy and told Ahab that he was the one who troubled Israel by allowing the worship of false gods. *"You and your family are the troublemakers, for you have refused to obey the commands of the LORD and have worshiped the images of Baal instead. Now summon all Israel to join me at Mount Carmel, along with the 450 prophets of Baal and the 400 prophets of Asherah who are supported by Jezebel."* (1 Kings 18: 18)

Elijah berated both the people of Israel and Ahab for their compromise and acquiescence in Baal worship. "How long will you go limping with two different opinions? If the Lord is God, follow him; but if Baal, then follow him." And the people were silent. 1 Kings 18:21 "And he urges them to say, "Let's have no wavering." Don't go on limping along or wavering between two opinions. Interestingly enough, the word that he uses here for limping or wavering is the same word used to describe the little shuffle

---

21   Blaiklock, E.M., Today's Handbook of Bible Characters, Bethany House Publishers, p. 209)

dance that the prophets of Baal will do later when they go around the altar calling upon Baal for hours on end. So, he's basically telling the people of God, 'Are you gonna act like those goofy prophets of Baal, shuffling along in their shuffle dance? Or are you going to worship Yahweh, the true God?'" [https://sharonrpc.org/1-kings-181746]

Elijah is known for his showdown with all the prophets of Baal, in which he challenged them to a duel. Two oxen were provided for sacrifice, one for Baal and one for Elijah's God. The prophets of Baal cried out for fire to come and consume their sacrifice, with wild dancing and chanting. Of course, nothing happened. So, Elijah stepped up and, mocking them, and then he made a moat around the sacrifice and filled it with water. Then he called out for the God of Abraham, Isaac, and Jacob to burn up the sacrifice, and fire came from heaven and consumed his sacrifice.

Elijah, the rugged, powerful prophet, serves as a forerunner to John the Baptist. He was a fearless, bold reformer, a man who rebuked kings, a mighty intercessor divinely honored by God. He was always ready to obey and trust God.

WORSHIP LEADER TYPE PROFILE

ELIJAH

BACKGROUND

- **Political Conditions:**
  - The kingdom of Judah faced its greatest crisis in history. Jezebel led the royal court to abandon itself to Phoenician ways.
  - Ahab - Ahaziah is now king of Israel.
- **Social Conditions:**
  - "King Ahab advertised the prosperity of his reign with elaborate building projects. However, the country's small farmers and laborers had only a marginal share in this prosperity. In Israel, as in the southern kingdoms, before Jehoshaphat's reforms, the gains of conquest and trade were enjoyed almost exclusively by the upper classes."[22]
  - Drought and famine.
- **Religious Conditions:**
  - Ahab led the Israelites into sin against God in the worship of Baal and Asherah poles.

---

22 <u>Great People of the Bible and How They Lived</u>, Reader's Digest Association Inc., Pleasantville, NY.1974, p. 198

FACTORS IN THE EQUIPPING FOR THE TASK

Intimate relationship with the Lord - Elijah truly knew the Lord and could hear Him clearly, He knew the Lord; therefore God was able to use him; 1 Kings 17, Matthew 17:3, Mark 9:4, Luke 9:30

> "Now Elijah, the Tishbite, from Tishbe in Gilead, said to Ahab,
> 'As the Lord, the God of Israel lives, whom I serve, there will be neither dew nor rain in the
> next few years except at my word'"
> *1 Kings 17:1*

ELIJAH'S PERSONALITY

Obedient - Elijah faithfully obeyed God and everything He instructed him to do; 1 Kings 17:2-5,8-10, 18:1-2, 19:15-19, 21:17-20.

> "Later on, in the third year of the drought, the Lord said to Elijah, 'Go and present yourself
> to King Ahab. Tell him that I will soon send rain!' So, Elijah went to appear before Ahab.
> Meanwhile, the famine had become very severe in Samaria."
> *1 Kings 18:1-2*

Confident in the Lord - Elijah was more confident in the Lord that He could do anything, and therefore spoke and preached in that confidence; 1 Kings 17:1, 19-21, 18:13-15, 23-24, 30-37.

> "Now bring two bulls. The prophets of Baal may choose whichever one they wish and cut
> it into pieces and lay it on the wood of their altar, but without setting fire to it.
> I will prepare the other bull and lay it on the wood on the altar, but not set fire to it.
> Then call on the name of your god, and I will call on the name of the Lord.
> The god who answers by setting fire to the wood is the true God!'
> And all the people agreed."
> *1 Kings 18:23-24*

ELIJAH'S RELATIONSHIP WITH GOD

Very intimate - God loved Elijah, and Elijah knew the heart and voice of God; 1 Kings 17:1, 2 Kings 1:9-12. It was quite an honor for Moses and Elijah, long deceased, to travel through time and be seen with Jesus; Matthew 17:3, Mark 9:4, Luke 9:30.

> "Then Elijah cried out to the Lord, 'O Lord my God, why have
> You brought tragedy to this widow who has opened her home to me,
> causing her son to die?'"
> *1 Kings 17:20*

THE REVELATION OF GOD THAT ELIJAH RECEIVED AND CARRIED TO THE PEOPLE OF GOD

Elijah told King Ahab about the drought and famine coming; 1 Kings 17:1

> "Now Elijah, who was from Tishbe in Gilead, told King Ahab,
> 'As surely as the Lord lives, the God of Israel,
> lives the God I serve there will be no dew or rain during
> the next few years until I give the word!'"
> *1 Kings 17:1*

Blessing the widow - Elijah blessed the widow's home so that she and her son would not run out of food during the famine; 1 Kings 17:14

> "For this is what the Lord, the God of Israel, says: There will always be
> flour and olive oil left in the containers until the time when
> the Lord sends rain and the crops grow again!"
> *1 Kings 17:14*

God is the one and only true, living God - Elijah made it known before all of the people of Israel through the test on Mount Carmel that God is the only true God; 1 Kings 18:36-39

> "And when all the people saw it,
> they fell face down on the ground and cried out,
> 'The Lord He is God! Yes, the Lord is God!'"
> *1 Kings 18:38*

Rain - Elijah told King Ahab about rain returning to the land; 1 Kings 18:41

> "Then Elijah said to Ahab, 'Go get something
> to eat and drink, for I hear a mighty rainstorm coming!'"
> *1 Kings 18:41*

Sin will be judged - Elijah gave the king's messengers the Lord's message concerning the judgment for the sins of him and his wife; 1 Kings 21:21-24

> "So now the Lord says, 'I will bring disaster on you and consume you.
> I will destroy every one of your male descendants, slave and free alike, anywhere in Israel!'"
> *1 Kings 21:21*

Ahaziah will die - Elijah was sent to tell Ahaziah that he would die; 2 Kings 1:3-4,16.

> "Now, therefore, this is what the Lord says: You will never leave the bed you are lying on;
> you will surely die.' So, Elijah went to deliver the message."
> *Kings 1:4*

LESSONS LEARNED FROM THIS WORSHIP LEADER TYPE

Trust God, He loves us and takes complete care of us - God took complete care of Elijah; he didn't have to worry about where his food or protection was coming from; 1 Kings 17:3-6, 9, 11-16.

> "The ravens brought him bread and meat each morning and evening,
> and he drank from the brook."
> *1 Kings 17:6*

Obey with courage - Elijah obeyed God, even though it may have potentially cost him his life. He didn't let anyone discourage him from obeying God's instructions; 1 Kings 18:13-15

> "Has no one told you, my lord, about the time when Jezebel was trying to kill the Lord's prophets? I hid 100 of them in two caves and supplied them with food and water. And now you say, 'Go and tell your master, 'Elijah is here.'
> 'Sir, if I do that, Ahab will certainly kill me.' But Elijah said, 'I swear by the Lord Almighty,
> in whose presence I stand, that I will present myself to Ahab this very day.'"
> *1 Kings 18:13-15*

Sometimes, we will have to stand alone - Elijah had to stand, even though he was greatly outnumbered; 1 Kings 18:22, Romans 11:3

> "Then Elijah said to them, 'I am the only prophet of the Lord who is left,
> but Baal has 450 prophets."
> *1 Kings 18:22*

Love for the Lord
Faithfully served the Lord - Elijah faithfully served and obeyed the Lord; 1 Kings 19:10,14

> "Elijah replied, 'I have zealously served the Lord God Almighty. But the people of Israel
> have broken their covenant with You, torn down Your altars,
> and killed every one of Your prophets. I am the only one left,
> and now they are trying to kill me, too.'"
> *1 Kings 19:10*

Love for God's people
Widow's son - Elijah cried out for the widow's son for the Lord to revive and heal him; 1 Kings 17:20-21

> "And he stretched himself out over the child three
> times and cried out to the Lord, 'O Lord my God,
> please let this child's life return to him.'"
> *1 Kings 17:21*

Strongly desired the people of Israel to turn wholeheartedly to the Lord - Elijah urged the people to choose the Lord, not these false gods they had come to worship; 1 Kings 18:21

> "Then Elijah stood in front of them and said, 'How much longer will you waver,
> hobbling between two opinions? If the Lord is God,
> follow Him! But if Baal is God, follow him!'
> But the people were completely silent."
> *1 Kings 18:21*

Zeal for the Lord
Slaughter of the prophets of Baal - After the test between the prophets on Mount Carmel, Elijah had all of Baal's prophets killed; 1 Kings 18:40

> "Then Elijah commanded, 'Seize all the prophets of Baal.
> Don't let a single one escape!' So, the people seized them all,
> and Elijah took them down to the Kishon Valley
> and killed them there."
> *1 Kings 18:40*

Examples of Prayer

Intercession - Elijah interceded for the life of the widow's son; 1 Kings 17:20-21

> "And he stretched himself out over the child
> three times and cried out to the Lord, 'O Lord my God,
> please let this child's life return to him.'"
> *1 Kings 17:21*

Rain - Elijah prayed for the rain to both cease and return and the Lord answered him; 1 Kings 18:41-44, James 5:17-18

> "Elijah was as human as we are, and yet when he prayed earnestly
> that no rain would fall, none fell for three and a half years!
> Then, when he prayed again,
> the sky sent down rain and the earth began to yield its crops."
> *James 5:17-18*

Prayer of fear and insecurity - Elijah prayed to the Lord, desiring to give up out of fear and his time seeming to come to an end; 1 Kings 19:4

> "Then he went on alone into the wilderness, traveling all day.
> He sat down under a solitary broom tree and prayed that he might die.
> 'I have had enough, Lord,' he said. 'Take my life, for I am no better than
> my ancestors who have already died.'"
> *1 Kings 19:4*

ELIJAH'S ABILITY TO HEAR AND RESPOND TO THE LORD

Obedience - Elijah's response of obedience to the Lord is evidence of him hearing the Lord clearly; 1 Kings 17:4-6, 9-11, 18:1-2, 19:15-19, 21:17-20

> "'Go and live in the village of Zarephath, near the city of Sidon.
> I have instructed a widow there to feed you.'
> So, he went to Zarephath. As he arrived at the gates of the village,
> he saw a widow gathering sticks, and he asked her,
> 'Would you please bring me a little water in a cup?'"
> *1 Kings 17:9-10*

WORSHIP LEADER TYPES

Dialogue - Elijah had a conversational prayer life with the Lord; 1 Kings 19:10-17

> "He replied again, 'I have zealously served the Lord God Almighty.
> But the people of Israel have broken
> their covenant with You, torn down Your altars,
> and killed every one of Your prophets.
> I am the only one left,
> and now they are trying to kill me, too.'"
> *1 Kings 19:14*

PRESENTER/REPRESENTATIVE OF THE LORD

Performed the miracles of God - Elijah performed different miracles; 1 Kings 17:12-23

> "The Lord heard Elijah's prayer,
> and the life of the child returned, and he revived!"
> *1 Kings 17:22*

God's mouthpiece - Elijah said everything that God said; 1 Kings 17:1,14-16,24, 18:41, 21:21-24, 2 Kings 1:3-4,16, 2 Chronicles 21:12-15

> "For this is what the Lord, the God of Israel,
> says: There will always be flour and
> olive oil left in your containers until the time
> when the Lord sends rain
> and the crops grow again!"
> *1 Kings 17:14*

REVELATIONS GIVEN TO ELIJAH FROM THE LORD

God is our provider; 1 Kings 17:4-6,11-16

> "So, Elijah did as the Lord told him and camped beside Kerith Brook,
> east of the Jordan. The ravens brought him bread and
> meat each morning and evening,
> and he drank from the brook."
> *1 Kings 17:5-6*

God is our protector; 2 Kings 1:9-12

> "But Elijah replied to the captain, 'If I am a man of God,
> let fire come down from heaven and
> destroy you and your fifty men!'
> Then fire fell from heaven and killed them all."
> *2 Kings 1:10*

FAITH/TRUST IN THE LORD

Obedient - Elijah trusted the Lord, therefore he was obedient to everything the Lord told him to do; 1 Kings 17:4-6, 9-11, 18:1-2, 19:15-19, 21:17-20.

> "Later on, in the third year of the drought, the Lord said to Elijah,
> 'Go and present yourself to King Ahab. Tell him that I will soon send rain!' So,
> Elijah went to appear before Ahab. Meanwhile,
> the famine had become very severe in Samaria."
> *1 Kings 18:1-2*

Obeyed with courage - Elijah obeyed God, even though it may have potentially cost him his life; 1 Kings 18:13-15

> "Has no one told you, my lord, about the time when Jezebel
> was trying to kill the Lord's prophets? I hid 100 of them in two caves
> and supplied them with food and water. And now you say,
> 'Go and tell your master, "Elijah is here." Sir, if I do that, Ahab will certainly kill me.'
> But Elijah said, 'I swear by the Lord Almighty,
> in whose presence I stand, that I will present myself to Ahab this very day.'"
> *1 Kings 18:13-15*

CHAPTER 9
REVIEW QUESTIONS
Elijah

1. What were the political conditions during Elijah's day?

2. What were the social conditions during Elijah's day?

3. What were the religious conditions during Elijah's day?

4. Name some factors in the equipping of Elijah for the task at hand.

5. What were the three miracles Elijah performed?

6. Describe the significance of the worship event between Elijah and the prophets of Baal.

10

Asa

Asa was, according to the Hebrew Bible, the third king of the Kingdom of Judah and the fifth king of the House of David. The Hebrew Bible gives the period of his reign as forty-one years. His reign is dated between 913-910 BC to 873-869 BC. He was succeeded by Jehoshaphat, his son. According to Thiele's chronology,[23] when Asa became very ill, he made Jehoshaphat co-regent. Asa died two years into the co-regency.

Asa was zealous in maintaining the traditional worship of YHWH, and in rooting out idolatry, with its accompanying immoralities. Abijam, a wise man and prophet exhorted Asa, to reinforce strict national observance of the law. Asa did what was right in the eyes of the Lord, "as did David, his father." (David was not really his father, but his highly esteemed ancestor.) Asa's father and predecessor was Abijah. King Asa removed all the idols his father, Abijah had made, and even removed his mother, Maachah, as queen, because she had made an idol in a grove. When the transition from Asherah worship to worship of YHWH took place, after Asa's 15th year of reigning, a great feast was held at Solomon's Temple.

Taking advantage of the thirty-five years of peace, Asa revamped and reinforced the fortress cities built by his grandfather Rehoboam. During this time, Asa's men defeated the Egyptian backed invader, the Ethiopian Zerah.

Asa obtained an alliance with the King of Syria by giving away the gold and silver treasures of the house of the Lord. For this grievous sin, Hanani the seer rebuked Asa. In his latter years, Asa developed a severe illness of his feet, (probably gout) and he named his son, Jehoshaphat as co-regent. He died two years later.

---

23 Thiele, Edwin, <u>The Mysterious Numbers of the Hebrew Kings</u>, 1965, (3rd edition) Eerdmans

WORSHIP LEADER TYPE PROFILE

ASA

BACKGROUND

- **Political Conditions:**
  - Judah and Israel are now split into two kingdoms. The first decades after the division provided a severe test of Judah's ability to survive. Attacked several times by Israel and Egypt, the country's leaders neglected domestic problems and as a result social and religious conditions gradually deteriorated.
- **Social Conditions:**
  - The gap between rich and poor grew wider than ever, and the erosion of religious principles continued almost unchecked. The moral authority of Judaism was restored, however, with the rise of King Asa and his son, Jehoshaphat.
  - Ten years of peace. They defeated the Egyptian invaders.
- **Religious Conditions:**
  - The downturn of morality finally was stopped when Asa became king. Asa led the people to faithfully serve God. He condemned the worship of Asherah and restored temple worship.

FACTORS IN THE EQUIPPING FOR THE TASK

He was the King; 1 Kings 15:9, 2 Chronicles 14:1

> "Asa began to rule over Judah in the twentieth year
> of Jeroboam's reign in Israel."
> *1 Kings 15:9*

God-given rest in the land; 2 Chronicles 14:1, 6-7

> "During those peaceful years, he was able to build up the fortified towns throughout
> Judah. No one tried to make war against him at this time,
> for the Lord was giving him rest from his enemies."
> *2 Chronicles 14:6*

ASA'S PERSONALITY

Asa was righteous - Asa followed after David's example in living a life pleasing to the Lord; 1 Kings 15:11, 2 Chronicles 14:2-5

> "Asa did what was pleasing and good in the sight of the Lord his God."
> 2 Chronicles 14:2

Asa was faithful - Asa remained faithful to the Lord; 1 Kings 15:14, 2 Chronicles 15:17

> "Although the pagan shrines were not removed from Israel, Asa's heart remained completely faithful throughout his life."
> 2 Chronicles 15:17

ASA'S RELATIONSHIP WITH GOD

Asa loved the Lord - Asa was very passionate for the Lord; 2 Chronicles 14:2-5

> "He removed the foreign altars and the pagan shrines. He smashed the sacred pillars and cut down the Asherah poles."
> 2 Chronicles 14:3

THE REVELATION OF GOD ASA RECEIVED AND CARRIED TO THE PEOPLE OF GOD

Serve God and God alone - God is the Lord and Him alone; 1 Kings 15:12, 2 Chronicles 14:3, 5, 15:8.

> "Asa also removed the pagan shrines, as well as the incense altars from every one of Judah's towns. So, Asa's kingdom enjoyed a period of peace."
> 2 Chronicles 14:5

Warrior - God is a warrior and fights against those who try to stand against Him; 2 Chronicles 14:8-15

> "So, the Lord defeated the Ethiopians in the presence of Asa and the army of Judah, and the enemy fled."
> 2 Chronicles 14:12

LESSONS LEARNED FROM THIS WORSHIP LEADER TYPE

Rely fully and completely on God. - God is to be our everything; Depend on Him at all times; 2 Chronicles 14:11-12

> "Then Asa cried out to the Lord his God, 'O Lord,
> no one but you can help the powerless against the mighty!
> Help us, O Lord our God, for we trust in you alone.
> It is in your name that we have come against this vast horde.
> O Lord, you are our God; do not let mere men prevail against you!'"
> *2 Chronicles 14:11*

God is to be reverently worshiped from the heart - God is seeking fervent and diligent worship from the heart; 2 Chronicles 15:12-15

> "Then they entered into a covenant to seek the Lord,
> the God of their ancestors, with all their heart and soul."
> *2 Chronicles 15:12*

Don't forget God - Asa forgot God and put his trust in man, therefore he ended up defeated in the end; 2 Chronicles 16:1-3,7-9.

> "At that time Hanani the seer came to King Asa and told him, 'Because you have put your trust in the king of Aram instead of in the Lord your God, you missed your chance to destroy the army of the king of Aram."
> *2 Chronicles 16:7*

Asa destroyed idolatry and pagan worship in the land; 1 Kings 15:12, 2 Chronicles 14:3,5, 15:8.

> "He removed the foreign altars and the pagan shrines.
> He smashed the sacred pillars and cut down the Asherah poles."
> *2 Chronicles 14:3*

Asa led all of the people to faithfully seek and serve God; 2 Chronicles 14:4

> "He commanded the people of Judah to seek the Lord,
> the God of their ancestors, and to obey his law and his commands."
> *2 Chronicles 14:4*

Destroyed idolatry and pagan worship in the land; 1 Kings 15:12, 2 Chronicles 14:3,5, 15:8.

> "When Asa heard this message from Azariah the prophet, he took courage and removed all the detestable idols from the land of Judah and Benjamin and in the towns he had captured in the hill country of Ephraim. And he repaired the altar of the Lord, which stood in front of the entry room of the Lord's Temple."
> *2 Chronicles 15:8*

Decreed that ALL were to worship the Lord - Asa made it so that all who did not worship the Lord would be put to death; 2 Chronicles 15:13

> "They agreed that anyone who refused to seek the Lord, the God of Israel, would be put to death - whether young or old, man or woman."
> *2 Chronicles 15:13*

Removed his grandmother from queenship - Asa removed his own grandmother from her queenship because she practiced worshipping other gods; 1 Kings 15:13, 2 Chronicles 15:16

> "King Asa even deposed his grandmother Maacah from her position as queen mother because she had made an obscene Asherah pole. He cut down her obscene pole, broke it up, and burned it in the Kidron Valley."
> *2 Chronicles 15:16*

EXAMPLE OF BEING A WORSHIPPER

Very passionate - Asa led the people alongside himself in true, passionate worship of God; 2 Chronicles 15:9-15

> "They shouted their oath of loyalty to the Lord with trumpets blaring and rams' horns sounding."
> *2 Chronicles 15:14*

Man of Prayer
Cried out to God in time of need - Asa went before the Lord when his kingdom faced war; 2 Chronicles 14:11

> "Then Asa cried out to the Lord his God, 'O Lord, no one but you can help the powerless against the mighty! Help us, O Lord our God, for we trust in you alone. It is in your name that we have come against this vast horde. O Lord, you are our God; do not let mere men prevail against you!'"
> *2 Chronicles 14:11*

Doer of the Word
Destroyed idolatry and pagan worship in the land; 1 Kings 15:12, 2 Chronicles 14:3, 5, 15:8.

> "He banished the male and female shrine prostitutes from the land and got rid of all the idols his ancestors had made."
> *1 Kings 15:12*

ASA'S ABILITY TO HEAR AND RESPOND TO THE LORD

Obedience - Asa responded to the voice of the Lord in obedience; 2 Chronicles 15:8

> "When Asa heard this message from Azariah the prophet, he took courage and removed all the detestable idols from the land of Judah and Benjamin and in the towns he had captured in the hill country of Ephraim. And he repaired the altar of the Lord, which stood in front of the entry room of the Lord's Temple."
> *2 Chronicles 15:8*

PRESENTER/REPRESENTATIVE OF THE LORD

Violent love - God loves us with a passionate and violent love. He fights for us and is jealous for us, King Asa also loved God with a violent love, so much so that anyone who did not fervently seek the Lord was to be put to death; 2 Chronicles 15:11-16

> "They agreed that anyone who refused to seek the Lord, the God of Israel, would be put to death whether young or old, man or woman."
> *2 Chronicles 15:13*

REVELATIONS GIVEN TO ASA FROM THE LORD

Seek the Lord, and you will find him; 2 Chronicles 15:1-4

> "And he went out to meet King Asa as he was returning from the battle. 'Listen to me, Asa!' he shouted. 'Listen, all you people of Judah and Benjamin! The Lord will stay with you as long as you stay with him! Whenever you seek him, you will find him. But if you abandon him, he will abandon you."
> *2 Chronicles 15:2*

God will reward good and faithful deeds done unto Him; 2 Chronicles 15:7

> "But as for you, be strong and courageous,
> for your work will be rewarded."
> *2 Chronicles 15:7*

We are to put our trust in God alone. It is only with and through Him that we are victorious or successful; 2 Chronicles 16:7-9

> "At that time Hanani the seer came to King Asa and told him, 'Because you have put your trust in the king of Aram instead of in the Lord your God, you missed your chance to destroy the army of the king of Aram.'"
> *2 Chronicles 16:7*

ASA'S FAITH/TRUST IN THE LORD

Relied on God for victory - Asa trusted God's faithfulness and mighty arm to save and protect them; 2 Chronicles 14:11

> "Then Asa cried out to the Lord his God, 'O Lord, no one but you can help the powerless against the mighty! Help us, O Lord our God, for we trust in you alone. It is in your name that we have come against this vast horde. O Lord, you are our God; do not let mere men prevail against you!'"
> *2 Chronicles 14:11*

Put his trust in man - Asa forgot God and turned to other kings to save him from his enemies; 1 Kings 15:18-19, 2 Chronicles 16:1-3

> "Let there be a treaty between you and me like the one
> between your father and my father. See, I am sending you silver and gold.
> Break your treaty with King Baasha of Israel so that he will leave me alone."
> *2 Chronicles 16:3*

CHAPTER 10
REVIEW QUESTIONS
Asa

1. What were the political conditions of Asa's time?

2. What were the social conditions?

3. What were the religious conditions?

4. What were the characteristics of Asa that assisted him in his tasks?

5. What can we learn from this Asa as a worship leader?

6. What were Asa's reforms?

7. Why did the prophet, Hanani, rebuke Asa?

11

Jehoshaphat

Jehoshaphat, also called Josaphat, Hebrew Yehoshaphat, was king (c. 873–c. 849 bc) of Judah during the reigns in Israel of Ahab, Ahaziah, and Jehoram, with whom he maintained close political and economic alliances. Jehoshaphat was 35 years old when he became king of Judah and he reigned for 25 years.[24]

His claim to fame is probably when he, Jehoshaphat, went to visit the king of Israel, the other half of the kingdom that was divided after king Solomon's reign, and the King of Israel asked, *"Will you go with me to fight against Ramoth Gilead?" Jehoshaphat replied to the king of Israel, "I am as you are, my people as your people, my horses as your horses." (1 Kings 22:4)* So, according to a covenant in which you declare that whatever I have is yours, they joined forces. The funny thing about this story follows. Jehoshaphat asked the king of Israel if there was anyone, a prophet for example, whom they might consult as to the mind of God. The king of Israel said, "There is still one prophet through whom we can inquire of the Lord, but I hate him because he never prophesies anything good about me, but always bad. He is Micaiah son of Imlah."

"The king should not say such a thing." Jehoshaphat replied.

So, the two kings sat side by side on their royal thrones, and the prophets came before them to say their piece and when Micaiah started to speak, the king of Israel said, "See what I told you? He never prophesies anything good about me, but only bad."

The incident that stands out in the context of worship leading is when Jehoshaphat appointed men to sing to the Lord and praise Him "for the splendor of His holiness" as they went out at the head of the army. They sang this song:

> "Give thanks to the Lord,
> For His love endures forever."

---

24 Britannica, The Editors of Encyclopedia. "Jehoshaphat" Encyclopedia Britannica, 23 Jul. 2010, https://www.britannica.com/biography/Jehoshaphat. Accessed 4 July 2021.

As a result of this tactic, the armies that were coming for the Israelites fought with each other and were completely destroyed so God Himself averted the battle, seemingly. So, it pays to worship, even when it seems an inappropriate response to the crisis at hand!

Jehoshaphat was succeeded by his son Jeroboam.

WORSHIP LEADER TYPE PROFILE

JEHOSHAPHAT

BACKGROUND

- **Political Conditions:**
  - Israel has divided into two kingdoms: Israel and Judah
  - Jehoshaphat is king, following another faithful king, his father, Asa.
- **Social Conditions:**
  - The kingdom of Judah enjoyed a great measure of peace and prosperity even though the armies of the Moanbites, Ammonites and some of the Meunites declared war on Jehoshophat. According to 2 Chronicles, YAHWEH annihilated this Gentile coalition.
- **Religious Conditions:**
  - Judah faithfully follows the Lord.

FACTORS IN THE EQUIPPING FOR THE TASK

Jehoshophat was King; 1 Kings 15:24, 22:41-42, 2 Chronicles 17:1

> "Then Jehoshaphat, Asa's son, became the next king.
> He strengthened Judah to stand against any attack from Israel."
> *2 Chronicles 17:1*

Jehoshophat was blessed - God was with Jehoshaphat, and greatly blessed him; 2 Chronicles 17:3, 5, 10.

> "The Lord was with Jehoshaphat because he followed the example of his
> father's early years and did not worship the images of Baal."
> *2 Chronicles 17:3*

Jehoshophat was wealthy - Jehoshaphat accumulated much wealth during his kingship; 2 Chronicles 17:5,11-12, 18:1.

> "So, the Lord established Jehoshaphat's control over the kingdom of Judah.
> All the people of Judah brought gifts to Jehoshaphat,
> so he became very wealthy and highly esteemed."
> *2 Chronicles 17:5*

JEHOSHAPHAT'S PERSONALITY

Wise - Jehoshaphat was wise to follow the godly example of his father, not his ungodly ways; 2 Chronicles 17:3

> "The Lord was with Jehoshaphat because he followed the example of his father's early
> years and did not worship the images of Baal."
> *2 Chronicles 17:3*

Righteous - Jehoshaphat lived to please the Lord; 1 Kings 22:43, 2 Chronicles 17:3-4, 18:4, 20:32

> "Jehoshaphat was a good king, following the ways of his father, Asa.
> He did what was pleasing in the Lord's sight."
> *2 Chronicles 20:32*

Discerning - Jehoshaphat knew the voice of the Lord in the midst of lies; 1 Kings 22:6-7, 2 Chronicles 18:4-6

> "But Jehoshaphat asked, 'Is there not also a prophet of the Lord here?
> We should ask him the same question.'"
> *2 Chronicles 18:6*

JEHOSHAPHAT'S RELATIONSHIP WITH GOD

Loved the Lord - Jehoshaphat sought after God, His Word, and His ways; 2 Chronicles 17:4, 19:3.

> "He sought his father's God and obeyed His commands instead of following the evil
> practices of the kingdom of Israel."
> *2 Chronicles 17:4*

Committed to the Lord - He removed pagan worship in Judah; 1 Kings 22:46, 2 Chronicles 17:6

> "He was deeply committed to the ways of the Lord.
> He removed the pagan shrines and Asherah poles from Judah."
> 2 Chronicles 17:6

THE REVELATIONS OF GOD THAT JEHOSHAPHAT RECEIVED AND CARRIED TO THE PEOPLE OF GOD

God hears - When Jehoshaphat stood to pray before Judah, and also led everyone to fast and pray, he was showing the people that God does hear His people; 2 Chronicles 20:5-12

> "They said, 'Whenever we are faced with any calamity such as war, plague, or famine, we can come to stand in your presence before this Temple where your name is honored. We can cry out to you to save us, and you will hear us and rescue us.'"
> 2 Chronicles 20:9

God is mighty to save - Jehoshaphat knew and acknowledged the power and might of God and shared that with the people of Judah during his prayer; 2 Chronicles 20:12

> "O our God, won't You stop them? We are powerless against this mighty army that is about to attack us. We do not know what to do, but we are looking to You for help."
> 2 Chronicles 20:12

LESSONS LEARNED FROM THIS WORSHIP LEADER TYPE

Do not join yourself with haters of God - We must be careful with whom we choose to join ourselves to and build relationships with. God will oppose those who oppose Him and if we are not careful, we will be guilty along with them; 1 Kings 22:8, 17-23, 2 Chronicles 18:1,7, 19:2, 20:35-37

> "Then Eliezer son of Dodavahu from Mareshah prophesied against Jehoshaphat. He said, 'Because you have allied yourself with King Ahaziah, the Lord will destroy your work.' So, the ships met with disaster and never put out to sea."
> 2 Chronicles 20:37

Know and heed God's voice, regardless of others - Jehoshaphat knew that the prophets that King Ahab called on were not speaking from the Lord, and therefore called for a true prophet - We are to know God's voice, when He is speaking and when He is not; 1 Kings 22:6-7, 2 Chronicles 18:5-6,16-22,31-32

> "So, the king of Israel summoned the prophets, 400 of them, and asked them, 'Should we go to war against Ramoth-gilead, or should I hold back?' They all replied, 'Yes, go right ahead! God will give the king victory.' But Jehoshaphat asked, 'Is there not also a prophet of the Lord here? We should ask him the same question.'"
> *2 Chronicles 18:5-6*

Trust God, and God alone - When Jehoshaphat saw that he and his people were in trouble, he went straight to God, knowing and acknowledging that God was their only hope - We need to realize, know, and actively acknowledge that God is our only hope, our everything; 2 Chronicles 20:1-4

> "Jehoshaphat was terrified by this news and begged the Lord for guidance. He also ordered everyone in Judah to begin fasting."
> *2 Chronicles 20:3*

Worship before the battle is won - When God spoke through Jehaziel of Judah's victory in battle, Jehoshaphat's immediate response was bowing before the Lord and worshiping Him - before the battle was won; 2 Chronicles 20:18

> "Then King Jehoshaphat bowed low with his face to the ground. And all the people of Judah and Jerusalem did the same, worshiping the Lord."
> *2 Chronicles 20:18*

Worship and praise to God are our warfare - God is the one who fights our battles; our responsibility is to praise and worship Him through it all; 2 Chronicles 20:21-24

> "At the very moment they began to sing and give praise, the Lord caused the armies of Ammon, Moab, and Mount Seir to start fighting among themselves."
> *2 Chronicles 20:22*

Love for the Lord

Removed pagan worship - Jehoshaphat worshiped the Lord and only the Lord; 1 Kings 22:46, 2 Chronicles 17:6

> "He was deeply committed to the ways of the Lord. He removed the pagan shrines and Asherah poles from Judah."
> *2 Chronicles 17:6*

Sought the Lord in decision making - Jehoshaphat went to the Lord in making his decisions; 1 Kings 22:5, 2 Chronicles 18:4

> "Then Jehoshaphat added, 'But first let's find out what the Lord says.'"
> *2 Chronicles 18:4*

Love for His people
Led and encouraged them to seek and return to God - Jehoshaphat led the people to continue seeking God with all of their hearts; 2 Chronicles 19:4-7

> "Jehoshaphat lived in Jerusalem, but he went out among the people, traveling from Beersheba to the hill country of Ephraim, encouraging the people to return to the Lord, the God of their ancestors."
> *2 Chronicles 19:4*

Love of God's Word
Taught the Word throughout the kingdom - Jehoshaphat appointed several officials and Levites to go out throughout the kingdom of Judah and teach the Word of God; 2 Chronicles 17:7-9

> "They took copies of the Book of the Law of the Lord and traveled around through all the towns of Judah, teaching the people."
> *2 Chronicles 17:9*

EXAMPLE OF BEING A PRAISER AND WORSHIPPER

Praised God after their victory - Jehoshaphat praised God, along with the people of Judah, on their way back from a victorious battle; 2 Chronicles 20:27-28

> "They marched into Jerusalem to the music of harps, lyres, and trumpets, and they proceeded to the Temple of the Lord."
> *2 Chronicles 20:28*

Worshipper
Removed pagan worship - Jehoshaphat worshiped God and God alone; 1 Kings 22:46, 2 Chronicles 17:6

> "He was deeply committed to the ways of the Lord. He removed the pagan shrines and Asherah poles from Judah."
> *2 Chronicles 17:6*

Response to the word of victory - When God spoke through Jehaziel of Judah's victory in battle, Jehoshaphat's immediate response was bowing before the Lord and worshiping Him before the battle was won; 2 Chronicles 20:18

> "Then King Jehoshaphat bowed low with his face to the ground. And all the people of
> Judah and Jerusalem did the same, worshiping the Lord."
> *2 Chronicles 20:18*

Man of Prayer
Called out to God in time of need - Jehoshaphat ran to God when he was in need or in trouble; 1 Kings 22:32-33, 2 Chronicles 18:31-32, 20:1-12

> "So, when the Aramean chariot commanders saw Jehoshaphat in his royal robes,
> they went after him. 'There is the king of Israel!' they shouted.
> But Jehoshaphat called out, and the Lord saved him.
> God helped him by turning the attackers away from him."
> *2 Chronicles 18:31*

Doer of the Word
Removed pagan worship - Jehoshaphat got rid of pagan shrines and Asherah poles in the land; 1 Kings 22:46, 2 Chronicles 17:6

> "He was deeply committed to the ways of the Lord.
> He removed the pagan shrines and Asherah poles from Judah."
> *2 Chronicles 17:6*

JEHOSHAPHAT'S ABILITY TO HEAR AND RESPOND TO THE LORD

Knew God's voice - Jehoshaphat knew the voice of the Lord and therefore sought the Lord for guidance; 1 Kings 22:5, 2 Chronicles 18:4

> "Then Jehoshaphat added, 'But first let's find out what the Lord says.'"
> *2 Chronicles 18:4*

REVELATIONS GIVEN TO JEHOSHAPHAT FROM THE LORD

Protector - God repeatedly protected Jehoshaphat and his people, especially during battle; 1 Kings 22:32-33, 2 Chronicles 18:31-32, 19:1.

> "When King Jehoshaphat of Judah arrived safely home in Jerusalem,"
> 2 Chronicles 19:1

Warrior - God fought the battle against the Arameans for Judah; 2 Chronicles 20:22-24, 29-30.

> "When all the surrounding kingdoms heard that the Lord Himself had fought against the enemies of Israel, the fear of God came over them."
> 2 Chronicles 20:29

JEHOSHAPHAT'S FAITH/TRUST IN THE LORD

Cried out to God for every fear, concern, and worry - Jehoshaphat called out to God constantly, knowing that God would answer and save him; 2 Chronicles 18:31-32, 20:1-12.

> "O our God, won't You stop them? We are powerless against this mighty army that is about to attack us. We do not know what to do, but we are looking to You for help."
> 2 Chronicles 20:12

Believed God's word - Jehoshaphat went out to war against the Arameans believing and trusting God at His word that He would give him the victory; 2 Chronicles 20:20

> "Early the next morning the army of Judah went out into the wilderness of Tekoa. On the way Jehoshaphat stopped and said, 'Listen to me, all you people of Judah and Jerusalem! Believe in the Lord your God, and you will be able to stand firm. Believe in His prophets, and you will succeed.'"
> 2 Chronicles 20:20

CHAPTER 11
REVIEW QUESTIONS
Jehoshaphat

1. What were the political, social and religious conditions of Jehoshaphat's time?

2. What were the factors in the equipping for the task for Jehoshaphat?

3. What were the characteristics of his personality?

4. What can we learn from the story of Jehoshaphat?

5. In his worship leader role, what did Jehoshapat do when he learned that a "vast enemy army was approaching?"

6. What did God say in answer to Jehoshaphat's prayer?

7. In his worship leadership of the people, What did Jehoshaphat do when he learned that "a vast enemy was approaching?"

8. What did God say in answer to Jehoshaphat's prayer?

9. What strategy did God give to Jehoshaphat that led to a victory?

*Rest assured that God delights
to show everyone who searches for Him,
who He is when they seek Him
with all their hearts.*

12

Joash/Jehoash

Joash, or Jehoash interchangeably, was crowned as king when he was seven years old, and he ruled for forty years. 2 Kings 12 tells us Jehoash's mother was Zibiah from Beersheba. His grandmother, Athaliah, ordered the massacre of the royal family after her son, Ahaziah the king, died from an accident. Jehoash was the sole survivor, saved and whisked away to be hidden in the Temple for years.

"According to the Hebrew Bible, following the death of his father, Ahaziah, Jehoash was spared from the rampages of Ahaziah's mother, Athaliah, by Jehoash's paternal aunt, Jehosheba, who was married to the high priest, Jehoiada. After hiding him in the Temple for seven years, Jehoiada had Jehoash crowned and anointed as the true king in a *coup d'état* against Athaliah, who had usurped the Throne of David. Athaliah was killed during the coup." [25]

What an awful thing to live with! Your own grandmother wipes out your family to gain power, and then after your aunt hides you away for seven years, and after your evil grandmother is killed and a coup takes place, it's your turn to be king! Talk about trauma!

According to the account in 2 Kings 12, Jehoash "did what was right in the eyes of the Lord as long as he listened to the priest Jehoiada." Another translation says, "Jehoash did what was pleasing in the Lord's sight throughout the lifetime of Jehoiada the priest." This indicates that King Jehoash did not have a particularly intimate walk with God, nor was he particularly a righteous man on his own. Still, he heeded what his advisor Jehoiada told him. He did what was right because the priest instructed him.

After being hidden for seven years, and after his grandmother Athaliah, the queen, was slain by the prophet Jehoiada, King Jehoash was anointed to rule Judah. The reign of Jehoash brought material prosperity to Judah and the influence of Baal worship declined.

---

25 Sperling, S.D., Encyclopedia Judaica, Joash, second edition, vol. 11, p. 343

But when Jehoiada died, Jehoash lapsed into idolatry, encouraged a revival of Canaanite worship, and erected a number of pagan religious shrines.

During his reign, King Jehoash oversaw the restoration of the temple, which was financed by taxing the people.

> "Then a proclamation was sent throughout Judah and Jerusalem,
> telling the people to bring to the Lord the tax that Moses, the servant of God,
> had required of the Israelites in the wilderness."
> *2 Chronicles 24:9*

The work on the temple progressed until King Hazael of Syria marched on Jerusalem. Then King Joash surrendered all the remaining gold from the treasuries, which had been meant for the continuing repair of the temple and forestalled an attack by giving it all to King Hazael. According to the account in 2 Chronicles, the Syrian army 'destroyed all the leaders of the people from among the people and sent all their spoil to the king of Damascus'.

2 Chronicles 24, narrates how Jehoash's son-in-law, the prophet Zechariah, Jehoiada's son and successor, rebuked him for forsaking God, which resulted in Jehoash ordering his execution by stoning.

Zechariah's last words as he died were, "May the Lord see what they are doing and avenge my death." Later, the Aramean army invaded Judah and Jerusalem and killed all the leaders.

WORSHIP LEADER TYPE PROFILE

JOASH/JEHOASH

BACKGROUND

- **Political Conditions:**
  - The kingdoms of Israel and Judah have split.
  - Jehoash is the king of Judah.
- **Social Conditions:**
  - The reign of Jehoash brought material prosperity to Judah and the influence of Baal worship declined.
- **Religious Conditions:**
  - The people were wavering in their walk with the Lord.

FACTORS IN EQUIPPING FOR THE TASK

JOASH/JEHOASH'S PERSONALITY

Joash was unfaithful - In that he had no genuine relationship with the Lord. ; 2 Kings 12:2-3, 2 Chronicles 24:2,17-18.

> "But after Jehoiada's death, the leaders of Judah came and bowed before King Jehoash and persuaded him to listen to their advice. They decided to abandon the Temple of the Lord, the God of their ancestors, and they worshiped Asherah poles and idols instead! Because of this sin, divine anger fell on Judah and Jerusalem."
> *2 Chronicles 24:17-18*

JOASH/JEHOASH'S RELATIONSHIP WITH GOD

Impersonal - Joash's relationship with the Lord and his own lack of integrity depended on someone else's integrity. 2 Kings 12:2, 2 Chronicles 24:2.

> "All his life Joash did what was pleasing in the Lord's sight because Jehoiada the priest instructed him."
> *2 Kings 12:2*

LESSONS LEARNED FROM THIS WORSHIP LEADER TYPE

Have a personal relationship with God – Joash/Jehoash did not have or maintain a personal relationship with the Lord, which led to his downfall; 2 Kings 12:2, 2 Chronicles 24:2.

> "Jehoash did what was pleasing in the Lord's sight throughout the lifetime of Jehoiada the priest."
> *2 Chronicles 24:2*

Don't listen to everyone – Only listen to those who will give you godly counsel.

> "After the death of Jehoiada, the officials of Judah came and paid homage to the king, and he listened to them. They abandoned the temple of the Lord, the God of their ancestors, and worshiped Asherah poles and idols. Because of their guilt, God's anger came on Judah and Jerusalem."
> *2 Chronicles 24:17-18*

EXAMPLE OF BEING A WORSHIPPER

Joash did what was right in the eyes of the Lord - He oversaw the restoration of the Temple; 2 Chronicles 24:4-5, 13-14.

> "At one point Joash decided to repair and restore the Temple of the Lord."
> *2 Chronicles 24:4*

Doer of the Word - Joash followed the law of Moses by collecting taxes for the Temple; 2 Chronicles 24:8-9.

> "Then a proclamation was sent throughout Judah and Jerusalem, telling the people to bring to the Lord the tax that Moses, the servant of God, had required of the Israelites in the wilderness."
> *2 Chronicles 24:9*

Portrayed God as an avenger; 2 Chronicles 24:21-26

> "That was how King Jehoash repaid Jehoiada for his loyalty - by killing his son. Zechariah's last words as he died were, 'May the Lord see what they are doing and avenge my death!' In the spring of the year the Aramean army marched against Joash. They invaded Judah and Jerusalem and killed all the leaders of the nation. Then they sent all the plunder back to their king in Damascus."
> *2 Chronicles 24:22-23*

JOASH/JEHOASH'S FAITH AND TRUST IN THE LORD

He was not completely faithful - Faith depended on someone else; 2 Kings 12:2-3, 2 Chronicles 24:2, 17-18.

> "All his life Jehoash did what was pleasing in the Lord's sight because Jehoiada the priest instructed him. Yet even so, he did not destroy the pagan shrines, and the people still offered sacrifices and burned incense there."
> *2 Kings 12:2-3*

CHAPTER 12
REVIEW QUESTIONS
Joash/Jehoash

1. How old was Joash/Jehoash when he became king? What does this speak to you about God?

2. What was the significant event that happened when Joash/Jehoash was a baby?

3. Who was King Joash/Jehoash's closest advisor?

4. What was the significant work Joash/Jehoash accomplished?

5. How was this financed?

6. How did Joash/Jehoash die?

7. What can we learn from Joash/Jehoash's life?

God gave a beautiful promise through the prophet Jeremiah when He said, "You will seek me and find me when you seek me with all your heart."
—Jeremiah 29: 13

13

Hezekiah

"Hezekiah was twenty-five years of age when he came to Judah's throne, and his reign of almost thirty years was one of the finest of all Jerusalem's Kings. Under King Ahab, the land had gone astray. The old, strong, stern religion, which has ennobled Jewish life, had decayed before those exotic cults, which demanded less in clean and upright living but instead made rituals of carnality and vice. It is part of an evil bent in man to welcome release from discipline."[26]

For the most part, King Hezekiah faithfully walked with God (2 Chronicles 31:20), and *"there was no one like him among all the kings of Judah, either before him or after him"* (2 Kings 18:5). He was compared to King David in 2 Kings 18:3. After his wicked father's reign, Hezekiah committed himself to set things right again in Judah.

King Hezekiah enacted sweeping religious reforms, including a strict mandate for the sole worship of Yahweh and a prohibition on venerating other deities within the Temple of Jerusalem.

To appease the Assyrians, Hezekiah paid King Sennacherib 300 silver talents and 30 gold. Later, Hezekiah became seriously ill. Hezekiah reminded God of his obedience and then wept bitterly. So, God healed him, adding 15 years to his life.

God had answered supernaturally, and all King Hezekiah had to do was to allow God to bring the victory. He did not have to do anything but have complete trust and faith in God Almighty. And in this way all glory and praise were to the LORD.

So, to sum up, Hezekiah was a righteous king. He did what was right in the eyes of the Lord after ruling behind the evil Ahab. He instituted religious reforms. He also faced a terrible situation with an evil king who threatened to attack and kill an entire population of people. God intervened, and Sennacherib never attacked again, even though he reigned for another 20 years.

---

26 Blaiklock, E.M. Today's Handbook of Bible Characters, Bethany House Publishers, Minneapolis, MN. 1979, p. 242

WORSHIP LEADER TYPES

WORSHIP LEADER TYPE PROFILE

HEZEKIAH

BACKGROUND

- **Political Conditions:**
  - The kingdoms of Israel and Judah have split.
  - The Assyrians were threatening to attack and take everyone into slavery if they were not killed in the battle. The Assyrians were a very cruel people.
  - Hezekiah is the king of Judah.
- **Social Conditions:**
  - The carnality of the cults around them had eroded life. Jerusalem's temple had been abandoned and was filled with rubbish.
- **Religious Conditions**
  - Spiritual revival to the Lord began in the first month of his reign when he cleansed the temple. Hezekiah called on the people to cleanse their own lives as well.

FACTORS IN THE EQUIPPING FOR THE TASK

Hezekiah was righteous - He lived to please the Lord; 2 Kings 18:3, 5, 2 Chronicles 29:2

"He did what was pleasing in the Lord's sight, just as his ancestor David had done."
2 Kings 18:3

Faithful - He was loyal in serving the Lord; 2 Kings 18:6

"He remained faithful to the Lord in everything, and he carefully obeyed all the commands the Lord had given Moses."
2 Kings 18:6

Obedient - He did what the Lord told him to do; 2 Kings 18:6

"He remained faithful to the Lord in everything, and he carefully obeyed all the commands the Lord had given Moses."
2 Kings 18:6

Peace-seeker - Hezekiah sought to avoid war and conflict; 2 Kings 18:13-16

> "King Hezekiah sent this message to the king of Assyria at Lachish:
> 'I have done wrong. I will pay whatever tribute money you demand if you will only
> withdraw.' The king of Assyria then demanded a settlement of more than
> eleven tons of silver and one ton of gold."
> *2 Kings 18:14*

HEZEKIAH'S RELATIONSHIP WITH GOD

Trusted in the Lord - He turned to the Lord in times of need and followed His ways; 2 Kings 18:5, 19:1,14-19, 2 Chronicles 32:7-8

> "Hezekiah trusted in the Lord, the God of Israel.
> There was no one like him among all the kings of Judah,
> either before or after his time."
> *2 Kings 18:5*

Sought to please the Lord - Hezekiah desired to live a life pleasing to the Lord; 2 Chronicles 31:20-21

> "In all that he did in the service of the Temple of God and
> in his efforts to follow God's laws and commands, Hezekiah sought his God
> wholeheartedly. As a result, he was very successful."
> *2 Chronicles 31:21*

THE REVELATION OF GOD THAT HEZEKIAH HAD RECEIVED AND CARRIED TO THE PEOPLE OF GOD

Defender; 2 Kings 19:7, 32-37, 2 Chronicles 32:21-22

> "And the Lord sent an angel who destroyed the Assyrian army
> with all its commanders and officers. So, Sennacherib was forced to return home in
> disgrace to his own land. And when he entered the temple of his god,
> some of his own sons killed him there with a sword."
> *2 Chronicles 32:21*

WORSHIP LEADER TYPES

God is in complete control; 2 Kings 19:23-28

> "But have you not heard? I decided this long ago. Long ago I planned it, and now I am making it happen. I planned for you to crush fortified cities into heaps of rubble."
> *2 Kings 19:25*

LESSONS LEARNED FROM THIS WORSHIP LEADER TYPE

Be faithful - Hezekiah's faith was honored by the Lord; 2 Kings 18:5-7

> "He remained faithful to the Lord in everything,
> and he carefully obeyed all the commands the Lord had given Moses."
> *2 Kings 18:6*

Trust in the Lord - Hezekiah turned to the Lord in times of need, knowing that He is the only one that saves; 2 Kings 19:1,14-19, 2 Chronicles 32:7-8

> "After Hezekiah received the letter from the messengers and read it,
> he went up to the And Hezekiah prayed this prayer before the Lord:
> "O Lord, God of Israel, You are enthroned between the mighty cherubim!
> You alone are God of all the kingdoms of the earth. You alone created the heavens and the earth. Bend down, O Lord, and listen! Open Your eyes, O Lord, and see! Listen to Sennacherib's words of defiance against the living God."
> *2 Kings 19:14-16*

> "'Be strong and courageous! Don't be afraid or discouraged because of the king of Assyria or his mighty army, for there is a power far greater on our side!
> He may have a great army, but they are merely men.
> We have the Lord our God to help us and to fight our battles for us!'
> Hezekiah's words greatly encouraged the people."
> *2 Chronicles 32:7-8*

Nationwide revival - He led the entire kingdom in spiritual revival to the Lord; 2 Chronicles 29:3-11, 30:6-9.

> "In the very first month of the first year of his reign, Hezekiah reopened the doors of the Temple of the Lord and repaired them."
> *2 Chronicles 29:3*

He removed idolatry - Hezekiah eliminated idols and pagan worship throughout the nation; 2 Kings 18:4, 2 Chronicles 31:1

"He removed the pagan shrines, smashed the sacred pillars, and cut down the Asherah poles. He broke up the bronze serpent that Moses had made, because the people of Israel had been offering sacrifices to it. The bronze serpent was called Nehushtan."
2 Kings 18:4

"When the festival ended, the Israelites who attended went to all the towns of Judah, Benjamin, Ephraim, and Manasseh, and they smashed all the sacred pillars, cut down the Asherah poles, and removed the pagan shrines and altars. After this, the Israelites returned to their own towns and homes."
2 Chronicles 31:1

EXAMPLE OF BEING A PRAISER AND WORSHIPPER

Temple's re-dedication - Praised God after having restored and rededicated the Temple and its functions; 2 Chronicles 29:36

"And Hezekiah and all the people rejoiced because of what God had done for the people, for everything had been accomplished so quickly."
2 Chronicles 29:36

Revival - Hezekiah praised God for and/or in revival to the Lord; 2 Chronicles 31:2

"Hezekiah then organized the priests and Levites into divisions to offer the burnt offerings and peace offerings, and to worship and give thanks and praise to the Lord at the gates of the Temple."
2 Chronicles 31:2

Temple's re-dedication - He restored and re-dedicated the Temple and its functions; 2 Chronicles 29:18-36

"Then the Levites went to King Hezekiah and gave him this report: 'We have cleansed the entire Temple of the Lord, the altar of burnt offering with all its utensils, and the table of the Bread of the Presence with all its utensils. We have also recovered all the items discarded by King Ahaz when he was unfaithful and closed the Temple. They are now in front of the altar of the Lord, purified and ready for use.'"
2 Chronicles 29:18-19

Passover celebration - Hezekiah restarted the Passover celebration in memory of the Exodus from Egypt; 2 Chronicles 30:15-25

"On the fourteenth day of the second month, one month later than usual the people
slaughtered the Passover lamb. This shamed the priests and Levites,
so they purified themselves and brought burnt offerings to the Temple of the Lord.
Then they took their places at the Temple as prescribed in the Law of Moses, the man of God.
The Levites brought the sacrificial blood to the priests,
who then sprinkled it on the altar."
2 Chronicles 30:15-16

Prayer and Supplication
Hezekia sought the Lord for his needs; 2 Kings 19:15-19, 2 Chronicles 32:20

"Then King Hezekiah and the prophet Isaiah son of Amoz cried out in prayer to God in heaven."
2 Chronicles 32:20

On his deathbed - Hezekiah cried out to the Lord in his illness; 2 Kings 20:2-3, 2 Chronicles 32:24

"About that time Hezekiah became deathly ill. He prayed to the Lord,
who healed him and gave him a miraculous sign."
2 Chronicles 32:24

Intercession - He prayed for others for grace during the Passover; 2 Chronicles 30:18-20

"Most of those who came from Ephraim, Manasseh, Issachar,
and Zebulun had not purified themselves. But King Hezekiah prayed for them,
and they were allowed to eat the Passover meal anyway, even though this was contrary to
the requirements of the Law. For Hezekiah said,
'May the Lord, who is good, pardon those who decide to follow the Lord,
the God of their ancestors, even though they are not properly cleansed for the ceremony.'
And the Lord listened to Hezekiah's prayer and healed the people."
2 Chronicles 30:18-20

REVELATIONS GIVEN TO HEZEKIAH FROM THE LORD

God is a Warrior; 2 Kings 19:35-37

> "That night the angel of the Lord went out to the Assyrian camp and killed 185,000 Assyrian soldiers. When the surviving Assyrians woke up the next morning, they found corpses everywhere."
> *2 Kings 19:35*

God is a Healer; 2 Kings 20:5-7, 2 Chronicles 32:24

> "Then Isaiah said, 'Make an ointment from figs.' So Hezekiah's servants spread the ointment over the boil, and Hezekiah recovered!"
> *2 Kings 20:7*

God is a Defender; 2 Kings 20:6

> "'I will add fifteen years to your life, and I will rescue you and this city from the king of Assyria. I will defend this city for My own honor and for the sake of My servant David.'"
> *2 Kings 20:6*

HEZEKIAH'S FAITH/TRUST IN THE LORD

Trusted in the Lord - He turned to the Lord in times of need and followed His ways; 2 Kings 18:5, 19:1, 14-19, 2 Chronicles 32:7-8

> "Hezekiah trusted in the Lord, the God of Israel. There was no one like him among all the kings of Judah, either before or after his time."
> *2 Kings 18:5*

CHAPTER 13
REVIEW QUESTIONS
Hezekiah

1. What was the political situation at this time?

2. What was the religious condition at this time?

3. What were the social conditions at this time?

4. What were the factors that helped Hezekiah accomplish the tasks before him?

5. Name some of the characteristics of Hezekiah.

14

Josiah

Josiah was faithful to God during his reign and was known for purifying the Israelites' worship. He is also known for re-instating the Mosaic law as written in a manuscript that was found while restoring the temple. Josiah came from an extensive line of kings, some who compromised and some who gave in to the pressure of other pagan nations.

Josiah's grandfather was Manasseh, who re-introduced pagan forms of worship, including the veneration of celestial bodies, the adoration of Astarte, and the encouragement of the detestable Baal cults, as well as the worship of Moloch, in which children were sacrificed by being burned. Even so, Josiah was a righteous king who destroyed all these practices and restored the worship of Jehovah. He then turned his attention to repairing the temple.

During the course of the renovations, Hilkiah the high priest discovered a copy of the ancient law, and it was brought to the king. On hearing the contents read aloud, Josiah was overcome with remorse because of the way in which the divine precepts had been ignored in previous days.

After his deportation to Babylon, Manasseh returned with a seeming repentant heart, for he instituted religious reformations in Judah. Manasseh's son, Amon, Josiah's father, also worshipped pagan gods at the beginning of his reign, and after two years of ruling, he was murdered in a palace conspiracy in the year 640 B.C.

Josiah showed a very pious side from an early age and from the time he was eight years old, he reigned until the year 609 B.C. At the age of twenty, he turned with vigor to the cleansing of the land.

"Perhaps it has some significance that the last of Assyria's great imperial monarchs died about this time-about 632 B.C., and this freed the young king of Judah from the fear of foreign reprisals if he took firm action against the Assyrian pagan cults which were rife in the land. It was also in the thirteenth year of Josiah's reign 26 B.C. that Jeremiah commenced his prophetic ministry."[27]

---

27 Blaiklock, E.M., Today's Handbook of Bible Characters, Bethany House Publishers, Minneapolis, MN., 1979, p. 249

Josiah ruled for 31 years. He died tragically and unnecessarily in his middle thirties, in an encounter with Pharaoh Necho the Second. He died at Megiddo when He refused to allow the Pharaoh to pass through the only place where he could get to the battle at Assyria. However, Josiah had lived as a man of conviction, action, and swift decisiveness on the battlefield, which served him well as ruler of Judah. He left an indelible mark on the land of Judah and the history of a people.

WORSHIP LEADER TYPES PROFILE

JOSIAH

BACKGROUND

- **Political Conditions:**
  - The kingdoms of Israel and Judah have split.
  - Josiah is king of Judah.
- **Social Conditions:**
  - Before Josiah, the land was weary of the evil of the two preceding reigns. During Josiah's reign, peace and prosperity flourished again.
- **Religious Conditions:**
  - Spiritual revival broke out after Josiah took the throne and found the scroll that had been buried in the rubble of the temple. He re-enacted the law from Deuteronomy.
  - Elimination of detestable pagan practices. Re-establishment of the Passover and the Law.

FACTORS IN THE EQUIPPING FOR THE TASK

JOSIAH'S PERSONALITY

Josiah was righteous - He lived a life pleasing life to the Lord; 2 Kings 22:2, 2 Chronicles 34:2

> "He did what was pleasing in the Lord's sight and followed the example of his ancestor David. He did not turn away from doing what was right."
>
> *2 Kings 22:2*

Faithful - He faithfully followed and served the Lord; 2 Kings 22:2, 23:4-20,24, 2 Chronicles 34:2-7

> "He did what was pleasing in the Lord's sight and followed the example of his ancestor David. He did not turn away from doing what was right."
> *2 Chronicles 34:2*

Obedient - Josiah obeyed the Word of the Lord; 2 Kings 23:25

> "Never before had there been a king like Josiah, who turned to the Lord with all his heart and soul and strength, obeying all the laws of Moses. And there has never been a king like him since."
> *2 Kings 23:25*

JOSIAH'S RELATIONSHIP WITH GOD

Feared the Lord - Josiah had a proper fear of the Lord when he realized he and the people had sinned; 2 Kings 22:11-13, 2 Chronicles 34:19-21

> "Go to the Temple and speak to the Lord for me and for the people and for all Judah. Inquire about the words written in this scroll that has been found. For the Lord's great anger is burning against us because our ancestors have not obeyed the words in this scroll. We have not been doing everything it says we must do."
> *2 Kings 22:13*

Loved the Lord wholeheartedly - His heart remained turned toward the Lord; 2 Kings 22:2

> "He did what was right in the eyes of the Lord and followed completely the ways of his father David, not turning aside to the right or to the left."
> *2 Kings 22:2*

THE REVELATION OF GOD THAT JOSIAH RECEIVED AND CARRIED TO THE PEOPLE OF GOD

The Word of God; 2 Kings 23:2, 2 Chronicles 34:30

> "And the king went up to the Temple of the Lord with all the people of Judah and Jerusalem, along with the priests and the Levites all the people from the greatest to the least. There the king read to them the entire Book of the Covenant that had been found in the Lord's Temple."
> *2 Chronicles 34:30*

LESSONS LEARNED FROM THIS WORSHIP LEADER TYPE

Repentance - Josiah repented immediately when he discovered from the Word of God, that he and his people had sinned; 2 Kings 22:11-13, 23:3, 2 Chronicles 34:19-21

> "Go to the Temple and speak to the Lord for me and for all the remnant of Israel and Judah. Inquire about the words written in the scroll that has been found. For the Lord's great anger has been poured out on us because our ancestors have not obeyed the word of the Lord. We have not been doing everything this scroll says we must do."
> *2 Chronicles 34:21*

Leading by example - The revival that Josiah led in the Kingdom started with him; He only required the people to do what he was doing; 2 Kings 23:2-3, 2 Chronicles 34:31-33.

> "The king took his place of authority beside the pillar and renewed the covenant in the Lord's presence. He pledged to obey the Lord by keeping all His commands, laws, and decrees with all his heart and soul. In this way, he confirmed all the terms of the covenant that were written in the scroll, and all the people pledged themselves to the covenant."
> *2 Kings 23:3*

Wholehearted worship - Josiah held nothing back in his turning to the Lord; 2 Kings 23:25, 2 Chronicles 34:33.

> "So Josiah removed all detestable idols from the entire land of Israel and required everyone to worship the Lord their God. And throughout the rest of his lifetime, they did not turn away from the Lord, the God of their ancestors."
> *2 Chronicles 34:33*

Love for the Lord
Josiah wholeheartedly worshiped God and was unswerving in his pledge to obey Him. He held nothing back in his walk with the Lord; 2 Kings 23:3, 25, 2 Chronicles 34:31

> "The king took his place of authority beside the pillar and renewed the covenant in the Lord's presence. He pledged to obey the Lord by keeping all his commands, laws, and decrees with all his heart and soul. He promised to obey all the terms of the covenant that were written in the scroll."
> *2 Chronicles 34:31*

Love for God's People
Revival - Josiah led the people in spiritual revival to God; 2 Kings 23:2-3, 2 Chronicles 34:31-33.

> "The king took his place of authority beside the pillar and renewed the covenant in the Lord's presence. He pledged to obey the Lord by keeping all his commands, laws, and decrees with all his heart and soul. He promised to obey all the terms of the covenant that were written in the scroll. And he required everyone in Jerusalem and the people of Benjamin to make a similar pledge. The people of Jerusalem did so, renewing their covenant with God, the God of their ancestors."
> *2 Chronicles 34:31-32*

Zeal for the Lord
Removed idolatry - Josiah destroyed all idols; 2 Kings 23:4-20, 24, 2 Chronicles 34:3-7, 33.

> "Then the king instructed Hilkiah the high priest and the priests of the second rank and the Temple gatekeepers to remove from the Lord's Temple all the articles that were used to worship Baal, Asherah, and all the powers of the heavens. The king had all these things burned outside Jerusalem on the terraces of the Kidron Valley, and he carried the ashes away to Bethel."
> *2 Kings 23:4*

Love of His Word
Immediate repentance and obedience - Josiah repented immediately when he realized the scroll that was discovered, included terms of the covenant that the people were not following. 2 Kings 22:11-13, 18-20, 23:3, 24, 2 Chronicles 34:19-21, 31-33.

> "You were sorry and humbled yourself before the Lord when you heard what I said against this city and its people - that this land would be cursed and become desolate. You tore your clothing in despair and wept before me in repentance. And I have indeed heard you, says the Lord. So I will not send the promised disaster until after you have died and been buried in peace. You will not see the disaster I am going to bring on this city."
> *2 Kings 22:19-20*

EXAMPLE OF BEING A WORSHIPPER

Removed idolatry - Destroyed all idols, acknowledging the Lord as the one true God; 2 Kings 23:4-20, 24, 2 Chronicles 34:3-7, 33.

> "Josiah also got rid of the mediums and psychics, the household gods, the idols,
> and every other kind of detestable practice, both in Jerusalem and throughout the land of
> Judah. He did this in obedience to the laws written in the scroll that
> Hilkiah the priest had found in the Lord's Temple."
> *2 Kings 23:24*

Passover - Josiah celebrated the Passover; 2 Kings 23:23, 2 Chronicles 35:1, 16.

> "Then Josiah announced that the Passover of the Lord would be celebrated in Jerusalem,
> and so the Passover lamb was slaughtered on the fourteenth day of the first month."
> *2 Chronicles 35:1*

Removed idolatry - Destroyed all idols; 2 Kings 23:4-20, 24, 2 Chronicles 34:3-7, 33.

> "He ordered that the altars of Baal be demolished and that the incense altars which stood
> above them be broken down. He also made sure that the Asherah poles,
> the carved idols, and the cast images were smashed and scattered over the graves of
> those who had sacrificed to them."
> *2 Chronicles 34:4*

PRESENTER/REPRESENTATIVE OF THE LORD

Grieved over sin - Josiah was torn up over the sins of his people; 2 Kings 22:11, 2 Chronicles 34:19.

> "When the king heard what was written in the Book of the Law,
> he tore his clothes in despair."
> *2 Kings 22:1*

CHAPTER 14
REVIEW QUESTIONS
Josiah

1. What were the political conditions during Josiah's time?

2. What were the social conditions?

3. What were the religious conditions?

4. What were the factors that helped Josiah complete his tasks?

5. List at least three lessons we can learn from Josiah.

6. What major campaign did Josiah launch during his reign?

7. What major construction did Josiah undertake during his reign?

Our revelation of God will determine the depth and quality of our response in our intimate worship relationship with Him.

15
Ezra

Ezra seemed to be in an official position in the Persian state organization. He may have been a "commissioner for Jewish affairs in an empire accustomed to the government of subject peoples...To read the letter of commission given by Artaxerxes to Ezra is to gain some insight into his standing with the Shah."[28] He was known as Ezra the Scribe. So, he had a high position with his captors. The first chapter of the book of Ezra states the task given to Ezra. The king of Persia was moved upon by the spirit of God that he should let the Israelites go back to build up the temple. This is how it read:

> "In the first year of Cyrus king of Persia, in order to fulfill the word of
> the Lord spoken by Jeremiah, the Lord moved the heart of Cyrus king of Persia
> to make a proclamation throughout his realm and also to put it in writing:
>
> 'This is what Cyrus king of Persia says:
> "'The Lord, the God of heaven, has given me all the kingdoms of the earth
> and he has appointed me to build a temple for him at Jerusalem in Judah.
> Any of his people among you may go up to Jerusalem in
> Judah and build the temple of the Lord, the God of Israel,
> the God who is in Jerusalem, and may their God be with them."
> *Ezra 1:1-3, NIV*

Those who chose to face the dangers of one hundred miles of land occupied by armed bandits took off to Jerusalem in the distance. Ezra refused to accept an armed guard. Ezra was not presuming on God, but instead he showed his earnest determination by fasting and prayer. His dependence on God was rewarded by safe passage.

---

28 Blaiklock, E.M. Today's Handbook of Bible Characters, Bethany House Publishers, Minneapolis, MN., 1979, p. 280

WORSHIP LEADER TYPES

Worship Leader Type Profile

EZRA

BACKGROUND

- **Political Conditions:**
  - Israelites were in and out of captivity under the Babylonians.
- **Social Conditions:**
  - The exiles in Babylon returned to Judah on the order of King Cyrus. Then, they return to rebuild the temple.
- **Religious Conditions:**
  - Rebuilding the Temple became especially important. Ezra, on returning to those who had been left in Jerusalem, found that many Jews had intermarried with non-Jews, and he determined to dissolve these marriages.

FACTORS IN THE EQUIPPING FOR THE TASK

Ezra had favor with King Cyrus - The Israelites were given special consideration when they were allowed to go and rebuild the walls in Jerusalem.; Ezra 1

> "Any of you who are His people may go to Jerusalem in Judah to rebuild this Temple of the Lord, the God of Israel, who lives in Jerusalem. And may your God be with you!"
>
> *Ezra 1:3*

He was a scribe who had favor with King Artaxerxes - Ezra 7:6

> "This Ezra was a scribe who was well versed in the Law of Moses, which the Lord, the God of Israel, had given to the people of Israel. He came up to Jerusalem from Babylon, and the king gave him everything he asked for, because the gracious hand of the Lord his God was on him."
>
> *Ezra 7:6*

EZRA'S PERSONALITY

Ezra was studious who diligently read and studied the Word; Ezra 7:6,10, Nehemiah 8:13-14

> "This was because Ezra had determined to study and obey the Law of the Lord and to teach those decrees and regulations to the people of Israel."
>
> *Ezra 7:10*

Ezra was wise - Ezra had God-given wisdom; Ezra 7:25

"And you, Ezra, are to use the wisdom your God has given you to appoint magistrates and judges who know your God's laws to govern all the people in the province west of the Euphrates River. Teach the law to anyone who does not know it."
Ezra 7:25

EZRA'S RELATIONSHIP WITH GOD

Feared the Lord - Ezra had a trembling reverence of the Lord; Ezra 9:6-15

"But even so, we are again breaking Your commands and intermarrying with people who do these detestable things. Won't Your anger be enough to destroy us, so that even this little remnant no longer survives?"
Ezra 9:14

THE REVELATION OF GOD THAT EZRA RECEIVED AND CARRIED TO THE PEOPLE OF GOD

The Word of God; Ezra 7:10, Nehemiah 8:2-3

"So, on October 8, Ezra the priest brought the Book of the Law before the assembly, which included the men and women and all the children old enough to understand. He faced the square just inside the Water Gate from early morning until noon and read aloud to everyone who could understand. All the people listened closely to the Book of the Law."
Nehemiah 8:2-3

God is a protector; Ezra 8:21-23

"So, we fasted and earnestly prayed that our God would take care of us, and He heard our prayer."
Ezra 8:23

He renewed the festival shelters; Nehemiah 8:14-17

"As they studied the Law, they discovered that the Lord had commanded through Moses that the Israelites should live in shelters during the festival to be held that month."
Nehemiah 8:14

LESSONS LEARNED FROM THIS WORSHIP LEADER TYPE

Know the Word - Ezra read, studied, and knew the Word of God; Ezra 7:6, 10, Nehemiah 8:13-14

"This Ezra was a scribe who was well versed in the Law of Moses, which the Lord, the God of Israel, had given to the people of Israel. He came up to Jerusalem from Babylon, and the king gave him everything he asked for, because the gracious hand of the Lord his God was on him."
Ezra 7:6

Trust in the Lord - Ezra did not trust in a king's armies, but in the arm of God Almighty; Ezra 8:21-23

"So, we fasted and earnestly prayed that our God would take care of us, and He heard our prayer."
Ezra 8:23

Deal with/treat sin as sin - Ezra understood the seriousness of sin and the urgency of repenting and correcting it; Ezra 9:3-15, 10:1,6.

"While Ezra prayed and made this confession, weeping and lying face down on the ground in front of the Temple of God, a very large crowd of people from Israel—men, women, and children— gathered and wept bitterly with him."
Ezra 10:1

Obedience - Ezra did and said everything he was commanded to and taught the people the Word of God; Ezra 7:10

"This was because Ezra had determined to study and obey the Law of the Lord and to each those decrees and regulations to the people of Israel."
Ezra 7:10

Led repentance - Ezra led the people back into righteousness through repentance; Ezra 10:10-12

"So now confess your sin to the Lord, the God of your ancestors, and do what He demands. Separate yourselves from the people of the land and from these pagan women."
Ezra 10:11

Grieved and enraged by sin - He was distraught at the sins of the people; Ezra 9:3-15, 10:1, 6

> "When I heard this, I tore my cloak and my shirt, pulled hair from my
> head and beard, and sat down utterly shocked."
> *Ezra 9:3*

Bible scholar and teacher - Ezra treasured the Word of God, reading and studying daily to know and teach it to others; Ezra 7:6, 10, Nehemiah 8:13-14.

> "This was because Ezra had determined to study and obey the Law of the Lord and to
> teach those decrees and regulations to the people of Israel."
> *Ezra 7:10*

EXAMPLE OF BEING A PRAISER

Favor with King Artaxerxes - Ezra praised God for favor with the King; Ezra 7:27-28.

> "Praise the Lord, the God of our ancestors, who made the king want
> to beautify the Temple of the Lord in Jerusalem! And praise Him for demonstrating such
> unfailing love to me by honoring me before the king, his council,
> and all his mighty nobles! I felt encouraged because
> the gracious hand of the Lord my God was on me.
> And I gathered some of the leaders of Israel to return with me to Jerusalem."
> *Ezra 7:27:28*

Praised in response to the reading of God's Word; Nehemiah 8:6

> "Then Ezra praised the Lord, the great God, and all the people chanted, 'Amen! Amen!'
> as they lifted their hands. Then they bowed down and worshiped
> the Lord with their faces to the ground."
> *Nehemiah 8:6*

Prayer
Fasting and supplication - Ezra sought the Lord for protection; Ezra 8:21-23

> "And there by the Ahava Canal, I gave orders for all of us to fast and humble
> ourselves before our God. We prayed that He would give us a safe
> journey and protect us, our children, and our goods as we traveled."
> *Ezra 8:21*

Confession and repentance - Ezra acknowledged and renounced the sins of his people; Ezra 9:6-15, 10:1.

> "O Lord, God of Israel, You are just. We come before You in our guilt as nothing but an escaped remnant, though in such a condition none of us can stand in Your presence."
> *Ezra 9:15*

PRESENTER/REPRESENTATIVE OF THE LORD

Teacher - Ezra taught the Word of God as Jesus did and Holy Spirit teaches us; Ezra 7:10

> "This was because Ezra had determined to study and obey the Law of the Lord and to teach those decrees and regulations to the people of Israel."
> *Ezra 7:10*

Grieved and enraged by sin - Ezra's heart was broken over the sins of God's people as God's heart is broken when we turn from Him and disobey; Ezra 9:3-15, 10:1,6.

> "While Ezra prayed and made this confession, weeping and lying face down on the ground in front of the Temple of God, a very large crowd of people from Israel—men, women, and children—gathered and wept bitterly with him."
> *Ezra 10:1*

Leading repentance - Ezra led the people in repentance to the Lord as Christ and His Spirit does; Ezra 10:10-12

> "So now confess your sin to the Lord, the God of your ancestors, and do what He demands. Separate yourselves from the people of the land and from these pagan women."
> *Ezra 10:11*

CHAPTER 15
REVIEW QUESTIONS
Ezra

1. What were the political conditions during Ezra's time?

2. What were the social conditions?

3. What were the religious conditions?

4. What were the factors that equipped Ezra for the task?

5. What were some of Ezra's characteristics?

6. Name at least three lessons learned from this worship leader type.

7. What were some revelations given to the people by the Holy Spirit?

"In worship, we offer our whole selves to God, presenting our hopes, fears, joys, and sorrows, knowing that He is the only one who can truly satisfy our souls."
—Timothy Keller

16

Nehemiah

Nehemiah was a trusted senior servant of Artaxerxes. As such, he had access to power. This was advantageous to him when Hanani, Nehemiah's brother, told him during a visit of the bad state of affairs in Jerusalem where the walls were torn down and the gates were burned. Being a man of prayer, Nehemiah fell to his knees and called out to the "God of heaven." Instead of blaming the people of Jerusalem for their lack of righteousness and deciding they deserved what they got, Nehemiah identified with them. If they were judged, then he was judged. This is one sign of a great leader, one who says, "The buck stops here."

Nehemiah brought wine to the king, the man who had power over life and death, and when the king asked him why he was so sad, Nehemiah told him about Jerusalem. The king might well have said, "Why should I care about your problems? I am the greatest man for miles around and I could have you put to death for bothering me with this." But he did not. Here is what Nehemiah said.

> "I was very much afraid, but I said to the king,
> "May the king live forever! Why should my face not
> look sad when the city where my ancestors are buried lies in ruins,
> and its gates have been destroyed by fire?"
> *Nehemiah 2:2b*

The king then asked, "What do you want?" Nehemiah stated his desire to go back and supervise the rebuilding of the temple, and the king who held Nehemiah's life in his hands, agreed to let him go. Nehemiah was even given letters from the king to ensure safe passage and to obtain timber from the king's forest for the gates and walls of Jerusalem. Accompanied by a military escort, Nehemiah traveled back to Jerusalem.

One scholar puts it this way, "...Nehemiah, a highly placed Jewish official in the Persian court, was informed of the privations that had overtaken the returned exiles. When he learned of the desolation and helplessness of Judea he was greatly distressed and sought permission of Artaxerxes to go to Jerusalem and rebuild the ruined portions of the city. In keeping with the tolerance towards other religions that characterized the Persian rulers as a whole, Artaxerxes appointed Nehemiah as governor of Judea and furnished him with the necessary documents establishing his authority."[29]

There, he took a lay of the land. He probably needed to know whom he could trust. And then, he ran into Sanballat, the satrap of Samaria, a rival, who harassed him during the work God called him to do. Sanballat mocked him and the people who worked on the wall. This ambitious man hoped to control Jerusalem himself, so when Nehemiah came along with his ability to inspire the people to rebuild the walls, Sanballat was threatened and tried to ally himself with others to attack those who were building the walls. But, anticipating such actions, Nehemiah made sure there were guards to protect the people who were re-building the walls. As governor, Nehemiah says that he didn't take advantage of food and land allotments that were allowed him due to his office, because there was already such a great burden on the people of his province (Nehemiah 5:14–19). He also made the other nobles and officials forgive all outstanding debts and ordered them to return all land and money that had been taken as taxes so the people would be able to feed themselves and their families. He also instituted extensive moral and liturgical reforms in rededicating the Jews to the worship of Yahweh. He was able to supervise the rebuilding of the wall in just 52 days.

"Once the city was safe from attack, the inhabitants were free to build their own houses and cultivate their lands without fear of outside interference. Nehemiah saw that the right time had now arrived for the reorganization of community life along spiritual times, and Ezra was summoned in 444 B.C. to proclaim the law to the people."[30]

---

29 Harrison, R.K., Old Testament Times, Hendrickson Publishers, Inc. Peabody, Massachusetts, 1970, p.282
30 Harrison, R.K., Old Testament Times, page 285

EXPLORING MUSICAL AND NON-MUSICAL BIBLE CHARACTERS

WORSHIP LEADER TYPE PROFILE

NEHEMIAH

BACKGROUND

- **Political Conditions:**
  - Many Israelites were taken into captivity under the Babylonians. Those who were left in Judah, struggled to return to a prosperous state, but they had a hard time growing things in the soil there. Since the walls had been torn down, they could not defend themselves from Samaritans and others who could rob, pillage, and steal from them. This is why it was important for Nehemiah to return to Judah and encourage others to re-build the wall.
  - King Artaxerxes was sympathetic to the request of Nehemiah to return and re-build the wall with the help of his fellow countrymen.
- **Social Conditions:**
  - "For some years, the expatriated Jews had experienced great hardship and the economy of the community was in a precarious state. The wealthier inhabitants were depriving the poorer ones of their holdings, while unscrupulous traders were profiting from the uncertain economic conditions. Intermarriage with surrounding peoples was rife and the resurgence of Canaanite idolatry was an ever-present threat to the spiritual life of the faithful Jews."[31]
  - Nehemiah was made a Cupbearer to the king.
- **Religious conditions:**
  - Israelites intermingling with foreign nations because of the forced migration to Babylon.
  - There was a lack of respect for the laws of Moses, especially in observing the Sabbath.[32]
  - The people were not supporting the work of the temple and misused the money.[33]

---

[31] Harrison, R.K., Old Testament Times, Hendrickson Publishers, 1970, p. 283
[32] Nehemiah 13:15
[33] Nehemiah 13:10, 12

FACTORS IN THE EQUIPPING FOR THE TASK

Nehemiah was divinely placed in a very close position to the king.

"Now, I was cupbearer to the king."
Nehemiah 1:11

Nehemiah had favor with the king – Nehemiah had favor with the King. He was peaceably released from his service to the king and was given royal protection for his journey.

"And I said to the king, "If it pleases the king, let letters be given me to the governors of the province Beyond the River, that they may let me pass through until I come to Judah, And the king granted me what I asked, for the good hand of my God was upon me."
Nehemiah 2:7-8

NEHEMIAH'S PERSONALITY

Patient – He waited on God for the opportune time to go back to Jerusalem.

"As soon as I heard these words I sat down and wept and mourned for days, and I continued fasting and praying before the God of heaven."
Nehemiah 1:4

Humble/meek – He served the king diligently; obeyed God completely.

Diligent – He worked until the task was complete

"So we built the wall. And all the wall was joined together to half its height, for the people had a mind to work."
Nehemiah 4:6

Determined – Nehemiah did not allow anyone to stop him from completing the task.

"And I looked and arose and said to the nobles and to the officials and to the rest of the people, "Do not be afraid of them. Remember the Lord, who is great and awesome, and fight for your brothers, your sons, your daughters, your wives, and your homes." When our enemies heard that it was known to us and that God had frustrated their plan, we all returned to the wall, each to his work. From that day on, half of my servants worked while the other half stood guard."
Nehemiah 4: 14-16

Leader - He was appointed governor over Jerusalem. The people listened to him as he encouraged them to rebuild the walls of the city.

Compassionate - He felt compassion for his fellow Israelites that had been left behind after the exile to Babylon.

Wise - He knew how to get people behind him and he knew how to keep Sanballat from taking over and even killing him. He refused to deal with Sanballat, even after he asked him to come and speak with him four times. Even when Sanballat tried to accuse Nehemiah of trying to overthrow his rule, he refused to go and speak to him, knowing he meant harm.

Man of faith - Nehemiah recounted the favor he received from God and encouraged the people with this:

> "And I told them of the hand of my God which had been good upon me, and also of the king's words which he had spoken to me. So they said, 'Let us rise up and build.'"
> *Nehemiah 2:18*

NEHEMIAH'S RELATIONSHIP WITH GOD

Nehemiah was trusting and he looked to God for his needs and desires. Nehemiah 1:4, 9

Nehemiah prayed to God, admitting that he and all the people had sinned but that he knew God would bless them and take care of them.

> "If you return to me and keep my commandments and do them, though your outcasts are in the uttermost parts of heaven, from there I will gather them and bring them to the place that I have chosen, to make my name dwell there.'
> *Nehemiah 1:9a*

> "As soon as I heard these words I sat down and wept and mourned for days, and I continued fasting and praying before the God of heaven. "
> *Nehemiah 1:4*

THE REVELATION OF GOD THAT NEHEMIAH RECEIVED AND CARRIED TO THE PEOPLE OF GOD

- God is a God of restoration. Nehemiah went back to restore the city of Jerusalem.
- God wants us to treat one another justly. He rebuked the wealthy of the city to take care of the poor and no longer enslave them. (Nehemiah 5)

LESSONS LEARNED FROM THIS LEADER TYPE

Love for the Lord

Prayer/intercession – Nehemiah showed his love for God by going to God first.

> "So it was, when I heard these words, that I sat down and wept, and mourned for many days; I was fasting and praying before the God of heaven."
> *Nehemiah 1:4*

Interceding for the people

> "And I became very angry when I heard their outcry and these words. After serious thought, I rebuked the nobles and rulers and said to them, "Each of you is exacting usury from his brother…will you even sell your brethren? Or should they be sold to us?"
> *Nehemiah 5:6-8*

Trusting God's Word and timing – Nehemiah waited to return to Jerusalem;

Patriotism – He led in the rebuilding of Jerusalem.

Wisdom in protection - He set guards around the wall.

> "So it was, from that time on, that half of my servants worked at construction, while the other half held the spears, the shields, the bows, and wore armor, and the leaders were behind all the house of Judah."
> *Nehemiah 4:16*

Zeal for the Lord

Nehemiah showed complete and immediate obedience when God spoke. He immediately left wealth and luxury behind.

Love of God's word

Nehemiah was faithful in seeking God's word. Nehemiah showed a reverence for God's word, reinforced God's law among the people.

EXAMPLE OF BEING A WORSHIPPER

Worshiper – Obedient in everything God told him to do.

> "And I told no one what my God had put into my heart to do for Jerusalem."
> *Nehemiah 2:12*

Encouraged the people by reminding them of God's protection and love for them.

> "Then as I looked over the situation, I called together the nobles and the rest of the people
> and said to them, "Don't be afraid of the enemy! Remember the Lord,
> who is great and glorious, and fight for your brothers, your sons,
> your daughters, your wives, and your homes!"
> *Nehemiah 4:14*

> "When you hear the blast of the trumpet, rush to wherever it is sounding.
> Then our God will fight for us!"
> *Nehemiah 4:20*

Prayer –sought the Lord for everything and waited for an answer "And I told them of the hand of my God that had been upon me for good," And we prayed to our God and set a guard as a protection against them day and night. – Nehemiah 2:18-20

Doer of the Word – reinforced God's law among the people

NEHEMIAH'S ABILITY TO HEAR AND RESPOND TO THE LORD

Nehemiah was in constant communion with the Lord.

> "Nehemiah said often, "And we prayed to our God", or "Remember the Lord who is great
> and awesome" or he gave credit to God for decisions he made. One example is when
> Sanballat sent a messenger to tell Nehemiah he was in danger and he should take refuge
> in the temple, with the intention of removing him as the leader of those who were building
> the wall. And Nehemiah said, "I understood and saw that God did not send him…"
> *Nehemiah 6:12*

> When questioned by the king about why he was so sad, he said, "With a prayer to the God
> of heaven, I replied, "If it please the king, and if you are pleased with me, your servant,
> send me to Judah to rebuild the city where my ancestors are buried."
> *Nehemiah 2:4, 5*

> I replied, "The God of heaven will help us succeed. We, his servants, will start rebuilding this wall."
> *Nehemiah 2:20*

CHAPTER 16
REVIEW QUESTIONS
Nehemiah

1. What were the political conditions of Nehemiah's time?

2. What were the social conditions?

3. What were the religious conditions?

4. What were some of the factors in the equipping of Nehemiah for his task?

5. Name at least six aspects of Nehemiah's personality.

6. How did Nehemiah show his love for the people?

7. How did Nehemiah show his love for God's interests?

17

Job

Who was Job from the Bible? We know that Job was a prophet who believed that worship before and during a trial was necessary and effective. God will fight our battles, according to this story. Job's story seems to defy the widely held idea that if one is good and follows the Law, one will be blessed and avoid suffering. The tale of Job opens with a description of his good life. Job had everything a person could ask for. He was an upright, wealthy man with grown-up offspring (seven sons and three daughters) and a great love for his family. Every day, his children would eat together in a great feast, with each of the seven sons alternating when they would host the party. When they were all eating together at the eldest brother's house, they were all killed, even the servants and livestock. So, Job lost all his family except his wife, and all of his wealth. Then, Job was afflicted with painful boils. His wife told him to "Curse God and die!" So, he found no comfort in his terrible grief, even from the one who should have been his greatest comfort at such a terrible time.

From Chapters 3 to 42, Job argues with his friends and then with God about what all this means. Why do good men suffer? Why was everything taken from him when he did everything right? These are the questions we humans ask when we find ourselves faced with the vagaries of life.

Ultimately, Job's prosperity was restored, and his last days were better than the first. So, who was Job? He was not an Israelite. He was a righteous man who had it all, lost it all, and was visited by three men known as Job's comforters. They tried to reason with him and themselves about what all this misery meant and why it was happening. Why do good men suffer? How does our righteousness affect our prosperity? Is prosperity a sign of a man's upright relationship with God? If a man is afflicted, does that mean he has committed sins he has not atoned for? All these questions are answered in the book of Job.

WORSHIP LEADER TYPE PROFILE
JOB

BACKGROUND

- The three conditions, political, religious and social, are not necessarily covered in the book of Job. It is the story of a man who is righteous yet is afflicted with the worst trials ever and then he must justify his position with a group of "friends" who try to tell him he must be sinning to have all this hardship thrust upon him. It is a philosophical argument about who must suffer in this world and why they are suffering?
- We do see the family of Job as a prosperous and close-knit family, all of whom took turns hosting the family get-together on a regular basis.

FACTORS IN THE EQUIPPING FOR THE TASK

Job was righteous - Job lived a life of righteousness, and his faith was set in God; Job 1:1, 8, 2:3, 27:3-6, Ezekiel 14:14

> "Even if Noah, Daniel, and Job were there, their righteousness
> would save no one but themselves,
> says the Sovereign Lord."
> *Ezekiel 14:14*

Blessed - God used Job through the abundant blessings He had given him; Job 1:2-3, 10, 42:12-17.

> "You have always put a wall of protection around him and his home and his property.
> You have made him prosper in everything he does. Look how rich he is!"
> *Job 1:10*

JOB'S PERSONALITY

A man of integrity - Job was completely honest in every way and everything he did; Job 1:1,8, 2:3.

> "Then the Lord asked Satan, 'Have you noticed My servant Job? He is blameless a man of
> complete integrity. He fears God and stays away from evil.'"
> *Job 1:8*

Righteous - Job lived a life of righteousness and his faith was set in God; Job 1:1,8, 2:3, 27:3-6, Ezekiel 14:14, 20

Faithful, loyal - Job was very loyal to the Lord and faithful in living a blameless and holy life; Job 1:22, 2:3, 6:10, 23:10-12, 27:3-6, James 5:11

> "As long as I live, while I have breath from God, my lips will speak no evil,
> and my tongue will speak no lies."
> *Job 27:3-4*

Humble - Job had a humble heart before the Lord; he knew his place in the eyes/presence of God; Job 7:7,20-21, 9:1-4,14-20, 21:22

> "So who am I, that I should try to answer God or even reason with Him?
> Even if I were right, I would have no defense. I could only plead for mercy."
> *Job 9:14-15*

JOB'S RELATIONSHIP WITH GOD

Feared the Lord - Job lived a life in a healthy fear and reverence of the Lord; Job 1:1, 8, 2:3, 13:15

> "There once was a man named Job who lived in the land of Uz. He was blameless a man
> of complete integrity. He feared God and stayed away from evil."
> *Job 1:1*

Friend of God - Job described that the presence of God was as that of a friend in his home; Job 29:4

> "When I was in my prime, God's friendship was felt in my home."
> *Job 29:4*

THE REVELATION OF GOD THAT JOB RECEIVED AND CARRIED TO THE PEOPLE OF GOD

God is Righteous; Job 9:2-4

> "Yes, I know all this is true in principle. But how can a person be declared
> innocent in God's sight? If someone wanted to take God to court,
> would it be impossible to answer Him even once in a thousand times?"
> *Job 9:2-3*

God Holds all wisdom; Job 9:4, 12:13, 21:22, 28:23-28, 38-39, 40:6-24, 41

"But true wisdom and power are found in God; counsel and understanding are His."
Job 12:13

God is Mighty; Job 9:4-13, 26:6-14.

"Without warning, He moves the mountains,
overturning them in His anger.
He shakes the earth from its place,
and its foundations tremble."
Job 9:5-6

God is our Advocate; Job 17:3-4

"You must defend my innocence, O God,
since no one else will stand up for me."
Job 17:3

God is in complete control; Job 23:13-14

"But once He has made His decision, who can change His mind?
Whatever He wants to do, He does.
So He will do to me whatever He has planned.
He controls my destiny."
Job 23:13-14

LESSONS LEARNED FROM THIS WORSHIP LEADER TYPE

Remained faithful - In the midst of everything Job went through, losing everything as well as being falsely accused of sin, he remained faithful to the Lord and refused to sin against Him; Job 2:3, 6:10, 23:10-12, 27:3-6, James 5:11

"Then the Lord asked Satan, 'Have you noticed My servant Job?
He is the finest man in all the earth. He is blameless a man
of complete integrity. He fears God and stays away from evil.
And he has maintained his integrity,
even though you urged Me to harm him without cause."
Job 2:3

All bad things that happen are not the result of sin - Job was suffering and even though he had not sinned, he was not being punished by God; Job 1:12-19, 2:6-8.

> "'All right, you may test him,' the Lord said to Satan.
> 'Do whatever you want with everything he possesses,
> but don't harm him physically.'
> So Satan left the Lord's presence."
> *Job 1:12*

In the midst of the storms of life, worship - Job worshiped the Lord immediately after he lost everything; He refused to turn away from God. Job 1:20

> "Job stood up and tore his robe in grief.
> Then he shaved his head and fell
> to the ground to worship."
> *Job 1:20*

Sometimes those closest to us will try to ***turn us away from God*** - Job's wife told him to curse God and die; Job 2:9

> "His wife said to him, 'Are you still trying to maintain your integrity? Curse God and die.'"
> *Job 2:9*

Finding no fault after self-examination according to the Lord's standard is not wrong. Job had examined himself and could genuinely say that he was not being punished because he hadn't sinned against God; Job 6:29-30, 16:17

> "Stop assuming my guilt, for I have done no wrong.
> Do you think I am lying? Don't I know the
> difference between right and wrong?"
> *Job 6:29-30*

Love for the Lord
Job feared the Lord - Job lived in a healthy fear and reverence of the Lord; Job 1:1, 8, 2:3, 13:15

> "There once was a man named Job who lived in the land of Uz.
> He was blameless a man of complete integrity.
> He feared God and stayed away from evil."
> *Job 1:1*

Offered sacrifices for his children - Job even offered sacrifices for his children just in case they had cursed God or sinned against Him at some point; Job 1:5

> "When these celebrations ended sometimes after several days Job would purify his children. He would get up early in the morning and offer a burnt offering for each of them. For Job said to himself, 'Perhaps my children have sinned and have cursed God in their heart.' This was Job's regular practice."
> *Job 1:5*

Did not blame God for his circumstances Job didn't turn on God or blame Him for his suffering; Job 1:22

> "In all of this, Job did not sin by blaming God."
> *Job 1:22*

Love for His people

Offered sacrifices for his children - Job offered sacrifices for his children just in case they had cursed God or sinned against Him at some point; Job 1:5

> "When these celebrations ended sometimes after several days Job would purify his children. He would get up early in the morning and offer a burnt offering for each of them. For Job said to himself, 'Perhaps my children have sinned and have cursed God in their heart.' This was Job's regular practice."
> *Job 1:5*

Encourager - Job had the heart to encourage others; Job 4:3-4, 16:5.

> "In the past you have encouraged many people; you have strengthened those who were weak. Your words have supported those who were falling; you encouraged those with shaky knees."
> *Job 4:3-4*

Compassion for those in need - Job showed active love towards people who needed help; Job 29:12-13, 15-16, 31:16-20.

> "I served as eyes for the blind and feet for the lame. I was a father to the poor and assisted strangers who needed help."
> *Job 29:15-16*

Lived blamelessly - Job lived an actively blameless life before the Lord; Job 1:1, 8, 2:3, 27:3-6.

> "I will maintain my innocence without wavering. My conscience is clear for as long as I live."
> *Job 27:6*

Faithful to the word of the Lord - Job never turned against or outside of the Word of God; Job 6:10, 23:12

> "At least I can take comfort in this: Despite the pain,
> I have not denied the words of the Holy One."
> *Job 6:10*

EXAMPLE OF BEING A PRAISER AND WORSHIPPER

Praised when he lost everything - Job turned and praised God when Satan struck his home and family; Job 1:21

> "He said, 'I came naked from my mother's womb, and I will be naked when I leave.
> The Lord gave me what I had, and the Lord has taken it away.
> Praise the name of the Lord!'"
> *Job 1:21*

Worshipper

Worshiped when he lost everything – Job stopped and worshipped God immediately when he had lost everything; Job 1:20-21

> "Job stood up and tore his robe in grief. Then he shaved his head and
> fell to the ground to worship. He said, 'I came naked from my mother's womb, and
> I will be naked when I leave. The Lord gave me what I had,
> and the Lord has taken it away. Praise the name of the Lord!'"
> *Job 1:20-21*

Worshiped despite his circumstances - Job worshipped God in the midst of everything: loss of his wealth, his family, and even his health; Job 19:25-27

> "But as for me, I know that my Redeemer lives, and He will stand upon the earth at last.
> And after my body has decayed, yet in my body I will see God! I will see Him for myself.
> Yes, I will see Him with my own eyes. I am overwhelmed at the thought!"
> *Job 19:25-27*

WORSHIP LEADER TYPES

Man of Prayer
Humble - Even though Job had not sinned, he still humbly went before God asking Him to examine him; Job 7:7, 20-21

> "If I have sinned, what have I done to You, O Watcher of all humanity?
> Why make me Your target? Am I a burden to You?"
> *Job 7:20*

Honest, transparent - Job was very honest in his prayers to God about how he was feeling, the questions he had, the preconceived thoughts he had about life and God; Job 7:11-21, 10, 14, 16:7-8, 30:20-23.

> "I cry to You, O God, but You don't answer. I stand before You, but You don't even look."
> *Job 30:20*

Genuinely questioned God and sought answers - Job had genuine questions for God during this difficult time in his life; Job 13:22-25, 24

> "Why do You turn away from me? Why do You treat me as Your enemy? Would You terrify a leaf blown by the wind? Would You chase dry straw?"
> *Job 13:24-25*

Spoke to God in a Dialogue - Job and the Lord spoke and responded to one another; Job 38-42:6

> "'Do you still want to argue with the Almighty? You are God's critic, but do you have the answers?' Then Job replied to the Lord, 'I am nothing how could I ever find the answers? I will cover my mouth with my hand.'"
> *Job 40:2-4*

Intercession - Job prayed for his friends after He answered him; Job 42:9-10

> "When Job prayed for his friends, the Lord restored his fortunes.
> In fact, the Lord gave him twice as much as before!"
> *Job 42:10*

Doer of the Word
Faithful to the word of the Lord - Job never sinned by going against the Word of God; Job 6:10, 23:12

"I have not departed from His commands, but have treasured His words more than daily food."
Job 23:12

JOB'S ABILITY TO HEAR AND RESPOND TO THE LORD

Dialogue - Job had a dialogue relationship with the Lord; Job 38-42:6

"'I have said too much already. I have nothing more to say.'
Then the Lord answered Job from the whirlwind:
'Brace yourself like a man, because I have some questions for you,
and you must answer them.'"
Job 40:5-7

PRESENTER/REPRESENTATIVE OF THE LORD

Righteous; Job 1:1, 8, 2:3, 27:3-6, Ezekiel 14:14, 20

"As surely as I live, says the Sovereign Lord, even if Noah, Daniel, and Job were there,
they wouldn't be able to save their own sons and daughters.
They alone would be saved by their righteousness."
Ezekiel 14:20

Faithful, loyal; Job 1:22, 2:3, 6:10, 23:10-12, 27:3-6, James 5:11

"I will maintain my innocence without wavering.
My conscience is clear for as long as I live."
Job 27:6

Chosen to suffer for the sake of righteousness; Job 1:7-12, 2:3-7, James 5:11

"We give great honor to those who endure under suffering.
For instance, you know about Job, a man of great endurance.
You can see how the Lord was kind to him at the end,
for the Lord is full of tenderness and mercy."
James 5:11

REVELATIONS GIVEN TO JOB FROM THE LORD

God is our only hope; Job 13:15

> "God might kill me, but I have no other hope. I am going to argue my case with Him."
> *Job 13:15*

God's wisdom is far beyond and outside of ours; Job 38-39, 40:6-24, 41, 42:5-6

> "Who kept the sea inside its boundaries as it burst from the womb,
> and as I clothed it with clouds and wrapped it in thick darkness?"
> *Job 38:8-9*

God is awesome and omnipotent; Job 38-39, 40:15-24, 41.

> "Take a look at Behemoth, which I made, just as I made you. It eats grass like an ox. See its powerful loins and the muscles of its belly. Its tail is as strong as a cedar. The sinews of its thighs are knit tightly together. Its bones are tubes of bronze. Its limbs are bars of iron. It is a prime example of God's handiwork, and only its Creator can threaten it."
> *Job 40:15-19*

God is entirely righteous and just; Job 40:8-14

> "Will you discredit My justice and condemn Me just to prove you are right?
> Are you as strong as God? Can you thunder with a voice like His?"
> *Job 40:8-9*

God is always good; Job 40:8-14, 42:10,12-17.

> "So the Lord blessed Job in the second half of his life even more than in the beginning.
> For now he had 14,000 sheep, 6,000 camels, 1,000 teams of oxen,
> and 1,000 female donkeys. He also gave Job seven more sons
> and three more daughters."
> *Job 42:12-13*

JOB'S FAITH/TRUST IN THE LORD

Never lost faith in the Lord - Job's faith never wavered during his time of trial and hardship; Job 1:22, 2:3, 6:10, 12:10, 13:16, 19:25-27, 23:10-12, 27:3-6

> "But as for me, I know that my Redeemer lives, and He will stand upon the earth at last.
> And after my body has decayed, yet in my body I will see God!
> I will see Him for myself. Yes, I will see Him with my own eyes.
> I am overwhelmed at the thought!"
> *Job 19:25-27*

Acknowledged that God is his only hope and is in complete control - Job continually confessed that God has all power and all authority and regardless of His reasonings He is right, and instead of becoming bitter at God he turned towards Him even more; Job 13:15, 17:3-4, 23:13-14.

> "You must defend my innocence, O God, since no one else will stand up for me."
> *Job 17:3*

CHAPTER 17
REVIEW QUESTIONS
Job

1. Where did Job live?

2. When did he live?

3. What factors or characteristics of Job helped him come through the terrible ordeal facing him?

4. What was Job's wife's advice to him?

5. What were some of the famous quotes in Job that revealed him as a man who praised in the midst of difficulty?

6. What does the book of Job reveal to us about Satan?

7. What commendable things does God say about Job to Satan?

18

Ezekiel

The author of the Book of Ezekiel presents himself as Ezekiel, the son of Buzzi, born into a priestly lineage. He was born around 622 BCE shortly after the call of Jeremiah to a prophetic ministry. Ezekiel's thirtieth year is given as five years after the exile of Judah's king Jehoiachim by the Babylonians. He lived during the reign of Josiah the king, the thirtieth year after Hilkiah the priest found the book of the law in the house of the sanctuary.

Ezekiel describes his 'call' from God this way: *"Now it came to pass in the thirtieth year, in the fourth month, in the fifth day of the month, as I was among the captives by the river of Chebar, that the heavens were opened, and I saw visions of God." (*Ezekiel 1:1). It further states that this was in the fifth year of the exile of King Jehoiachim.

Ezekiel was one of the four major prophets in the Old Testament along with Isaiah, Jeremiah and Daniel. Ezekiel, along with his wife, lived among the Jewish exiles in Babylon at a settlement along the river Chebar called Tel-abib (Ezekiel 3:15), less than one hundred miles south of Babylon. The invading Babylonians brought about ten thousand Jews to the village in 597 BC, including Ezekiel and the last king of Judah, Jehoiachim (2 Kings 24:8–14). *https://www.insight.org/resources/bible/the-major-prophets/ezekiel*

Ezekiel describes his calling to be a prophet by going into great detail about his encounter with God and four "living creatures" with four wheels that stayed beside the creatures. For the next five years he incessantly prophesied and acted out the destruction of Jerusalem and its temple, which was met with some opposition. However, Ezekiel and his contemporaries like Jeremiah, another prophet who was living in Jerusalem at that time, witnessed the fulfillment of their prophecies with the siege of Jerusalem by the Babylonians. On the hypothesis that the "thirtieth year" of Ezekiel 1:1 refers to Ezekiel's age, Ezekiel was fifty-years old when he had his final vision. Based on the dates given in the Book of Ezekiel, his span of prophecies can be calculated to have occurred over the course of about 22 years. The last recorded prophecy of Ezekiel dates to April 570 BCE.

WORSHIPER LEADER TYPE PROFILE

EZEKIEL

BACKGROUND

- **Political Conditions:**
  - Israelites in captivity by the Babylonians
- **Social Conditions:**
  - Being torn from your own land and home, and even having family ties severed is traumatic.
  - The separation of the exiles from their own familiar place and social setting changed people forever.
  - Being taken into the Babylonian culture meant being subjected to contrasting religious and moral beliefs.
- **Religious Conditions:**
  - Those who were exiled to Babylon were able to retain their own religious observances and their priests went along with them.
  - Idolatry was practiced in Babylon but the exiled Israelites were given freedom to worship as they wished.
  - "Having been cut off from Jerusalem and its Temple where alone Yahweh dwelled and could be worshipped, the deportees were faced with a crisis of faith and practice. Ezekiel attempted to sustain his fellow exiles by striving to keep alive their traditional religious beliefs and by fostering a spirit of unity with one another."[34]

FACTORS IN THE EQUIPPING FOR THE TASK

EZEKIEL'S PERSONALITY

Ezekiel was obedient - Ezekiel did and said all he was told to; Ezekiel 3:1-3, 22-23, 11:5-13, 12:7, 24:18, 37:4-7, 9-10.

> "The voice said to me, 'Son of man, eat what I am giving you eat this scroll! Then go and give its message to the people of Israel.' So I opened my mouth, and he fed me the scroll."
> *Ezekiel 3:1-2*

---

[34] Britannica, The Editors of Encyclopedia. "The Book of Ezekiel". Encyclopedia Britannica, 20 Jul. 1998, https://www.britannica.com/topic/The-Book-of-Ezekiel. Accessed 13 December 2021.

Faithful, unwavering - His heart steadfastly turned towards the Lord; Ezekiel 3:8-9

> "But look, I have made you as obstinate and hard-hearted as they are.
> I have made your forehead as hard as the hardest rock!
> So don't be afraid of them or fear their angry looks,
> even though they are rebels."
> *Ezekiel 3:8-9*

Humble - He did not see himself as above the different things God commanded him to do; Ezekiel 3:24-27, 4:1-13, 5:1-4, 12:1-7, 24:15-18.

> "Now lie on your left side and place the sins of Israel on yourself.
> You are to bear their sins for the number of days you lie there on your side.
> I am requiring you to bear Israel's sins for 390 days one day for each year of their sin.
> After that, turn over and lie on your right side for 40 days
> one day for each year of Judah's sin."
> *Ezekiel 4:4-6*

EZEKIEL'S RELATIONSHIP WITH GOD

Feared the Lord - Ezekiel had a trembling reverence for the Lord; Ezekiel 1:28, 3:23, 11:13

> "All around Him was a glowing halo, like a rainbow shining in the
> clouds on a rainy day. This is what the glory of the Lord looked like to me.
> When I saw it, I fell face down on the ground, and
> I heard someone's voice speaking to me."
> *Ezekiel 1:28*

THE REVELATION OF GOD THAT EZEKIEL RECEIVED AND CARRIED TO THE PEOPLE OF GOD

Righteous Judge; Ezekiel 5:5-17, 6, 7, 12:8-20, 13:1-3, 16:36-41, 59, 17:19-21, 20:4, 33-38, 21:1-5, 9-11, 24-32, 22:13-16, 19-22, 31, 23:22-49, 34:17-24

> "Because of your detestable idols, I will punish you like
> I have never punished anyone before
> or ever will again."
> *Ezekiel 5:9*

WORSHIP LEADER TYPES

There is only one Lord; Ezekiel 6, 14:3-11, 17:22-24

"I, the Lord, will answer all those, both Israelites and foreigners, who reject Me and set up idols in their hearts and so fall into sin, and who then come to a prophet asking for my advice. I will turn against such people and make a terrible example of them, eliminating them from among my people.
Then you will know that I am the Lord."
Ezekiel 14:7-8

Restorer; Ezekiel 11:16-17, 16:53-55, 60-63, 28:25-26, 34:25-31, 36

"Therefore, tell the exiles, 'This is what the Sovereign Lord says: Although I have scattered you in the countries of the world, I will be a sanctuary to you during your time in exile. I, the Sovereign Lord, will gather you back from the nations where you have been scattered, and I will give you the land of Israel once again.'"
Ezekiel 11:16-17

Faithful; Ezekiel 12:21-28

"For I am the Lord! If I say it, it will happen. There will be no more delays, you rebels of Israel. I will fulfill My threat of destruction in your own lifetime.
I, the Sovereign Lord, have spoken!"
Ezekiel 12:25

Faithful Lover of His people; Ezekiel 16

"But I came by and saw you there, helplessly kicking about in your own blood.
As you lay there, I said, 'Live!' And I helped you to thrive like a plant in the field.
You grew up and became a beautiful jewel. Your breasts became full, and your body hair grew, but you were still naked. And when I passed by again,
I saw that you were old enough for love. So I wrapped My cloak around you to cover your nakedness and declared My marriage vows.
I made a covenant with you, says the Sovereign Lord, and you became Mine."
Ezekiel 16:6-8

Jealous; Ezekiel 16:35-42

"I will punish you for your murder and adultery. I will cover you with blood in My jealous fury."
Ezekiel 16:38

Merciful; Ezekiel 16:60-63, 20:42-44

> "And I will reaffirm my covenant with you, and you will know that I am the Lord.
> You will remember your sins and cover your mouth in silent shame when
> I forgive you of all that you have done. I, the Sovereign Lord, have spoken!"
> *Ezekiel 16:62-63*

Holy; Ezekiel 20:39-41

> "As for you, O people of Israel, this is what the Sovereign Lord says: Go right ahead
> and worship your idols, but sooner or later you will obey Me and will stop
> bringing shame on My holy name by worshiping idols."
> *Ezekiel 20:39*

Rescuer; Ezekiel 34:10,22

> "This is what the Sovereign Lord says: I now consider these shepherds my enemies,
> and I will hold them responsible for what has happened to My flock. I will take away their
> right to feed the flock, and I will stop them from feeding themselves. I will rescue My flock
> from their mouths; the sheep will no longer be their prey."
> *Ezekiel 34:10*

Good Shepherd; Ezekiel 34:12-16, 31

> "I will be like a shepherd looking for His scattered flock. I will find My sheep and rescue
> them from all the places where they were scattered on that dark and cloudy day.
> I will bring them back home to their own land of Israel from among the peoples
> and nations. I will feed them on the mountains of Israel and
> by the rivers and in all the places where people live."
> *Ezekiel 34:12-13*

LESSONS LEARNED FROM THIS WORSHIP LEADER TYPE

Obey for others' sake - God was able to use Ezekiel mightily in the lives of others through his obedience; Ezekiel 24:18-24, 37:4-7, 9-10

> "So I spoke the message as He commanded me, and breath came into their bodies.
> They all came to life and stood up on their feet a great army."
> *Ezekiel 37:10*

Accountability is our responsibility - Ezekiel was responsible for warning the people, or else their sins and blood would be on his hands; Ezekiel 3:16-21, 33:7-9.

> "If I warn the wicked, saying, 'You are under the penalty of death,' but you fail to deliver the warning, they will die in their sins. And I will hold you responsible for their deaths."
> *Ezekiel 3:18*

Be open and available to the Lord - Ezekiel allowed his entire life - body, family - to be used by God; Ezekiel 3:24-27, 4:1-13, 5:1-4, 12:1-7, 24:15-18.

> "So now, son of man, pretend you are being sent into exile. Pack the few items an exile could carry, and leave your home to go somewhere else. Do this right in front of the people so they can see you. For perhaps they will pay attention to this, even though they are such rebels."
> *Ezekiel 12:3*

Ezekiel loved and feared the Lord – Ezekiel had a trembling reverence for the Lord; Ezekiel 1:28, 3:23, 11:13

> "While I was still prophesying, Pelatiah son of Benaiah suddenly died. Then I fell face down on the ground and cried out, 'O Sovereign Lord, are You going to kill everyone in Israel?'"
> *Ezekiel 11:13*

Obedient – Ezekiel did and said everything he was commanded to; Ezekiel 3:1-3, 22-23, 11:5-13, 24:18, 37:4-7, 9-10.

> "So I proclaimed this to the people the next morning, and in the evening my wife died. The next morning I did everything I had been told to do."
> *Ezekiel 24:18*

EZEKIEL'S ABILITY TO HEAR AND RESPOND TO THE LORD

Initial call - Ezekiel acknowledged and answered the initial call; Ezekiel 2:2

> "The Spirit came into me as he spoke, and he set me on my feet. I listened carefully to his words."
> *Ezekiel 2:2*

Obedient - He responded to the Lord's words in obedience; Ezekiel 3:1-3, 22-23, 11:5-13, 24:18, 37:4-7, 9-10.

"Then the Lord took hold of me and said, 'Get up and go out into the valley, and I will
speak to you there.'" So I got up and went, and there I saw the glory of the Lord,
just as I had seen in my first vision by the Kebar River.
And I fell face down on the ground."
Ezekiel 3:22-23

Dialogue - The Lord spoke, he responded, he spoke, the Lord responded, Ezekiel 37:3

"Then He asked me, 'Son of man, can these bones become living people again?'
'O Sovereign Lord,' I replied, "You alone know the
answer to that.'"
Ezekiel 37:3

PRESENTER/REPRESENTATIVE OF THE LORD

The Lord's mouthpiece - Ezekiel accurately relayed everything the Lord was saying to His people; Ezekiel 3:17, 5:5-17, 6, 7, 11:5-12,25, 12:8-28, 13, 14:4-11, 16, 17, 18, 20, 21:1-17, 22, 24:20-27, 25, 26, 27, 28, 29:1-16, 30:1-19, 31, 32:1-16, 33:1-20, 27-29, 34, 35, 36, 37:12-14, 38, 39:1-24

"Son of man, I have appointed you as a watchman for Israel.
Whenever you receive a message from Me,
warn people immediately."
Ezekiel 3:17

REVELATIONS GIVEN TO EZEKIEL FROM THE LORD

The four living beings; Ezekiel 1:1-25

"As I looked, I saw a great storm coming from the north,
driving before it a huge cloud that flashed with lightning and
shone with brilliant light. There was fire inside the cloud,
and in the middle of the fire glowed something like gleaming amber.
From the center of the cloud came four living beings that looked human,
except that each had four faces and four wings."
Ezekiel 1:4-6

WORSHIP LEADER TYPES

The glory of God; Ezekiel 1:26-28, 3:23, 10, 11:22-23, 43:1-6

"Above this surface was something that looked like a throne made of blue lapis lazuli. And on this throne high above was a figure whose appearance resembled a man. From what appeared to be His waist up, he looked like gleaming amber, flickering like a fire. And from His waist down, He looked like a burning flame, shining with splendor. All around Him was a glowing halo, like a rainbow shining in the clouds on a rainy day. This is what the glory of the Lord looked like to me. When I saw it, I fell face down on the ground, and I heard someone's voice speaking to me."
Ezekiel 1:26-28

Drought, famine were coming; Ezekiel 4:16-17

"Then He told me, 'Son of man, I will make food very scarce in Jerusalem. It will be weighed out with great care and eaten fearfully. The water will be rationed out drop by drop, and the people will drink it with dismay. Lacking food and water, people will look at one another in terror, and they will waste away under their punishment."
Ezekiel 4:16-17

Israel's idolatry; Ezekiel 8, 14:3

"Son of man, these leaders have set up idols in their hearts. They have embraced things that will make them fall into sin. Why should I listen to their requests?"
Ezekiel 14:3

Israel's judgment; Ezekiel 9, 14:21-23, 15:6-8, 18

"And I will make the land desolate because My people have been unfaithful to Me. I, the Sovereign Lord, have spoken!"
Ezekiel 15:8

The four cherubim; Ezekiel 10, 11:22-23

"The cherubim were standing at the south end of the Temple when the man went in, and the cloud of glory filled the inner courtyard. Then the glory of the Lord rose up from above the cherubim and went over to the entrance of the Temple. The Temple was filled with this cloud of glory, and the courtyard glowed brightly with the glory of the Lord."
Ezekiel 10:3-4

Israel's restoration; Ezekiel 11:18-21, 39:25-29

> "And I will give them singleness of heart and put a new spirit within them.
> I will take away their stony, stubborn heart and give them a tender,
> responsive heart, so they will obey My decrees and regulations.
> Then they will truly be My people,
> and I will be their God."
> *Ezekiel 11:19-20*

Israel's exile; Ezekiel 12:1-6

> "So now, son of man, pretend you are being sent into exile. Pack the few items an exile
> could carry, and leave your home to go somewhere else. Do this right in front of the
> people so they can see you. For perhaps they will pay attention to this,
> even though they are such rebels."
> *Ezekiel 12:3*

Judgment on false prophets; Ezekiel 13

> "This is what the Sovereign Lord says: What sorrow awaits the false
> prophets who are following their own imaginations
> and have seen nothing at all!"
> *Ezekiel 13:3*

Israel's kings/princes' funeral song; Ezekiel 19

> "Sing this funeral song for the princes of Israel:"
> *Ezekiel 19:1*

Insight into Israel's ways through Oholah and Oholibah; Ezekiel 23

After relaying the terrible story of the two sisters who were lewd and promiscuous, the explanation was that they were an example of how Israel had left the true God and righteousness to act in evil ways.

> "The Lord said to me, 'Son of man, you must accuse Oholah and Oholibah of all their
> detestable sins. They have committed both adultery and murder adultery
> by worshiping idols and murder by burning as sacrifices
> the children they bore to Me."
> *Ezekiel 23:36-37*

WORSHIP LEADER TYPES

Dry bones' revival; Ezekiel 37:4-14

> "Then He said to me, 'Speak a prophetic message to the winds, son of man.
> Speak a prophetic message and say, 'This is what the Sovereign Lord says:
> Come, O breath, from the four winds! Breathe into these dead bodies so they may live
> again.' So I spoke the message as He commanded me, and breath came
> into their bodies. They all came to life and stood up on their feet a great army."
> *Ezekiel 37:9-10*

Unification of Israel and Judah; Ezekiel 37:15-28

> "I will unify them into one nation on the mountains of Israel.
> One king will rule them all; no longer will they be divided
> into two nations or into two kingdoms."
> *Ezekiel 37:22*

Temple's complete restoration; Ezekiel 40, 41, 42, 43:13-27, 44, 46:19-24

> "I could see a wall completely surrounding the Temple area.
> The man took a measuring rod that was 10 1/2 feet
> long and measured the wall, and the wall was
> 10 1/2 feet thick and 10 1/2 feet high."
> *Ezekiel 40:5*

River of life; Ezekiel 47:1-12

> "There will be swarms of living things wherever the water of this river flows.
> Fish will abound in the Dead Sea, for its waters will become fresh.
> Life will flourish wherever this water flows."
> *Ezekiel 47:9*

CHAPTER 18
REVIEW QUESTIONS
Ezekiel

1. What were the political conditions of Ezekiel's time?

2. What were the social conditions of his time?

3. What were the religious conditions?

4. What were the factors Ezekiel had to equip him in the task given to him by God?

5. Name some of Ezekiel's character traits.

6. What lessons can we learn from Ezekiel's life?

7. What were some of the things that God allowed Ezekiel to see that were going on in the Temple?

8. What did God allow those who remained faith to Him to do?

*God chooses people, situations and places
that are off the beaten path,
people whose clan is the weakest and a
man who is the least in his family that
His glory might be seen.*

19
Daniel

Daniel was a descendant of the royal house of David. He was a handsome, intelligent, and gifted man who demonstrated courage and integrity. Daniel was known as a "wise man," and we know he was a dreamer and an interpreter of dreams. He is almost a copy of the Old Testament Joseph.

In the book of Daniel, we learn that Nebuchadnezzar, a cruel and evil king, defeated the Israelites and kidnapped some of the surviving young men for service to the King. One of the qualifications for this position was physical attractiveness, so we know Daniel had to be handsome. Another qualification was intelligence, so we know Daniel was no dummy. They also had to be able to learn many new things, including the language of the realm, Babylonian. Combined with those traits, Daniel possessed a gift of interpreting dreams.

Since we know Nebuchadnezzar was an evil man and possessed great power, it would not be surprising to learn that he had many troubling dreams. In Daniel's day, these dreams were not a sign of a troubled man; instead, they were a message from the supernatural world, from a god trying to tell the King something important. Otherwise, men came forth to interpret these dreams, but only Daniel succeeded, greatly pleasing the King.

Daniel showed great integrity when he and his three compatriots refused to eat the food provided for them. Instead, they asked to eat only the food allowed by their religion, and they promised that if they did not show signs of great health afterward, they would eat the food offered. Of course, these dietary rules were a large part of their laws and covenants with God, so it was important to stay true to them.

Daniel showed courage even though an edict was passed that no one could pray except to the King. Yet, Daniel continued praying three times a day to God. It was reported to King Darius that Daniel defined the order not to pray, and he was thrown into the lion's den. However, he was discovered unscathed and unhurt by these fearsome beasts. He stood for truth against fearsome odds, even in the face of death. This hero image of Daniel inspired the weak to be strong and gave courage to those living under impossible conditions. Daniel was faced with an existential pressure to conform and to compromise his own values and beliefs, yet he overcame these pressures.

Daniel's character represented the truest and best of Israel. Whether Daniel was a historical figure or a character used to illustrate certain essential character traits is unimportant here. Like David of the Old Testament, Daniel became greater as a symbol than he could ever have been as a historical personality. In conclusion, Daniel was a wise, handsome dreamer and interpreter of dreams who stood firm in the face of adversity and never wavered in his beliefs.

WORSHIP LEADER TYPE PROFILE

DANIEL

BACKGROUND

- **Political Conditions:**
  - Jehoiakim is king of Judah; King Nebuchadnezzar of Babylon has taken over Jerusalem.
  - Belshazzar becomes the king of Babylon,
  - Darius the Mede conquers Babylon and becomes king.
  - Cyrus the Persian becomes king.
- **Social Conditions:**
  - Israelites in captivity by the Babylonians.
- **Religious Conditions:**
  - Israelites had to deal with Babylon, a polytheistic/pagan nation that was in power. The Israelites had no freedom at all within this religious, social and political tyrannical system.

FACTORS IN THE EQUIPPING FOR THE TASK

Daniel was intelligent, strong and healthy - Daniel was physically healthy and strong, thus him being chosen to be taken into captivity; Daniel 1:4-6. He was was of the young Hebrews to serve in the royal palace.

> "'Select only strong, healthy, and good-looking young men,' he said. 'Make sure they are well versed in every branch of learning, are gifted with knowledge and good judgment, and are suited to serve in the royal palace. Train these young men in the language and literature of Babylon'...Daniel, Hananiah, Mishael, and Azariah were four of the young men chosen, all from the tribe of Judah."
> *Daniel 1:4-6*

Educated - Daniel, along with his three friends, were very educated, "qualifying" them to be chosen to be taken; Daniel 1:4-6

> "'Select only strong, healthy, and good-looking young men,' he said.
> 'Make sure they are well versed in every branch of learning, are gifted with knowledge and good judgment, and are suited to serve in the royal palace. Train these young men in the language and literature of Babylon'...Daniel, Hananiah, Mishael, and Azariah were four of the young men chosen, all from the tribe of Judah."
> *Daniel 1:4-6*

Favored and gifted by God - Daniel was favored by God in the sight of those in authority over him as well as gifted to with knowledge, understanding, and interpretation of dreams and visions; Daniel 1:9,17, 5:12,14, 6:3.

> "God gave these four young men an unusual aptitude for understanding every aspect of literature and wisdom. And God gave Daniel the special ability to interpret the meanings of visions and dreams."
> *Daniel 1:17*

HIS PERSONALITY

Faithful - Daniel was faithful to God in every position God placed him in; Daniel 1:8, 6:4

> "Then the other administrators and high officers began searching for some fault in the way Daniel was handling government affairs, but they couldn't find anything to criticize or condemn. He was faithful always responsible, and completely trustworthy."
> *Daniel 6:4*

Respectful - Daniel respected his authorities, he was not rude in refusing to eat the food the king provided; Daniel 1:8

> "But Daniel was determined not to defile himself by eating the food and wine given to them by the king. He asked the chief of staff for permission not to eat these unacceptable foods."
> *Daniel 1:8*

Wise, discerning - Daniel was gifted with godly wisdom, as well as simply exercised wisdom in life; Daniel 1:17-20, 2:14, 5:11,14.

> "When Arioch, the commander of the king's guard, came to kill them, Daniel handled the situation with wisdom and discretion."
> *Daniel 2:14*

Reliable and responsible - Daniel was known as very trustworthy with men as well as with God; Daniel 6:4

> "Then the other administrators and high officers began searching for some fault in the way Daniel was handling government affairs, but they couldn't find anything to criticize or condemn. He was faithful always responsible, and completely trustworthy."
> *Daniel 6:4*

Humble - Daniel was humble before the Lord; Daniel 10:12

> "Then he said, 'Don't be afraid, Daniel. Since the first day you began to pray for understanding and to humble yourself before your God, your request has been heard in heaven. I have come in answer to your prayer."
> *Daniel 10:12*

DANIEL'S RELATIONSHIP WITH GOD

Daniel feared, and revered the Lord - Daniel had a fear and reverence for the Lord that refused to dishonor Him; Daniel 1:8

> "But Daniel was determined not to defile himself by eating the food and wine given to them by the king. He asked the chief of staff for permission not to eat these unacceptable foods."
> *Daniel 1:8*

Daniel had a close relationship with the Father - Daniel was very close to the heart of God, communing with Him daily - multiple times a day; Daniel 6:10

> "But when Daniel learned that the law had been signed, he went home and knelt down as usual in his upstairs room, with its windows open toward Jerusalem. He prayed three times a day, just as he had always done, giving thanks to his God."
> *Daniel 6:10*

Daniel was very precious to the Lord - God tells Daniel multiple times how he is precious to Him; Daniel 9:23, 10:11,19

> "The moment you began praying, a command was given. And now I am here to tell you what it is, for you are very precious to God. Listen carefully so that you can understand the meaning of your vision."
> *Daniel 9:23*

THE REVELATION OF GOD THAT DANIEL CARRIED TO THE PEOPLE OF GOD

God is a Revealer of secrets; Daniel 2:27-30, 47

> "But there is a God in heaven who reveals secrets, and He has shown King Nebuchadnezzar what will happen in the future. Now I will tell you your dream and the visions you saw as you lay on your bed."
> *Daniel 2:28*

God is the One who elevates and brings down kings and kingdoms; Daniel 2:21, 37-44, 5:18-28, 11.

> "He controls the course of world events;
> He removes kings and sets up other kings.
> He gives wisdom to the wise and knowledge to the scholars."
> *Daniel 2:21*

Anyone who elevates themselves above God will be brought down; Daniel 4:24-26, 5:20-28.

> "But when his heart and mind were puffed up with arrogance, he was brought down from his royal throne and stripped of his glory."
> *Daniel 5:20*

God is our rescuer; Daniel 6:22

> "My God sent His angel to shut the lions' mouths so that they would not hurt me, for I have been found innocent in His sight. And I have not wronged you, Your Majesty."
> *Daniel 6:22*

LESSONS LEARNED FROM THIS WORSHIP LEADER TYPE

We must be determined in our hearts to obey God - Daniel's obedience was a decision already made and set in his heart; Daniel 1:8

> "But Daniel was determined not to defile himself by eating the food and wine given to them by the king. He asked the chief of staff for permission not to eat these unacceptable foods."
> *Daniel 1:8*

It is God who gifts us and elevates us - Daniel's favor with these different kings and special abilities and gifts of knowledge, wisdom, and interpretation came from God and God alone; Daniel 1:17-20, 6:2-3.

> "Daniel soon proved himself more capable than all the
> other administrators and high officers. Because of Daniel's great ability,
> the king made plans to place him over the entire empire."
> *Daniel 6:3*

Praise before the storm is over - Daniel praised God before the threat was ended; Daniel 2:19-23

> "That night the secret was revealed to Daniel in a vision.
> Then Daniel praised the God of heaven.
> He said, 'Praise the name of God forever and ever,
> for He has all wisdom and power."
> *Daniel 2:19-20*

Every revelation the Lord gives us to give others won't be pleasant - The interpretations that Daniel was given were very unpleasant; Daniel 4:19-27, 5:22-28.

> "This is the message that was written: MENE, MENE, TEKEL, and PARSIN.
> This is what these words mean: Mene means 'numbered' -
> God has numbered the days of your reign and has brought it to an end.
> Tekel means 'weighed' - you have been weighed on the balances
> and have not measured up. Parsin means 'divided' - your kingdom has been
> divided and given to the Medes and Persians."
> *Daniel 5:25-28*

True and faithful worship and praise of our God is infectious - Daniel's life of worship caused unbelieving kings to praise and honor the Lord; Daniel 2:47, 6:25-27

> "The king said to Daniel, 'Truly, your God is the greatest of gods,
> the Lord over kings, a revealer of mysteries,
> for you have been able to reveal this secret.'"
> *Daniel 2:47*

Remain faithful, no matter what - Daniel remained faithful to the Lord despite the consequences that he would suffer; Daniel 6:10-16

> "Then the officials went together to Daniel's house and found him praying and asking for God's help. So they went straight to the king and reminded him about his law. 'Did you not sign a law that for the next thirty days any person who prays to anyone, divine or human - except to you, Your Majesty - will be thrown into the den of lions?' 'Yes,' the king replied, 'that decision stands; it is an official law of the Medes and Persians that cannot be revoked.'"
>
> *Daniel 6:11-12*

We will suffer for righteousness - Daniel was thrown into a den of lions for praying to the Lord; Daniel 6:16-17

> "So at last the king gave orders for Daniel to be arrested and thrown into the den of lions. The king said to him, 'May your God, whom you serve so faithfully, rescue you.' A stone was brought and placed over the mouth of the den. The king sealed the stone with his own royal seal and the seals of his nobles, so that no one could rescue Daniel."
>
> *Daniel 6:16-17*

Love for the Lord
Feared, reverenced the Lord - Daniel had such a loving fear of the Lord that he simply refused to dishonor Him; Daniel 1:8

> "But Daniel was determined not to defile himself by eating the food and wine given to them by the king. He asked the chief of staff for permission not to eat these unacceptable foods."
>
> *Daniel 1:8*

Love for His people
Sought God to save him and his friends - Daniel did not only seek to save himself, but he also sought the Lord on behalf of his brethren; Daniel 2:18

> "He urged them to ask the God of heaven to show them His mercy by telling them the secret, so they would not be executed along with the other wise men of Babylon."
>
> *Daniel 2:18*

Had his friends promoted - Daniel had his friends promoted along with him after interpreting Nebuchadnezzar's dream; Daniel 2:49

> "At Daniel's request, the king appointed Shadrach, Meshach, and Abednego to be in charge of the affairs of the province of Babylon, while Daniel remained in the king's courts."
>
> *Daniel 2:49*

Pleading for repentance - Daniel begged King Nebuchadnezzar to repent at the Lord's warning; Daniel 4:19, 27

> "King Nebuchadnezzar, please accept my advice.
> Stop sinning and do what is right. Break from your wicked past and be
> merciful to the poor. Perhaps then you will continue to prosper."
> *Daniel 4:27*

Intercession - After reading the book of Jeremiah, Daniel pleads for the Lord to have mercy on His people; Daniel 9:3-20

> "In view of all Your faithful mercies, Lord, please turn your furious anger away from Your
> city Jerusalem, Your holy mountain. All the neighboring nations mock Jerusalem and Your
> people because of our sins and the sins of our ancestors."
> *Daniel 9:16*

Zeal for the Lord

Prayed and remained obedient despite consequences - Daniel knew the consequences of worshipping the Lord during this specific time but refused to let that stop him; Daniel 6:16-17

> "So at last the king gave orders for Daniel to be arrested and thrown into the den of lions.
> The king said to him, 'May your God, whom you serve so faithfully, rescue you.'
> A stone was brought and placed over the mouth of the den.
> The king sealed the stone with his own royal seal and the seals of his nobles,
> so that no one could rescue Daniel."
> *Daniel 6:16-17*

EXAMPLE OF BEING A MAN OF PRAISE AND PRAYER

Praised God for answering prayer - Daniel praised God for answering his prayer in revealing the meaning of Nebuchadnezzar's dream; Daniel 2:19-23

> "I thank and praise You, God of my ancestors, for You have given me wisdom and strength.
> You have told me what we asked of You and revealed to us what the king demanded."
> *Daniel 2:23*

A Man of Prayer

Sought God for help - Daniel went to the Lord when the lives of he and his friends were being threatened; Daniel 2:18, 6:11

> "Then the officials went together to Daniel's house and found him
> praying and asking for God's help."
> *Daniel 6:11*

Faithful in prayer life - Daniel prayed three times a day everyday faithfully; Daniel 6:10,13

> "But when Daniel learned that the law had been signed,
> he went home and knelt down as usual in his upstairs room, with its windows open
> toward Jerusalem. He prayed three times a day, just as he had always done,
> giving thanks to his God."
> *Daniel 6:10*

Continued to pray openly despite the law - Daniel continued to pray faithfully despite the King's law stating that no one could pray to or worship anyone else but him for 30 days; Daniel 6:10

> "But when Daniel learned that the law had been signed, he went home and knelt down as
> usual in his upstairs room, with its windows open toward Jerusalem.
> He prayed three times a day, just as he had always done,
> giving thanks to his God."
> *Daniel 6:10*

Confession and intercession - After reading the book of Jeremiah, Daniel immediately prayed, confessing the sins of he and his people and begging for mercy; Daniel 9:3-20

> "I went on praying and confessing my sin and the sin of my people,
> pleading with the Lord my God for Jerusalem, His holy mountain."
> *Daniel 9:20*

DANIEL'S ABILITY TO HEAR AND RESPOND TO THE LORD

Sought the Lord and received an answer - Daniel sought the Lord for help and God answered him; Daniel 2:18-19

> "He urged them to ask the God of heaven to show them His mercy by telling them the secret,
> so they would not be executed along with the other wise men of Babylon.
> "That night the secret was revealed to Daniel in a vision.
> Then Daniel praised the God of heaven."
> *Daniel 2:18-19*

Received visions from the Lord - Daniel received visions of the end times; Daniel 7, 8, 10, 11, 12

> "As my vision continued that night, I saw someone like a
> son of man coming with the clouds of heaven.
> He approached the Ancient One and was led into His presence."
> *Daniel 7:13*

PRESENTER/REPRESENTATIVE OF THE LORD

Pleading for repentance - Daniel pleads with Nebuchadnezzar to repent of his evil deeds and prideful heart, as Christ does during His time here on earth; Daniel 4:27

> "King Nebuchadnezzar, please accept my advice.
> Stop sinning and do what is right.
> Break from your wicked past and be merciful to the poor.
> Perhaps then you will continue to prosper."
> *Daniel 4:27*

Close relationship with the Father - Daniel had an intimate relationship with the Father, as Christ did; Daniel 6:10

> "But when Daniel learned that the law had been signed,
> he went home and knelt down as usual in his upstairs room,
> with its windows open toward Jerusalem. He prayed three times a day,
> just as he had always done, giving thanks to his God."
> *Daniel 6:10*

Persecuted for righteousness - Daniel was accused of evil for doing right and punished, as Christ suffered for righteousness; Daniel 6:16-17

> "So at last the king gave orders for Daniel to be arrested and
> thrown into the den of lions. The king said to him,
> 'May your God, whom you serve so faithfully, rescue you.'
> A stone was brought and placed over the mouth of the den.
> The king sealed the stone with his own royal seal and the seals of his nobles,
> so that no one could rescue Daniel."
> *Daniel 6:16-17*

REVELATIONS GIVEN TO DANIEL

God is the establisher and terminator of kings and kingdoms; Daniel 2:21, 11

"He controls the course of world events;
He removes kings and sets up other kings.
He gives wisdom to the wise and knowledge to the scholars."
Daniel 2:21

God is our rescuer; Daniel 6:22

"My God sent His angel to shut the lions' mouths
so that they would not hurt me,
for I have been found innocent in His sight.
And I have not wronged you, Your Majesty."
Daniel 6:22

God is the avenger; Daniel 6:24

"Then the king gave orders to arrest the men who had maliciously accused Daniel. He had
them thrown into the lions' den, along with their wives and children.
The lions leaped on them and tore them apart
before they even hit the floor of the den."
Daniel 6:24

Christ and the coming of His kingdom; Daniel 7

"As my vision continued that night, I saw someone like a son of man coming with the
clouds of heaven. He approached the Ancient One and was led into His presence.
He was given authority, honor and sovereignty over all the nations of the world, so that
people of every race and nation and language would obey Him.
His rule is eternal - it will never end. His kingdom will never be destroyed."
Daniel 7:13-14

End times; Daniel 8

"Then he said, 'I am here to tell you what will happen later in the time of wrath.
What you have seen pertains to the very end of time."
Daniel 8:19

Daniel

First coming of Christ; Daniel 9:24-27

> "Now listen and understand! Seven sets of seven plus sixty-two sets of seven will pass from the time the command is given to rebuild Jerusalem until a ruler - the Anointed One - comes. Jerusalem will be rebuilt with streets and strong defenses, despite the perilous times. After this period of sixty-two sets of seven, the Anointed One will be killed, appearing to have accomplished nothing, and a ruler will arise whose armies will destroy the city and the Temple. The end will come with a flood, and war and its miseries are decreed from that time to the very end."
> *Daniel 9:25-26*

Spiritual warfare; Daniel 10:13-14, 20-22

> "He replied, 'Do you know why I have come? Soon I must return to fight against the spirit prince of the kingdom of Persia, and after that the spirit prince of the kingdom of Greece will come."
> *Daniel 10:20*

Future events of kingdoms to come; Daniel 11

> "Now then, I will reveal the truth to you. Three more Persian kings will reign, to be succeeded by a fourth, far richer than the others. He will use his wealth to stir up everyone to fight against the kingdom of Greece."
> *Daniel 11:2*

DANIEL'S FAITH AND TRUST IN THE LORD

Obedient despite consequences - Daniel remained faithful and obedient to the Lord despite the consequences he would have to face; Daniel 6:10, 23

> "But when Daniel learned that the law had been signed, he went home and knelt down as usual in his upstairs room, with its windows open toward Jerusalem. He prayed three times a day, just as he had always done, giving thanks to his God."
> *Daniel 6:10*

Came out of the lions' den unharmed - Daniel was defended and saved because of his trust in the Lord; Daniel 6:23

> "The king was overjoyed and ordered that Daniel be lifted from the den. Not a scratch was found on him, for he had trusted in his God."
> *Daniel 6:23*

CHAPTER 19
REVIEW QUESTIONS
Daniel

1. What were the political and social conditions in Daniel's time?

2. What were the religious conditions?

3. Name three factors in the equipping of Daniel's task.

4. Name four aspects of Daniel's personality.

5. Name three events told in the book of Daniel that shows us important principles.

6. What were some of these principles?

7. Why was Daniel thrown into Lion's den?

8. Why was Daniel thrown into the Lion's den?

9. What lesson do we glean from Daniel's worship life to the Lord?

10. Name 3 specific ways that we can see Daniel's trust in God.

"Worship is not limited to a specific time or place; it is a continuous conversation with God, acknowledging His presence in every moment of our lives."
—Beth Moore

20
Shadrach, Meshach and Abednego

Who were these three young men who stood fearlessly and refused to bow to a false god? Much of the book of Daniel is about these young men, and they serve as examples of courage, standing strong in the face of oppression and just refusing to give way out of fear of the all-powerful Babylonians who captured them and took them into slavery.

If one is to be taken as a slave, the "three Hebrew boys" and Daniel had pretty cushy slave assignments. Their Hebrew names were Hananiah, Michael, and Azariah, but they were given Babylonian names, the three names we are familiar with in this story. They were described as 'without defect, handsome, intelligent, quick-witted and wise. With these qualities, they were taken into the palace to serve the king of Babylon.

These men showed remarkable courage when they refused to eat the food given to them and instead remained faithful to their people's dietary restrictions. Even when they deprived themselves of the delicacies of the Babylonian diet (or perhaps because of it), they stayed healthy and strong. At the end of ten days on their special diet, Daniel and his three friends "looked healthier and better nourished than the young men who had been eating the food assigned by the king." (Daniel 1:13)

The three young men (and Daniel, of course) were trained in the language and literature of Babylon. They had an unusual aptitude for understanding every aspect of literature and wisdom.

> "Select only strong, healthy, and good-looking young men," he said.
> "Make sure they are well versed in every branch of learning, are gifted with knowledge and good judgment, and are suited to serve in the royal palace. Train these young men in the language and literature of Babylon.[c]"
> *Daniel 1:4*

They also surpassed even the most revered wise men and advisors to the King and showed more aptitude for wisdom and discernment than these experienced and trusted advisors.

The three Hebrew boys, as they are known, were an example of courage, of uncompromising beliefs and trust in God, which was shown by their refusal to submit to the edicts of the kingdom to bow down to the golden idol. When they were thrown into the fiery furnace, they were not burned, and came out unscathed, prompting the might king of Babylon to commend them and make the decree that "If any people, whatever their race or nation or language, speak a word against the God of Shadrach, Meshach and Abednego, they will be torn limb from limb, and their houses will be turned into heaps of rubble. There is no other god who can rescue like this!"

Daniel 3:29

Worship Leader Type Profile

Shadrach, Meshach, & Abednego

BACKGROUND

- **Political Conditions:**
  - King Nebuchadnezzar seized Jerusalem.
- **Social Conditions:**
  - Hebrews are now in captivity.
- **Religious Conditions:**
  - Babylonians were polytheistic/pagans.

FACTORS IN THE EQUIPPING FOR THE TASK

The three Hebrew boys were healthy and strong - The three were chosen to be taken for their intellectual and physical health; Daniel 1:4-6

"'Select only strong, healthy, and good-looking young men,' he said. 'Make sure they are well versed in every branch of learning, are gifted with knowledge and good judgment, and are suited to serve in the royal palace. Train these young men in the language and literature of Babylon.'"

Daniel 1:4

Teachable - The three were chosen to serve in the royal palace. Daniel 1:4
Wise and discerning - The three were chosen to be taken for their wisdom; Daniel 1:4

> "'Select only strong, healthy, and good-looking young men,' he said.
> 'Make sure they are well versed in every branch of learning,
> are gifted with knowledge and good judgment,
> and are suited to serve in the royal palace.
> Train these young men in the language and literature of Babylon.'"
> *Daniel 1:4*

Gifted with understanding and wisdom from God - God increased their ability to learn, understand, and discern; Daniel 1:17-20

> "God gave these four young men an unusual aptitude for understanding every aspect of
> literature and wisdom. And God gave Daniel the special ability to
> interpret the meanings of visions and dreams."
> *Daniel 1:17*

SHADRACH, MESHACH, & ABEDNEGO PERSONALITIES

Faithful - The three remained faithful to the Lord with the way they behaved and conducted themselves, despite being in captivity; Daniel 1:12-15, 3:12-18.

> "The attendant agreed to Daniel's suggestion and tested them for ten days.
> At the end of the ten days, Daniel and his three friends looked
> healthier and better nourished than the young men
> who had been eating the food assigned by the king."
> *Daniel 1:14-15*

Obedient - The three remained obedient to the Lord despite being in captivity; Daniel 1:12-15, 3:12-18, 28.

> "But there are some Jews - Shadrach, Meshach, and Abednego -
> whom you have put in charge of the province of Babylon.
> They pay no attention to you, Your Majesty.
> They refuse to serve your gods and do not worship
> the gold statue you have set up."
> *Daniel 3:12*

SHADRACH, MESHACH, & ABEDNEGO RELATIONSHIPS WITH GOD

Loved and feared the Lord - The three very much loved the Lord and refused to dishonor Him; Daniel 1:12-15, 3:12-18, 28.

> "But there are some Jews - Shadrach, Meshach, and Abednego - whom you have put in charge of the province of Babylon. They pay no attention to you, Your Majesty. They refuse to serve your gods and do not worship the gold statue you have set up."
> *Daniel 3:12*

THE REVELATIONS OF GOD THEY RECEIVED AND CARRIED TO THE PEOPLE OF GOD

God is a rescuer and defender; Daniel 3:25-27

> "Then the high officers, officials, governors, and advisers crowded around them and saw that the fire had not touched them. Not a hair on their heads was singed, and their clothing was not scorched. They didn't even smell of smoke!"
> *Daniel 3:27*

God is the only living, true God; Daniel 3:26-29

> "Then the high officers, officials, governors, and advisers crowded around them and saw that the fire had not touched them. Not a hair on their heads was singed, and their clothing was not scorched. They didn't even smell of smoke! Then Nebuchadnezzar said, 'Praise to the God of Shadrach, Meshach, and Abednego! He sent His angel to rescue His servants who trusted in Him. They defied the king's command and were willing to die rather than serve or worship any god except their own God."
> *Daniel 3:27-28*

LESSONS LEARNED FROM THIS WORSHIP LEADER TYPE

Do not make compromises because of threats. The three did not waver or compromise in their worship of God. Daniel 3:12

> "But there are some Jews - Shadrach, Meshach, and Abednego - whom you have put in charge of the province of Babylon. They pay no attention to you, Your Majesty. They refuse to serve your gods and do not worship the gold statue you have set up."
> *Daniel 3:12*

Remain faithful, whatever the cost. The three remained faithful in refusing to worship or serve any other god but the Lord; Daniel 3:15-18

> "If we are thrown into the blazing furnace, the God whom we serve is able to save us. He will rescue us from your power, Your Majesty. But even if He doesn't, we want to make it clear to you, Your Majesty, that we will never serve your gods or worship the gold statue you have set up."
> *Daniel 3:17-18*

God does not abandon us in our trials. God manifested Himself in the fire with the three. He did not leave them - in fact, He drew closer to them than ever before; Daniel 3:23-25

> "But suddenly, Nebuchadnezzar jumped up in amazement and exclaimed to his advisers, 'Didn't we tie up three men and throw them into the furnace?' 'Yes, Your Majesty, we certainly did,' they replied. 'Look!' Nebuchadnezzar shouted. 'I see four men, unbound, walking around in the fire unharmed! And the fourth looks like a god!'"
> *Daniel 3:24-25*

God allows us to be thrown into the fire to display His glory and power through us; Daniel 3:25-29

> "Then the high officers, officials, governors, and advisers crowded around them and saw that the fire had not touched them. Not a hair on their heads was singed, and their clothing was not scorched. They didn't even smell of smoke! Then Nebuchadnezzar said, 'Praise to the God of Shadrach, Meshach, and Abednego! He sent His angel to rescue His servants who trusted in Him. They defied the king's command and were willing to die rather than serve or worship any god except their own God. Therefore, I make this decree: If any people, whatever their race or nation or language, speak a word against the God of Shadrach, Meshach, and Abednego, they will be torn limb from limb, and their houses will be turned into heaps of rubble. There is no other god who can rescue like this!'"
> *Daniel 3:27-29*

WORSHIP LEADER TYPES

Our lives of faithful worship draw others to the Lord. The faith and faithful worship of these three men to the Lord caused the king to praise their God. Daniel 3:28-29

"Praise to the God of Shadrach, Meshach, and Abednego!
He sent His angel to rescue His servants who trusted in Him.
They defied the king's command and were willing to die rather
than serve or worship any god except their own God.
Therefore, I make this decree: If any people, whatever their race or
nation or language, speak a word against the God of Shadrach, Meshach,
and Abednego, they will be torn limb from limb, and their houses will be turned into
heaps of rubble. There is no other god who can rescue like this!"
Daniel 3:28-29

Our faithfulness will be rewarded. The three were promoted after they were delivered out of the furnace. Daniel 3:30

"Then the king promoted Shadrach, Meshach, and Abednego to even higher positions in
the province of Babylon."
Daniel 3:30

Love for the Lord produces obedience - The three refused to dishonor the Lord; Daniel 1:12-15, 3:12-18.

"But there are some Jews - Shadrach, Meshach, and Abednego -
whom you have put in charge of the province of Babylon.
They pay no attention to you, Your Majesty. They refuse to serve your gods and do not
worship the gold statue you have set up."
Daniel 3:12

Willing to be martyred, out of their zeal for the Lord - The three were willing to die faithful rather than compromise and live; Daniel 3:14-18,28

"If we are thrown into the blazing furnace, the God whom we serve is able to save us.
He will rescue us from your power, Your Majesty. But even if He doesn't,
we want to make it clear to you, Your Majesty, that we will never serve your gods or
worship the gold statue you have set up."
Daniel 3:17-1

EXAMPLE OF BEING WORSHIPPERS

Refused idolatry. The three refused to obey in bowing down and worshiping Nebuchadnezzar's image; Daniel 3:12-18

> "But there are some Jews - Shadrach, Meshach, and Abednego - whom you have put in charge of the province of Babylon. They pay no attention to you, Your Majesty. They refuse to serve your gods and do not worship the gold statue you have set up."
> *Daniel 3:12*

Men of prayer sought God for help; Daniel 2:18

They did not demand that God deliver them. They knew that God could deliver them, but if He didn't the three refused to sin against God by worshiping another god or idol; Daniel 3:12-18.

> "If we are thrown into the blazing furnace, the God whom we serve is able to save us. He will rescue us from your power, Your Majesty. But even if He doesn't, we want to make it clear to you, Your Majesty, that we will never serve your gods or worship the gold statue you have set up."
> *Daniel 3:17-18*

Persecuted for righteousness - The three were punished for doing good, as Christ was ultimately put to death; Daniel 3:16-23.

> "So they tied them up and threw them into the furnace, fully dressed in their pants, turbans, robes, and other garments."
> *Daniel 3:21*

Their lives were used to display the righteousness, glory, and power of God. God used the punishment and deliverance of the three men as a witness to who He is and the power and authority He holds over all, as Christ was crucified and resurrected as a witness to the one true God; Daniel 3:25-29

> "Then the high officers, officials, governors, and advisers crowded around them and saw that the fire had not touched them. Not a hair on their heads was singed, and their clothing was not scorched. They didn't even smell of smoke! Then Nebuchadnezzar said, 'Praise to the God of Shadrach, Meshach, and Abednego! He sent His angel to rescue His servants who trusted in Him. They defied the king's command and were willing to die rather than serve or worship any god except their own God. Therefore, I make this decree:

> If any people, whatever their race or nation or language, speak a word against the God of Shadrach, Meshach, and Abednego, they will be torn limb from limb, and their houses will be turned into heaps of rubble. There is no other god who can rescue like this!'"
> *Daniel 3:27-29*

REVELATIONS GIVEN TO SHADRACH, MESHACH, & ABEDNEGO FROM THE LORD

Defender/Rescuer/Protector; Daniel 3:25-27

> "Then the high officers, officials, governors, and advisers crowded around them and saw that the fire had not touched them. Not a hair on their heads was singed, and their clothing was not scorched. They didn't even smell of smoke!"
> *Daniel 3:27*

God with us in the fire; Daniel 3:24-25

> "But suddenly, Nebuchadnezzar jumped up in amazement and exclaimed to his advisers, 'Didn't we tie up three men and throw them into the furnace?' 'Yes, Your Majesty, we certainly did,' they replied. 'Look!' Nebuchadnezzar shouted. 'I see four men, unbound, walking around in the fire unharmed! And the fourth looks like a god!'"
> *Daniel 3:24-25*

Faithful despite consequences - The three remained steadfast in the Lord, regardless of the cost; Daniel 3:12-18

> "If we are thrown into the blazing furnace, the God whom we serve is able to save us. He will rescue us from your power, Your Majesty. But even if He doesn't, we want to make it clear to you, Your Majesty, that we will never serve your gods or worship the gold statue you have set up."
> *Daniel 3:17-18*

Confident that God would save - The three had such a confidence in the Lord, that He would deliver them from the fire; Daniel 3:17

> "If we are thrown into the blazing furnace, the God whom we serve is able to save us. He will rescue us from your power, Your Majesty."
> *Daniel 3:17*

CHAPTER 20
REVIEW QUESTIONS
Shadrach, Meshach and Abednego

1. Name three attributes the three men showed, which caused them to be chosen to serve in the palace:

    a.

    b.

    c.

2. Name three lessons to learn from these three young men.

    a.

    b.

    c.

3. What does the story of the fiery furnace teach us?

4. Name three aspects of the young men's character.

    a.

    b

    c.

Obedience to the Lord brings change.

21

Hosea

Hosea is given a short biography in the first verses of the book of Hosea. Here is what it says:

"The word of the Lord that came to Hosea, son of Beeri, during the reigns of Uzziah, Jotham, Ahaz and Hezekiah, kings of Judah, and during the reign of Jeroboam son of Jehoash[a] king of Israel."

So, we know his lineage and we know when he lived and performed a sort of object lesson for the people of Israel. We also know from this verse that he heard God's voice and responded. We can assume that he was a righteous man as well as a creative and resourceful one because of the way he chose to teach the Israelites about their wrongdoing.

Hosea bought a prostitute named Gomer, and we are told her mother's name as well, so she is given a lineage and a sense of dignity. Hosea married her, according to God's instructions, as a message to the people of Israel, saying, *"For like an adulterous wife this land is guilty of unfaithfulness to the Lord."* Hosea 1:2. With the birth of his first son with the prostitute Gomer, he is instructed to name the child Jezreel. God says, *"Call him Jezreel, because I will soon punish the house of Jehu for the massacre at Jezreel, and I will put an end to the kingdom of Israel. In that day I will break Israel's bow in the Valley of Jezreel."* Hosea 1:4, 5

The next two births, first a girl, and then a boy, Hosea names them "Not loved" and "Not my people." Imagine how a child would be influenced knowing his name meant "not loved." Imagine in the context of today's preoccupation with names controlling our destiny, how a child would feel being called, "Not Loved." Wow. But we cannot get sidetracked by the meanness and insensitivity that God shows towards these poor, defenseless children. Rather, we should put emphasize the message God was giving to His people.

The final and the ultimate message was that God would take his people back, faithless Israel, as a man would take back an adulterous wife and love her with all His heart. God's message was ultimately about of His love for us. Hosea came for this and this alone, to give the Israelites a message from God, urging them to return and be faithful because He loved them.

WORSHIP LEADER TYPE PROFILE

HOSEA

BACKGROUND

- **Political Conditions:**
  - Uzziah, Jotham, Ahaz, Hezekiah were the kings of Judah.
  - Jeroboam was the king of Israel.
- **Social Conditions:**
  - "Hosea may have preached a little later than Amos, but it was still in the days round the middle of the eighth century before Christ, in the bright Indian summer of Israel's greatness, and just before the dark shadow of the imperialism of Assyria fell across the land."[35]
  - Hosea most likely came from a farming family of some standing, since he knew the countryside and was aware of political issues as well as the history of his people.[36]
- **Religious Conditions:**
  - Spiritual prostitution and idolatry were common.

FACTORS IN THE EQUIPPING FOR THE TASK

HOSEA'S PERSONALITY

Hosea was obedient - Hosea was obedient when God told him to marry a prostitute, Gomer, who became his wife and the mother of his children; Hosea 1:2-3, 3:1-2.

> "When the Lord first began speaking to Israel through Hosea, he said to him,
> 'Go and marry a prostitute, so that some of her children will be conceived in prostitution.
> This will illustrate how Israel has acted like a prostitute by turning against
> the Lord and worshiping other gods.' So Hosea married Gomer, the daughter of Diblaim,
> and she became pregnant and gave Hosea a son."
> Hosea 1:2-3

Courageous - Hosea was courageous enough to obey God in keeping an unfaithful prostitute; Hosea 1:2-3, 3:1-2

---

[35] Blaiklock, E.M., <u>Today's Handbook of Bible Characters,</u> Bethany House Publishers, Minneapolis, MN. 1979, p. 237
[36] Ibid

> "Then the Lord said to me, 'Go and love your wife again,
> even though she commits adultery with another lover. This will illustrate that the Lord still
> loves Israel, even though the people have turned to other gods
> and love to worship them.' So I bought her back for fifteen pieces of silver and
> five bushels of barley and a measure of wine."
> *Hosea 3:1-2*

HOSEA'S RELATIONSHIP WITH GOD

Fully devoted - Evidence of fully being devoted to God by allowing his entire family to be used in his prophetic ministry; Hosea 1:2-9, 3.

> "And the Lord said, 'Name the child Jezreel, for I am about to punish
> King Jehu's dynasty to avenge the murders he committed at Jezreel.
> In fact, I will bring an end to Israel's independence.'"
> *Hosea 1:4*

THE REVELATION THAT HOSEA RECEIVED AND CARRIED TO THE PEOPLE OF GOD

Our Heavenly Father is forgiving and will not forsake us; Hosea 1:10

> "Yet the time will come when Israel's people will be like the sands of the seashore too
> many to count! Then, at the place where they were told, 'You are not my people,'
> it will be said, 'You are children of the living God.'"
> *Hosea 1:10*

Jealous Husband; Hosea 2:2-13, 5:3, 9:1

> "I know what you are like, O Ephraim. You cannot hide yourself from Me, O Israel.
> You have left Me as a prostitute leaves her husband;
> you are utterly defiled."
> *Hosea 5:3*

Pursuing Husband; Hosea 2:14-23, 14:4-8

> "I will make you My wife forever, showing you righteousness and justice,
> unfailing love and compassion. I will be faithful to you and make You mine,
> and you will finally know Me as the Lord."
> *Hosea 2:19-20*

Holy One; Hosea 11:9

> "No, I will not unleash My fierce anger. I will not completely destroy Israel,
> for I am God and not a mere mortal. I am the Holy One living among you,
> and I will not come to destroy."
>
> *Hosea 11:9*

God is faithful; Hosea 13:4

> "I have been the Lord your God ever since I brought you out of Egypt.
> You must acknowledge no God but Me, for there is no other savior."
>
> *Hosea 13:4*

LESSONS LEARNED FROM THIS WORSHIP LEADER TYPE

Allow God to use you in any aspect of life - Hosea offered his entire life and family to be used of God by giving them specific names from the Lord symbolizing the Lord's message to Israel; Hosea 1:2-9, 3.

> "Soon Gomer became pregnant again and gave birth to a daughter.
> And the Lord said to Hosea, 'Name your daughter Lo-ruhamah
> "Not loved" for I will no longer show love to the people of Israel or forgive them."
>
> *Hosea 1:6*

Say what God says - Hosea spent his life simply saying what God said, not his opinions, nor self-formed beliefs; Hosea 4, 5, 8, 9.

> "Hear the word of the Lord, O people of Israel! The Lord has brought
> charges against you, saying: 'There is no faithfulness, no kindness,
> no knowledge of God in your land."
>
> *Hosea 4:1*

Repentance leads to redemption and healing - Hosea's final message to Israel: repentance is necessary for healing and redemption; Hosea 6:1-3, 14.

> "The Lord says, 'Then I will heal you of your faithlessness;
> My love will know no bounds, for My anger will be gone forever."
>
> *Hosea 14:4*

Love for the Lord
Obedient - Obeyed God by marrying a prostitute; Hosea 1:2-3, 3:1-2.

> "When the Lord first began speaking to Israel through Hosea, he said to him,
> 'Go and marry a prostitute, so that some of her children will be conceived in prostitution.
> This will illustrate how Israel has acted like a prostitute by turning against
> the Lord and worshiping other gods.' So Hosea married Gomer,
> the daughter of Diblaim, and she became pregnant and gave Hosea a son."
> *Hosea 1:2-3*

Love for His people
Calling for repentance - Pleaded with Israel to repent and return to their Father and Maker, the Lord; Hosea 6, 14:1-3

> "Come, let us return to the Lord. He has torn us to pieces; now He will heal us.
> He has injured us; now He will bandage our wounds. In just a short time He will restore us,
> so that we may live in His presence."
> *Hosea 6:1-2*

HOSEA'S ABILITY TO HEAR AND RESPOND TO THE LORD

Obedient - Obeyed God in marrying a prostitute; Hosea 1:2-3, 3:1-2. He obeyed everything God told him to do; 1:2-3, 3:1-2.

> "When the Lord first began speaking to Israel through Hosea, he said to him,
> 'Go and marry a prostitute, so that some of her children will be
> conceived in prostitution. This will illustrate how Israel has acted like a
> prostitute by turning against the Lord and worshiping other gods.'
> So Hosea married Gomer, the daughter of Diblaim, and she became
> pregnant and gave Hosea a son."
> *Hosea 1:2-3*

> "Then the Lord said to me, 'Go and love your wife again, even though she commits
> adultery with another lover. This will illustrate that the Lord still loves Israel,
> even though the people have turned to other gods and love to worship them.'
> So I bought her back for fifteen pieces of silver and
> five bushels of barley and a measure of wine."
> *Hosea 3:1-2*

God's mouthpiece concerning Israel's sins and judgment - Said everything God said concerning Israel's sin and redemption; Hosea 4-5, 8-9.

> "Hear this, you priests. Pay attention, you leaders of Israel.
> Listen, you members of the royal family. Judgment has been handed down against you.
> For you have led the people into a snare by worshiping
> the idols at Mizpah and Tabor."
> *Hosea 5:1*

PRESENTER/REPRESENTATIVE OF THE LORD

Married a prostitute - Hosea married a prostitute, symbolizing God's current relationship with Israel; Hosea 1:2-3, 3:1-2.

> "When the Lord first began speaking to Israel through Hosea, he said to him, 'Go and
> marry a prostitute, so that some of her children will be conceived in prostitution.
> This will illustrate how Israel has acted like a prostitute by turning against the Lord and
> worshiping other gods.' So Hosea married Gomer, the daughter of Diblaim,
> and she became pregnant and gave Hosea a son."
> *Hosea 1:2-3*

Calling God's people to repentance - As the Lord does, Hosea pleaded with the people of Israel to repent and return to God; Hosea 6:1-3, 14:1-3.

> "Return, O Israel, to the Lord your God, for your sins have brought you down.
> Bring your confessions, and return to the Lord. Say to Him,
> 'Forgive all our sins and graciously receive us,
> so that we may offer You our praises.'"
> *Hosea 14:1-2*

REVELATIONS GIVEN TO HOSEA FROM THE LORD

Israel's spiritual prostitution; Hosea 1:2, 2:1-8, 4, 7

> "Leave Israel alone, because she is
> married to idolatry."
> *Hosea 4:17*

Judgment on Israel; Hosea 1:4-6, 8-9, 2:9-13, 8, 9, 10, 12, 13

> "But though they have sold themselves to many allies,
> I will now gather them together for judgment.
> Then they will writhe under the burden of the great king."
> *Hosea 8:10*

Israel's redemption/return; Hosea 1:10-12, 2:14-23, 3:4-5, 11, 14

> "But afterward the people will return and devote themselves to the Lord their
> God and to David's descendant, their king. In the last days,
> they will tremble in awe of the Lord and of His goodness."
> *Hosea 3:5*

Sin and judgment of Israel's leaders; Hosea 5

> "Hear this, you priests. Pay attention, you leaders of Israel. Listen, you members of the
> royal family. Judgment has been handed down against you. For you have led the people
> into a snare by worshiping the idols at Mizpah and Tabor."
> *Hosea 5:1*

HOSEA'S FAITH/TRUST IN THE LORD

Obedient - Showed trust in the Lord through his obedience; Hosea 1:2-3, 3:1-2

> "When the Lord first began speaking to Israel through Hosea, he said to him,
> Go and marry a prostitute, so that some of her children will be conceived in prostitution.
> This will illustrate how Israel has acted like a prostitute by turning against the Lord and
> worshiping other gods.' So Hosea married Gomer, the daughter of Diblaim,
> and she became pregnant and gave Hosea a son."
> *Hosea 1:2-3*

CHAPTER 21
REVIEW QUESTIONS
Hosea

1. Who does Hosea represent? What does his name mean?

2. What were the religious conditions of Hosea's time?

3. Who does Gomer represent?

4. What were the factors in the equipping for Hosea's task?

5. What were the names of Hosea's children? What does each name mean and what message does it send to God's people?

6. What can we learn from the story of Hosea?

22

Habakkuk

Habakkuk might have been born around 630 B.C., around the time of Josiah's restoration of worship. The book of the law (possibly Deuteronomy) was discovered, and the result was a renewal of a great feeling of pride in the origins of the Israelite's history and a respect for the law. The hated and evil city of Ninevah was destroyed. But, as usual, things changed. This was also a time of extreme upheaval when Nebuchadnezzar captured whole populations into slavery to build his monuments.

Habakkuk expresses his dismay and despair as he calls on God to try and understand this disaster that has struck those around him. How has a pagan nation gained mastery over God's chosen people? How does one retain faith when such a terrible thing happens? Such was Habakkuk's wrestling with his own faith.

"It was a great soul which, in the hour of his people's twilight and terror, grasped the thought that it is a quality within the heart, a principle of endurance based on trust in God, which keeps a nation alive, and keeps men and women human when catastrophe falls on a land and on a person."[37]

This conclusion forms the basis for many struggles in the Old and New Testaments. How does evil seem to win out? How do evil men flourish and the righteous come to ruin? How is this possible when God always promises blessings to those who obey and live for Him? Even the final book of the Bible, Revelations, grapples with this seeming contradiction. Yet we find that in the long term, righteousness is rewarded, and the evildoers are punished. And so, we are comforted, as was Habakkuk.

---

37 Blaiklock, E.M., Today's Handbook of Bible Characters, Bethany House Publishers, Minneapolis, MN.1979 p. 265

WORSHIP LEADER TYPE PROFILE

HABAKKUK

BACKGROUND

- **Political Conditions**:
  - The state of Judah collapsed. All the leaders and people of intelligence were led into exile by the Babylonians.
- **Social Conditions**:
  - Those who were left behind had to carry on without the best of their men. They had to deal with life in a totally different way. Their institutions were gone, both political and religious.
- **Religious Conditions**:
  - The temple and the priests were led into captivity. The Southern Kingdom, Judah, began a rapid decline. Internal incoherence and external pressure from the burgeoning Babylonian empire resulted in Judah becoming a vassal state to Babylon.
  - Shortly afterward an ill-advised rebellion brought down the wrath of the Babylonians in 587 B.C., leading to the collapse of the state of Judah and the deportation of the elites to the center of the Babylonian empire (2 Kings 24-25).
  - In exile, the people of Israel had to work out how to be faithful while separated from their key religious institutions, the temple, the priesthood, even the land.[38]

FACTORS IN THE EQUIPPING FOR THE TASK

HABAKKUK'S PERSONALITY

Loved justice - Habakkuk longed for justice and righteousness; Habakkuk 1:2-4

> "How long, O Lord, must I call for help? But You do not listen!
> 'Violence is everywhere!' I cry, but You do not come to save.
> Must I forever see these evil deeds? Why must I watch all this misery? Wherever I look, I see destruction and violence. I am surrounded by people who love to argue and fight.
> The law has become paralyzed, and there is no justice in the courts.
> The wicked far outnumber the righteous, so that justice has become perverted."
> *Habakkuk 1:2-4*

---

[38] Faith and Work During the Exile—Nahum, Habakkuk, Zephaniah, *Bible Commentary / Produced by TOW Project*, p. 1.

HABAKKUK'S RELATIONSHIP WITH GOD

Intimate - He had a dear and trusting relationship with the Lord.

> "O Lord my God, my Holy One, You who are eternal surely You do not plan to wipe us out? O Lord, our Rock, You have sent these Babylonians to correct us, to punish us for our many sins. But You are pure and cannot stand the sight of evil. Will You wink at their treachery? Should You be silent while the wicked swallow up people more righteous than they?"
> *Habakkuk 1:12-13*

THE REVELATION OF GOD THAT HABAKKUK CARRIED TO THE PEOPLE OF GOD

God is Awesome; Habakkuk 3:1-16

> "I have heard all about You, Lord. I am filled with awe by Your amazing works.
> In this time of our deep need, help us again as You did in years gone by.
> And in Your anger, remember Your mercy."
> *Habakkuk 3:2*

LESSONS LEARNED FROM THIS WORSHIP LEADERSHIP TYPE

Pray - Habakkuk brought every thought of confusion, opinion, question, and concern to the Lord; Habakkuk 1, 2, 3

> "Are we only fish to be caught and killed? Are we only sea creatures that have no leader? Must we be strung up on their hooks and caught in their nets while they rejoice and celebrate?"
> *Habakkuk 1:14-15*

Wait on the Lord - Habakkuk waited for the Lord's answer, not the opinions of others; Habakkuk 2:1

> "I will climb up to my watchtower and stand at my guardpost. There I will wait to see what the Lord says and how He will answer my complaint."
> *Habakkuk 2:1*

Praise regardless of the circumstances - Habakkuk sang a prayer of praise to the Lord before the situation was over; Habakkuk 3:18-19

> "Yet I will rejoice in the Lord! I will be joyful in the God of my salvation. The Sovereign Lord
> is my strength! He makes me as surefooted as a deer,
> able to tread upon the heights."
> *Habakkuk 3:18-19*

Intercessor - Prayed for his people; Habakkuk 1:12-17

> "Are we only fish to be caught and killed? Are we only sea creatures that have no leader?
> Must we be strung up on their hooks and caught in their
> nets while they rejoice and celebrate?"
> *Habakkuk 1:14-15*

EXAMPLE OF BEING A PERSON OF PRAYER AND PRAISE

Dialogue with God - Habakkuk spoke, the Lord responded, the Lord spoke, Habakkuk responded; Habakkuk 1, 2

> "The law has become paralyzed, and there is no justice in the courts.
> The wicked far outnumber the righteous, so that justice has become perverted.
> The Lord replied, 'Look around at the nations; look and be amazed!
> For I am doing something in your own day, something you
> wouldn't believe even if someone told you about it."
> *Habakkuk 1:4-5*

Intercession - Prayed for his people; Habakkuk 1:12-17

> "Are we only fish to be caught and killed?
> Are we only sea creatures that have no leader?
> Must we be strung up on their hooks and caught
> in their nets while they rejoice and celebrate?"
> *Habakkuk 1:14-15*

Supplication - Sought the Lord for help; Habakkuk 3:2

> "I have heard all about You, Lord. I am filled with awe by Your amazing works.
> In this time of our deep need, help us again as You did in years gone by.
> And in Your anger, remember Your mercy."
> *Habakkuk 3:2*

Composer of songs

Habakkuk composed and sang a prayer song of praise to the Lord; Habakkuk 3

> "Yet I will rejoice in the Lord! I will be joyful in the God of my salvation.
> The Sovereign Lord is my strength! He makes me as surefooted as a deer,
> able to tread upon the heights."
> *Habakkuk 3:18-19*

REVELATIONS GIVEN TO HABAKKUK FROM THE LORD

God is our Avenger; Habakkuk 2:6-17

> "But soon their captives will taunt them. They will mock them, saying,
> 'What sorrow awaits you thieves! Now you will get what you deserve!
> You've become rich by extortion, but how much longer can this go on?'
> Suddenly, your debtors will take action. They will turn on you and take all you have, while
> you stand trembling and helpless."
> *Habakkuk 2:6-7*

God is Holy and is Almighty; Habakkuk 2:20

> "But the Lord is in His holy Temple. Let all the earth be silent before Him."
> *Habakkuk 2:20*

HABAKKUK FAITH/TRUST IN THE LORD

Prayed in faith to the Lord; Habakkuk 1, 2, 3

> "How long, O Lord, must I call for help? But You do not listen! 'Violence is everywhere!'
> I cry, but You do not come to save. Must I forever see these evil deeds?
> Why must I watch all this misery? Wherever I look, I see destruction and violence.
> I am surrounded by people who love to argue and fight.
> The law has become paralyzed, and there is no justice in the courts.
> The wicked far outnumber the righteous, so that justice has become perverted."
> *Habakkuk 1:2-4*

CHAPTER 22
REVIEW QUESTIONS
Habakkuk

1. What were the political conditions of this time?

2. What were the social conditions?

3. What were the religious conditions?

4. What were the factors that equipped Habakkuk for the task?

5. What were at least three lessons learned from this worship leader type?

6. From Habakkuk 3, what were the words of the song Habakkuk wrote and sang?

23
Zephaniah

Zephaniah's own name means "Yahweh has hidden," indicating that his birth may have taken place during Manasseh's reign of terror according to 2 Kings 21:16.[39] Zephaniah was the great-great-grandson of the reforming monarch of Judah, Hezekiah. Zephaniah was around twenty years old at the time of Josiah's religious reforms. Zephaniah carefully lays out his heritage, naming ancestors back four generations, so we know his bloodline was important.

Zephaniah seems to have written in a very distressed state of mind for the nation. His prophecies are full of visions of fire, smoke, and desolation. Zephaniah showed a great zeal for the truth and an indignation at the corruption he saw around him.

The prophecy of Zephaniah is one of reproof and judgment. "Zephaniah sees no way out of such departure from God than judgment, so he announces a day of the Lord, denounces idolaters, waverers and apostates, and pronounces doom on wrongdoers."[40] But even though he preached terrible judgment, his love for the people shows through in his pleading with them to repent and turn before it was too late. *"Gather before judgment begins...Act now before the fury of the Lord falls and the terrible day of the Lord begins."* (Zephaniah 2:2)

---

39 <u>Today's Handbook of Bible Characters,</u> E.M. Blaiklock, Bethany House Publishers, Minneapolis, MN. 1979, p. 254.
40 <u>All the Men of the Bible</u>, Herbert Lockyear, Zondervan Publishing House, Grand Rapids, MI 1958, p. 346.

Worship Leader Type Profile:

ZEPHANIAH

BACKGROUND

- **Political Conditions:**
  - The Kingdoms of Israel and Judah are split. The threat of the invading Chaldeans is real. Zephaniah 1:2-4
  - Josiah is king of Judah.
  - "Nahum, Habakkuk and Zephaniah were active during the period when the southern kingdom began a rapid decline. Internal incoherence and external pressure from the burgeoning Babylonian empire resulted in Judah becoming a vassal state to Babylon. Shortly afterwards, an ill-advised rebellion brought down the wrath of the Babylonians in 587 BC, leading to the collapse of the state of Judah and the deportation of the elites to the center of the Babylonian empire (2 Kings 24-25). In exile, the people of Israel had to work out how to be faithful while separated from their key religious institutions, the temple, the priesthood, even the land."[41]
- **Social Conditions:** (See above.)
  - Additionally, the people were experiencing economic and political disaster with the takeover by the Babylonian empire and the forced exile of people from Israel to live in Babylon and work for that empire.
  - "The punishment is of the people's own making. The people have been working faithlessly, turning good materials of stone, wood and metal into idols. Work that creates idols has no value, no matter how expensive the materials or well-crafted the results are."[42]

---

[41] Faith and Work During the Exile—Nahum, Habakkuk, Zephaniah *Bible Commentary / Produced by TOW Project*
[42] Faith and Work During the Exile—Nahum, Habakkuk, Zephaniah *Bible Commentary / Produced by TOW Project*

- **Religious Conditions:**
  - The alien worship of Baal and Astarte had infected the people. With it came customs of these pagan people and compromise was rampant. People also begin to re-learn how to work in faithful service to God during this period. This is fully explored in Theology of Work Project articles such as Jeremiah & Lamentations and Work and Daniel and Work, but is also hinted at here in the Book of the Twelve. The key point of this is that even in the wretched circumstances of the exile, it is still possible to be faithful."[43]
  - Idolatry, judgment: The people are told that their situation, of being overtaken by the Babylonians, is a result of their own godlessness and wickedness.
  - "The unifying theme of these prophets is that in God there is no split between the work of worship and the work of daily life. Nor is there a split between individual wellbeing and the common good. The people of Israel are faithful or unfaithful, in varying degrees, to God's covenant with them, and degree of their faithfulness is immediately apparent in their worship or their neglect to worship. The people's faithfulness, or lack of faithfulness, to God's covenant, is reflected in not only the spiritual environment, but also the social and physical environment, including the land itself. The people's degree of faithfulness is also visible in their ethics in life and work, which in turn determines the fruitfulness of their labor and their consequent prosperity or poverty. In the short term the wicked may prosper, but both God's discipline and the natural consequences of unjust work will eventually reduce the unjust to poverty and despair. But when people and societies work in faithfulness to God, he blesses them with an integrated spiritual-ethical-environmental health and prosperity."[44]

FACTORS IN THE EQUIPPING FOR THE TASK

Zephaniah was chosen by God; Zephaniah 1:1

> "The Lord gave this message to Zephaniah when Josiah son of
> Amon was king of Judah. Zephaniah was the son of Cushi, son of Gedaliah,
> son of Amariah, son of Hezekiah."
> *Zephaniah 1:1*

---

[43] Faith and Work During the Exile—Nahum, Habakkuk and Zephaniah
[44] The Twelve Prophets and Work, theologyofwork.org

ZEPHANIAH'S PERSONALITY

Obedient - Did everything he was told/led to do; Zephaniah 1, 2:4-15, 3:1-8

> "Because you have sinned against the Lord, I will make you grope around like the blind. Your blood will be poured into the dust, and your bodies will lie rotting on the ground."
> *Zephaniah 1:17*

Spoke and followed the Lord fearlessly and confidently; Zephaniah 1, 2:4-15, 3:1-8.

> "And what sorrow awaits you Philistines who live along the coast and in the land of Canaan, for this judgment is against you, too! The Lord will destroy you until not one of you is left."
> *Zephaniah 2:5*

Feared the Lord - Sought repentance immediately; Zephaniah 2:1-3

> "Seek the Lord, all who are humble, and follow His commands. Seek to do what is right and to live humbly. Perhaps even yet the Lord will protect you - protect you from His anger on that day of destruction."
> *Zephaniah 2:3*

Heart aligned with God - Spoke from the heart of God; Zephaniah 2:1-3

> "Gather before judgment begins, before your time to repent is blown away like chaff. Act now, before the fierce fury of the Lord falls and the terrible day of the Lord's anger begins."
> *Zephaniah 2:2*

THE REVELATION OF GOD THAT ZEPHANIAH CARRIED TO THE PEOPLE OF GOD

God is jealous; Zephaniah 1:4-6, 8-9, 18, 3:8

> "'Therefore, be patient,' says the Lord. 'Soon I will stand and accuse these evil nations. For I have decided to gather the kingdoms of the earth and pour out My fiercest anger and fury on them. All the earth will be devoured by the fire of My jealousy.'"
> *Zephaniah 3:8*

God is a judge; Zephaniah 1:7,12-18, 2:5, 9-13, 3:8

"Stand in silence in the presence of the Sovereign Lord, for the awesome day of the Lord's judgment is near. The Lord has prepared His people for a great slaughter and has chosen their executioners."
Zephaniah 1:7

God is also a restorer and a redeemer; Zephaniah 2:6-7, 3:9-20

"The remnant of the tribe of Judah will pasture there. They will rest at night in the abandoned houses in Ashkelon. For the Lord their God will visit His people in kindness and restore their prosperity again."
Zephaniah 2:7

God is an avenger; Zephaniah 3:19

"And I will deal severely with all who have oppressed you.
I will save the weak and helpless ones; I will bring together those who were chased away. I will give glory and fame to
My former exiles, wherever they have been mocked and shamed."
Zephaniah 3:19

God rejoices over His people; Zephaniah 3:17

"The Lord your God is with you, the Mighty Warrior who saves.
He will take great delight in you; in his love he will no longer rebuke you, but will rejoice over you with singing."
Zephaniah 3:17

LESSONS LEARNED FROM THIS WORSHIP LEADER TYPE

Intimacy with God is important - Zephaniah was enabled to live as the Lord's mouthpiece out of his personal and intimate relationship with the Lord; Zephaniah 1, 2, 3

"I will sweep away people and animals alike. I will sweep away the birds of the sky and the fish in the sea. I will reduce the wicked to heaps of rubble, and I will wipe humanity from the face of the earth,' says the Lord."
Zephaniah 1:3

Obedience to the voice of God - Zephaniah obeyed the Lord in speech and in life, regardless of what he had to say or do; Zephaniah 1, 2:4-15, 3.

> "'Now, as surely as I live,' says the Lord of Heaven's Armies, the God of Israel, 'Moab and Ammon will be destroyed - destroyed as completely as Sodom and Gomorrah. Their land will become a place of stinging nettles, salt pits, and eternal desolation. The remnant of My people will plunder them and take their land.'"
> *Zephaniah 2:9*

Zephaniah love and feared the Lord – He sought repentance immediately. Zephaniah 2:1-3

> "Seek the Lord, all who are humble, and follow His commands. Seek to do what is right and to live humbly. Perhaps even yet the Lord will protect you - protect you from His anger on that day of destruction."
> *Zephaniah 2:3*

Zephaniah pleaded with the people to repent and return to the Lord; Zephaniah 2:1-3

> "Gather before judgment begins, before your time to repent is blown away like chaff. Act now, before the fierce fury of the Lord falls and the terrible day of the Lord's anger begins."
> *Zephaniah 2:2*

EXAMPLE OF BEING A WORSHIPPER

He was the Lord's mouthpiece – He used to say everything the Lord told him to say; Zephaniah 1, 2:4-15, 3.

> "The Lord gave this message to Zephaniah when Josiah son of Amon was king of Judah. Zephaniah was the son of Cushi, son of Gedaliah, son of Amariah, son of Hezekiah."
> *Zephaniah 1:1*

ZEPHANIAH'S ABILITY TO HEAR AND RESPOND TO THE LORD

Obedience - Zephaniah responded to the Lord with obedience; Zephaniah 1, 2:4-15, 3

> "'On that day,' says the Lord, 'a cry of alarm will come from the Fish Gate and echo throughout the New Quarter of the city. And a great crash will sound from the hills.'"
> *Zephaniah 1:10*

PRESENTER/REPRESENTATIVE OF THE LORD

Lord's mouthpiece – He spoke what the Lord was saying; Zephaniah 1, 2:4-15, 3

> "'I will sweep away everything from the face of the earth,' says the Lord."
> *Zephaniah 1:2*

REVELATIONS GIVEN TO ZEPHANIAH FROM THE LORD

God's anger is terrible; Zephaniah 1, 2:4-5, 9-13, 3:6-8

> "It will be a day when the Lord's anger is poured out - a day of terrible distress and anguish, a day of ruin and desolation, a day of darkness and gloom, a day of clouds and blackness, a day of trumpet calls and battle cries. Down go the walled cities and the strongest battlements!"
> *Zephaniah 1:15-16*

God's anger doesn't last forever; Zephaniah 2:6-7, 3:9-20

> "For the Lord will remove His hand of judgment and will disperse the armies of your enemy. And the Lord Himself, the King of Israel, will live among you! At last your troubles will be over, and you will never again fear disaster."
> *Zephaniah 3:15*

HAVE FAITH AND TRUST IN THE LORD

Confidently and fearlessly obeyed the Lord; Zephaniah 1, 2, 3:1-8

> "And what sorrow awaits you Philistines who live along the coast and in the land of Canaan, for this judgment is against you, too! The Lord will destroy you until not one of you is left."
> *Zephaniah 2:5*

CHAPTER 23
REVIEW QUESTIONS
Zephaniah

1. What were the political, social and religious conditions of the time of Zephaniah?

2. With whom was Zephaniah a contemporary?

3. What notable person was Zephaniah descended from?

4. What was the unusual thing about Zephaniah's ministry?

5. Zephaniah was the first prophet to mention whom?

6. Name a few of the images that Zephaniah talks about that are also seen in the book of Revelation.

7. What are four images that prefigure Christ?

8. Which verse in Zephaniah 3 gives us an amazing way God views us?

24

The Wise Men

"Magi, the singular Magus, also called Wise Men, in the Christian tradition, the noble pilgrims "from the East" who followed a miraculous guiding star to Bethlehem, where they paid homage to the infant Jesus as king of the Jews (Matthew 2:1–12)."[45]

Who were the wise men? Tradition numbers them at three, probably because of the three gifts mentioned: gold, frankincense, and myrrh. But earlier traditions claimed there were twelve. They are often called "kings," but they were not called that in the original telling of the tale. It is possible they were called kings because of the prophecy that said kings would bow down to the savior.

"Despite their familiarity, they only appear once in the New Testament, in Matthew 2:1-12. If you carefully read Matthew's account of Jesus' birth, you may be surprised that many of the details people assume about the magi are actually absent. In fact, much of what people think they know about the magi comes from later Christian legends rather than from the Bible."[46]

According to tradition, the magi's names were Bithisarea, Melichior, and Gathaspa, taken from a chronicle known as the Excerpta Latina barbari. They have become known most commonly as Balthasar, Melchior, and Gaspar (or Casper).

The word for wise men was *magoi* and it meant, more accurately, astrologers or magicians. It can specifically refer to priests of the Zoroastrian religion, which was an Iranian tradition. These priests were experts in interpreting the night sky. This seems to be more evidence that the wise men were from Iran.

Regardless of the facts referring to the wise men from the east who followed a star and then bowed down to worship the child, Jesus, bringing valuable gifts of gold, frankincense, and myrrh, they are a compelling part of the tradition of the birth of Jesus Christ and will remain a fascinating subject for further study.

---

45   Britannica, The Editors of Encyclopedia. "Magi". Encyclopedia Britannica, 9 Dec. 2020, https://www.britannica.com/topic/Magi.
46   https://www.bibleodyssey.org/en/passages/related-articles/magi

WORSHIP LEADER TYPE PROFILE
THE MAGI

BACKGROUND

- **Political Conditions:** Herod is king of Judea.
- **Social Conditions:** The paranoid ruler of Judea and Jerusalem, Herod, had to be dealt with in a wise manner. The three men possibly by camel caravan and lived as people of Jesus' time, making the ground their bed and bearing the rigors of travel. It has been suggested by Bible scholars that the wise men were from Babylon and had been influenced by Daniel's prophecy regarding the star leading them to the coming messiah.
- **Religious Conditions:** Jesus has come.

FACTORS IN THE EQUIPPING FOR THE TASK

The Magi were most likely scholars who devoted their lives to studying the about God; Matthew 2:4-6

> "He called a meeting of the leading priests and teachers of religious law and asked,
> 'Where is the Messiah supposed to be born?' 'In Bethlehem in Judea,' they said,
> 'for this is what the prophet wrote: "And you, O Bethlehem in the land of Judah,
> are not least among the ruling cities of Judah, for a ruler will come
> from you who will be the shepherd for my people Israel."'
> *Matthew 2:4-6*

THE MAGI'S PERSONALITIES

They had wisdom; Matthew 2:1

> "Jesus was born in Bethlehem in Judea, during the reign of King Herod.
> About that time some wise men from eastern lands arrived in Jerusalem…"
> *Matthew 2:1*

Dedicated their lives to the Lord; Matthew 2:1-2, 9-11

> "Jesus was born in Bethlehem in Judea, during the reign of King Herod.
> About that time some wise men from eastern lands arrived in Jerusalem, asking,
> 'Where is the newborn king of the Jews? We saw his star
> as it rose, and we have come to worship him.'"
> *Matthew 2:1-2*

Obeyed the voice of the Lord; Matthew 2:12

> "When it was time to leave, they returned to their own country by another route,
> for God had warned them in a dream not to return to Herod."
> *Matthew 2:12*

THE MAGI'S RELATIONSHIP WITH GOD

Passionate - Actively loved and adored the Lord; Matthew 2:1-2, 9-11

> "They entered the house and saw the child with his mother, Mary, and they bowed down
> and worshiped him. Then they opened their treasure chests and gave him gifts of gold,
> frankincense, and myrrh."
> *Matthew 2:11*

THE REVELATION OF GOD THAT THEY CARRIED TO THE PEOPLE OF GOD

Promise Keeper; Matthew 2:4-5

> "When he had called together all the people's chief priests and
> teachers of the law, he asked them where the Messiah was to be born.
> "In Bethlehem in Judea," they replied, "for this is what the prophet has written..."
> *Matthew 2:4-5*

Jesus King of the Jews; Matthew 2:2

> "Where is the newborn king of the Jews? We saw his star as it rose,
> and we have come to worship him."
> *Matthew 2:2*

Jesus the Messiah; Matthew 2:4-6

> "He called a meeting of the leading priests and teachers of religious law and asked,
> 'Where is the Messiah supposed to be born?' 'In Bethlehem in Judea,'
> they said, 'for this is what the prophet wrote: "And you, O Bethlehem in the land of Judah,
> are not least among the ruling cities of Judah, for a ruler will come from you who will be
> the shepherd for my people Israel.'"
> *Matthew 2:4-6*

LESSONS LEARNED FROM THIS WORSHIP LEADER TYPE

Know and study the Word - The Word led them to a revelation of Christ; Matthew 2:4-6

> "He called a meeting of the leading priests and teachers of religious law and asked, 'Where is the Messiah supposed to be born?' 'In Bethlehem in Judea,' they said, 'for this is what the prophet wrote: "And you, O Bethlehem in the land of Judah, are not least among the ruling cities of Judah, for a ruler will come from you who will be the shepherd for my people Israel."'
> *Matthew 2:4-6*

Worship is costly - Their worship consisted of long-term travel and actual gifts to the Lord; Matthew 2:11

> "They entered the house and saw the child with his mother, Mary, and they bowed down and worshiped him. Then they opened their treasure chests and gave him gifts of gold, frankincense, and myrrh."
> *Matthew 2:11*

Listen for and follow God's voice - They followed the voice of the Lord directing them to return home a different way; Matthew 2:12

> "When it was time to leave, they returned to their own country by another route, for God had warned them in a dream not to return to Herod."
> *Matthew 2:12*

They Left their homes, bringing gifts, to express adoration of the Lord; Matthew 2:2,10-11

> "When they saw the star, they were filled with joy! They entered the house and saw the child with his mother, Mary, and they bowed down and worshiped him. Then they opened their treasure chests and gave him gifts of gold, frankincense, and myrrh."
> *Matthew 2:10-11*

Be inquirers and pursuers of the Lord; Matthew 2:1-2,9-11.

> 'Where is the newborn king of the Jews? We saw his star as it rose, and we have come to worship him.'"
> *Matthew 2:1-2*

EXAMPLE OF BEING WORSHIPPERS

Left their home, bringing gifts, to express adoration of/to the Lord; Matthew 2:11

"They entered the house and saw the child with his mother, Mary, and they bowed down
and worshiped him. Then they opened their treasure chests and
gave him gifts of gold, frankincense, and myrrh."
Matthew 2:11

THE MAGI'S ABILITY TO HEAR AND RESPOND TO THE LORD

Obedience - Obeyed the voice of the Lord; Matthew 2:12

"When it was time to leave, they returned to their own country by another route, for God
had warned them in a dream not to return to Herod."
Matthew 2:12

PRESENTER/REPRESENTATIVE OF THE LORD

The entire mission of the Magi was to find the Messiah, the infant who was sent to save the world. In everything they did, following the star, bearing gifts to honor the child and even hearing God warn them not to return to Herod was evidence that they represented the Lord.

REVELATIONS GIVEN TO THEM FROM THE LORD

Herod's plot - The Lord revealed Herod's intent to kill Jesus; Matthew 2:12

"When it was time to leave, they returned to their own country by another route,
for God had warned them in a dream not to return to Herod."
Matthew 2:12

THE MAGI'S FAITH/TRUST IN THE LORD

Left their home, by faith in the Word, to find Jesus; Matthew 2:1-2,9-11.

"Jesus was born in Bethlehem in Judea, during the reign of King Herod.
About that time some wise men from eastern lands arrived in Jerusalem, asking,
'Where is the newborn king of the Jews? We saw his star as it rose,
and we have come to worship him.'"
Matthew 2:1-2

Trusted the Lord in obedience to His direction; Matthew 2:12

"When it was time to leave, they returned to their own country by another route, for God had warned them in a dream not to return to Herod."
Matthew 2:12

CHAPTER 24
REVIEW QUESTIONS
The Wise Men

1. What were the political conditions of this time?

2. What were the social conditions?

3. What were the religious conditions?

4. What were the factors contributing to the accomplishment of the task?

5. Explain how the worship of Jesus by the Magi was costly.

6. Name some attributes of the Magi from what the Bible tells of their journey to find the Messiah.

7. What is the significance of each of the gifts given to Jesus by the Magi? (Gold, frankincense and myrrh.)

"Worship is not about impressing God with our words or actions; it is about humbling ourselves before Him, recognizing His greatness and our utter dependence on Him."
–Max Lucado

25

Peter

Peter was the first of the twelve disciples who was called to follow Jesus in the three years of his earthly ministry. When Jesus told him to leave his nets and follow Him, Peter did just that. Then he took his brother, Andrew, along with him. *"Passing alongside the Sea of Galilee, he saw Simon and Andrew the brother of Simon casting a net into the sea, for they were fishermen. And Jesus said to them,"Follow me, and I will make you become fishers of men. And immediately they left their nets and followed him." Mark 1:16-18*

He was fiercely independent, a fisherman by trade, and in business for himself, alongside his father, named Jona or Jonah. His livelihood depended on his hard work, and he answered to no one but himself and his father. We know Peter was physically strong because we know what was required of a fisherman in the time of Christ. Fishing required enormous strength to haul in the nets and to row the ship out to sea. Fishermen had to be robust and energetic to be successful.

Peter expresses the confusion of all the disciples when he asks Jesus what he meant by saying it did not matter what a person ate, but what did matter was what came out of his mouth, for it expressed the heart. Whereas all the disciples were confused, Peter dared to ask the question.

Peter was fiercely loyal to Jesus. When Jesus told his disciples what would happen to him, that he would be tried and convicted and put to a cruel death on the cross, Peter protested! When the soldiers came by night to take Jesus away, Peter drew his sword and cut off the ear of one of the men.

We know Peter as the impulsive, independent, proud, and perhaps overly confident fisherman who swore never to fail his master, Jesus. Yet, he denied Him three times before the rooster crowed, as was prophesied. Imagine how he felt when Jesus told him exactly what he would do, and then he denied his Lord, not just once in a short time, but three times back-to-back! Yet Peter owned up to his failure, and we can imagine the sorrow he experienced when he realized what he had done.

According to tradition, Peter was the source of the story in the gospel of Mark, and he spares no detail of his shameful wrongdoing. Perhaps he hoped others would learn something from his failure. Peter had sworn that even if he were to die at Jesus' side, he would never betray him. Yet he gave in to fear, as most of us would have.

The church's missionary outreach began with Peter, the great leader who held the community of believers together by the strength of his leadership and the firmness of his testimony regarding Jesus' life, death, and resurrection. Along with the other disciples and believers, he was an eyewitness of the most extraordinary miracle of all time, the death and resurrection of Jesus Christ.

Ultimately, Peter is chiefly recalled for recognizing Jesus as the Son of God and the foundational rock of the church. Jesus referred to Peter as the "stone" or "small rock" while identifying the church as the "cornerstone" in Ephesians 2:20, underscoring Jesus as the foundation and standard of the church.

WORSHIP LEADER TYPE PROFILE

PETER

BACKGROUND

Peter was one of the first disciples called to follow Jesus. Andrew brought him to Jesus (John 1:41-42).

- **Political Conditions:**
  - The political situation in Palestine was intense, and Jewish resentment of Roman rule grew stronger by the day. The Hebrew people lived under brutal, sadistic and decadent King Herod who was a puppet of foreign pagan interests and a tool of the Romans. Those in power did not care about the Hebrew people or any of the poor and powerless people they ruled over.
- **Social Conditions:**
  - The people lived simply, many in one humble one room dwellings, with extended work and living spaces either outside or on the rooftop. The diet consisted of many varieties of vegetables, grains, nuts and fruits. Meat was a rarity, saved for celebrations. Clothing was made from homespun cloth and was made by hand. Travel was mostly on foot, with the wealthy traveling on camels or donkeys.
- **Religious Conditions:**
  - Even under the oppressive Roman rule, the Jews observed the holy days and attended temple to study the Torah. They made the annual pilgrimage to Jerusalem for Passover. Religious practice was woven into the fabric of everyday life.

FACTORS IN THE EQUIPMENT FOR THE TASK

Peter was a fisherman – He was fearless, possibly because of many storms at sea which he had survived. Jesus was going to teach Peter for what he did in the natural as a fisherman to be a 'fisher of men'.

Peter was an ordinary man – He was an example and an encouragement to others. He seemed to have been accustomed to hardships, from being an eyewitness to many miracles of Jesus:

- Jesus healed the paralytic, Mark 2
- Heals the man with the withered hand, Mark 3
- Jesus calms the storm, Mark 4
- Jesus heals the man with demons, Mark 5
- Heals the woman with a flow of blood, Mark 5
- Jesus brings back to life Jairus' 12-year-old daughter, Mark 5
- Jesus heals the deaf man and heals blind Bartimaeus, Mark 10
- Jesus heals the sick in Genessaret, walks on water and feeds the 5000+, Mark 6
- Jesus curses the fig tree, Mark 11

PETER'S PERSONALITY

Peter was often arrogant, cocky, vigorous and quick tempered. He seems to always be putting his foot in his mouth.

He was naturally impulsive; Matthew 14:28 and John 21:7.

> "That disciple whom Jesus loved therefore said to Peter, "It is the Lord!"
> When Simon Peter heard that it was the Lord, he got out of the boat, and threw himself
> into the sea, ultimately walked on the water."
> *John 21:7, ESV*

He was tenderhearted and teachable. When Jesus attempted to serve the disciples by washing their feet, Peter jumped in and let it be known that he was in need of cleansing in more ways than the physical. Matthew 26:25 and John 13:9

> "Simon Peter said to him, "Lord, not my feet only but also my hands and my head!""
> *John 13:9*

He was gifted with spiritual insight, according to John 6:68.

> "Simon Peter answered him, "Lord, to whom shall we go? You have the words of eternal life…"
> *John 6:68, ESV*

But sometimes Peter was slow to understand the deeper truths as seen when he questions Jesus about the difference between avoiding unclean food and keeping the inner self pure and clean as seen in Matthew 15:15.

> "Peter said to him, "Explain the parable to us." ¹⁶ And he said,
> "Are you also still without understanding?"
> *Matthew 15:13-16*

In John 13, when Jesus washes disciples' feet, Peter protests saying, "No, you shall never wash my feet."

He was quick to repent. Peter said in Luke 5:8 - "Go away from me Lord; I am a sinful man!" In this statement, it seems he recognized his own failings.

> Showing his passionate side, Peter said, "We have left everything to follow you!"
> *Mark 10:28*

After seeing Jesus tortured and killed and then witnessing his ascension, Peter changes radically and we see a humble, willing, obedient servant of the Lord. Through it all, Jesus saw something wonderful in Peter. After all, in Matthew 16:18, it says, Jesus gave him the "keys to the kingdom." Jesus saw something in Peter that was not always apparent to others, and He saw qualities that could have been overshadowed by Peter's impulsiveness and his lack of tact.

PETER'S RELATIONSHIP WITH GOD

Disciple/Follower of Jesus, one of Jesus' twelve, "Brother" of Jesus

> "For whoever does the will of my Father in heaven is my brother and sister and mother"
> *Matthew 12:50*

> "And I tell you that you are Peter, and on this rock I will build my church,
> and the gates of Hades will not overcome it"
> *Matthew 16:18*

Friend, one of Jesus' closest friends/disciples. Peter was a good friend. Even though he faltered when Jesus was crucified. He still found his footing again and received forgiveness and restoration.

Jesus takes Peter and two others to Gethsemane when he prayed. Matt. 26: 36-46
Jesus only took Peter, James, and John with him to raise a dead girl. Mark 5
Jesus sent Peter and John to prepare for the Passover, Luke 22:8

Peter loved Jesus with everything He had within him.
Peter was among the three on the mount of transfiguration.

> "Lord, why can't I follow you now? I will lay down my life for you."
> *John 13: 37*

THE REVELATION OF GOD THAT PETER RECEIVED AND CARRIED TO THE PEOPLE OF GOD

As the leader of the disciples, Peter went on to sum up what had happened, how Judas acted in accordance with the fulfillment of the Holy Scriptures to "fulfill what the Holy Spirit had foretold," and to explain that Judas Ascariot needed to be replaced. He then put forth two men for their consideration.

> "Now on one of those days Peter arose among the brethren,
> the whole number of whom gathered together was about a hundred and twenty."
> *Acts 1:15*

The revelation that Peter communicated to the early church was that the sick would be healed, the blind would see, and the lame would walk.

- Peter went on to perform signs and wonders, Acts 2:43
- Peter heals a lame beggar, Acts 3:1-10
- Peter raises Tabitha from dead, Acts 9
- Peter's Vision, Acts 10

The great revelation that Peter had was that God's redemptive plan is for everyone, not just the Jews. We are all a part of a holy priesthood. 1 Peter 2:9

LESSONS LEARNED FROM THIS WORSHIP LEADER TYPE

When Jesus calls, we need to answer immediately.

God has a purpose for your lives.

God wants to develop a close relationship with us - Jesus said "follow me" - inviting Peter to be His disciple.

God plays no favorites - Jesus was walking by the Sea of Galilee to find his disciples- fishermen- they were ordinary men.

We need to be diligent in our work - Peter was working when Jesus called him, Peter was a fisherman and knew how to endure hardships

We must deny ourselves, take up the cross and follow Him. Acts 5:41

> "Then the apostles left the Sanhedrin, rejoicing because they had been
> counted worthy of suffering disgrace for the Name."
> *Acts 5:41*

Peter was willing to give up his life for Jesus. Matthew 26:35

> "But Peter declared, "Even if I have to die with you, I will never disown you."
> And all the other disciples said the same."
> *Matthew 26:35*

Love for God's people
Peter wrote the letters which became 1 and 2 Peter for the persecuted church. In 1 Peter, he speaks tenderly to the believers, calling them "a royal priesthood, a holy nation" and says *"Having purified your souls by your obedience to the truth for a sincere brotherly love, love one another earnestly from a pure heart,"* His advice is that of a loving father that wants the best for his children. In these letters, Peter gave loving and sound advice to the believers.

> "You were cleansed from your sins when you obeyed the truth, so now you must show
> sincere love to each other as brothers and sisters. Love each other deeply with all your eart."
> *1 Peter 1:22*

Peter gives sound advice to the church, speaking to them as a loving father. He advises them to obey the governing authorities, knowing that if they do not, the penalties will be severe. He instructs the men to love their wives, the wives to submit to their husbands and the children to respect their parents. These tender admonitions reveal Peter's deep affection for the believers, old and new.

> "Submit yourselves for the Lord's sake to every human authority: whether to the emperor,
> as the supreme authority, or to governors, who are sent by him to punish those who do
> wrong and to commend those who do right. For it is God's will that by doing good you
> should silence the ignorant talk of foolish people. Live as free people, but do not use your
> freedom as a cover-up for evil; live as God's slaves. Show proper respect to everyone, love
> the family of believers, fear God, honor the emperor.'
> *1 Peter 2:13-17*

EXAMPLE OF BEING A PRAISER AND WORSHIPPER

Peter as a man of Praise:
Peter always began his letters with greetings which emphasized thanksgiving for all God had done.

> "Praise be to the God and Father of our Lord Jesus Christ!"
> *1 Peter 1:3*

Peter and Paul sang praises when they were beaten, put in stocks, and locked up in the innermost section of the prison. This would probably have been the place most of us would complain, weep and moan rather than praise. And seemingly, their praise set them free!

Peter as a Worshipper:
Matt. 28:17 After Jesus' resurrection, He appeared to the eleven disciples, (which would include Peter). Jesus told them to "Go into the world and preach the gospel." The response of the disciples was this: "When they saw him, they worshiped Him..."

Man of Prayer:
The apostle Peter prayed three times a day. In Acts 2:15, he prayed with the church at the third hour which would be 9:00 AM. In Acts 3:1, Peter and John went up together to the temple at the hour of prayer, the ninth hour, which would be 3:00 PM. And in Acts 10:9, Peter went up to the housetop to pray at the sixth hour of the day, which would be noon.

(www.thebiblicalfoundation.com)

Peter heard Jesus pray often.
The entire chapter of John 17 is Jesus praying a very long prayer. In Matthew 6 - The Lord's prayer" came because of 'one of the disciples' asking Jesus to show them how to pray.

Peter advised the people to be sober minded and self-controlled so their prayers would not be hindered. Perhaps he was looking back on his own life for the times he was not sober-minded nor self-controlled and saw the importance of building these character traits so their faith would not be hindered by their own guilt and shame over their lack of self-control.

Doer of the Word
Peter suffered for Jesus' cause.

> "But if you suffer for doing good and you endure it, this is commendable before God. To this you were called because Christ suffered for you, leaving you an example, that you should follow in his steps."
> *1 Peter 2:20-21*

> "However, if you suffer as a Christian, do not be ashamed, but praise God that you bear the name."
> *1 Peter 4:16*

Peter preached the Word and sought to continue and complete Christ's earthly ministry.

In the sermon Peter preached to those who came from many different countries as well as the Jews and people of Jerusalem, he explained that the phenomenon they were witnessing was not a result of too much alcohol but was the Holy Spirit falling upon the crowd of people. He went on to outline the purpose of God in sending Jesus as well as the death and resurrection, all of which were part of the divine plan for humankind. He then told the ones who asked, "What shall we do?" that they must repent and believe (Acts 2:14-42).

PETER'S ABILITY TO HEAR AND RESPOND TO THE LORD

Jesus called the disciples to be fishers of men. When Peter heard the Lord's call, he didn't hesitate and immediately left his nets. (Mark 1:17, Luke 5:9-11)

When Jesus called Peter out of the boat, to come onto the water with him, again Peter did not hesitate. Matthew 14:22-33

Peter learned humility. The fact that Peter remained with Jesus even after such a harsh rebuke that shows Peter was teachable and humble. (Mark 8:31-33)

When Peter did not understand Jesus' death, he took matters into his own hands. Peter, being a man of action, recoiled from the idea that Jesus would be delivered up to the authorities in Jerusalem, and he vehemently protested the idea. (Matthew 16:21-13) And when the men came to arrest Jesus, of course, he drew his sword, to fight for his friend. (Matthew 26:47-52) Yet, in both of these actions he was rebuked by Jesus. So, taking matters into his own hands was not always the best course of action.

In John 20, Peter ran to the empty tomb but still did not fully understand that Jesus had risen. We cannot be too hard on Peter since we would also have great difficulty facing the horrible torture and death of this great man whom we had grown to love, who had 'the words of life' and who truly was the 'Holy One of God.' These two realities were almost impossible to reconcile. So, when Peter ran from the tomb, he was still reeling from the inconceivable fact that his Lord had been raised from the grave.

Peter was a man of action. Further, we see the disciples, still in shock from the death of Jesus, probably lingering around trying to make sense of it all, when Peter says, true to form, "I'm going fishing." (John 21:1-3) Going out into the boat, the men see Jesus on the shore, though they still don't recognize him. As soon as they know it is him, impulsive Peter, jumps into the water, heading towards his friend. In the words of the Bible, he 'threw himself into the sea'. This is truly Peter, a man of action, on full display. (John 21:7-9)

Peter reinstated by Jesus. In John 21, Jesus reinstates Peter by asking him three times, "Do you love me?" This was a painful reminder of Peter's three denials. In response, Peter answers each question in the affirmative, and then Jesus tells him to go and "feed my sheep." So, Peter is given his assignment, and understands that he has been forgiven and fully restored in his relationship with Jesus.

All of this emboldened Peter to become one of the early church's most fearless spokesmen. (John 21:15-19)

PRESENTER/REPRESENTATIVE OF THE LORD

As a representative of the Lord, one of his first acts was to choose Matthias to replace Judas.

> [15] In those days Peter stood up among the brothers (the company of persons was in all about 120) and said, [16] "Brothers, the Scripture had to be fulfilled, which the Holy Spirit spoke beforehand by the mouth of David concerning Judas, who became a guide to those who arrested Jesus. [17] For he was numbered among us and was allotted his share in this ministry.
>
> [21] So one of the men who have accompanied us during all the time that the Lord Jesus went in and out among us, [22] beginning from the baptism of John until the day when he was taken up from us one of these men must become with us a witness to his resurrection. [26] And they cast lots for them, and the lot fell on

Matthias, and he was numbered with the eleven apostles."
Acts 1:15-17, 21-26

Peter was the first one to preach on the day of Pentecost. (Acts 2:14-41)

But Peter, standing with the eleven, lifted up his voice and addressed them: "Men of Judea and all who dwell in Jerusalem, let this be known to you, and give ear to my words.
Acts 2:14

Peter called for repentance. In Acts 3, after healing the lame beggar, Peter spoke to the crowd and explained that the man had been healed by the power of God. He spoke about Jesus, how he had been crucified even though he was a righteous man, and that his death was a fulfillment of what the prophets had spoken.

"Now when they heard this they were cut to the heart, and said to Peter and the rest of the apostles, "Brothers, what shall we do?" [38] And Peter said to them, "Repent and be baptized every one of you in the name of Jesus Christ for the forgiveness of your sins, and you will receive the gift of the Holy Spirit. [39] For the promise is for you and for your children and for all who are far off, everyone whom the Lord our God calls to himself." [40] And with many other words he bore witness and continued to exhort them, saying, "Save yourselves from this crooked generation." [41] So those who received his word were baptized, and there were added that day about three thousand souls."
Acts 3:37-41

Peter spoke bold in the Spirit. After Peter and John are questioned by the Sanhedrin, Peter responds boldly:

"Then Peter, filled with the Holy Spirit, said to them, "Rulers and elders of our people, are we being questioned today because we've done a good deed for a crippled man? Do you want to know how he was healed? Let me clearly state to all of you and to all the people of Israel that he was healed by the powerful name of Jesus Christ the Nazarene, the man you crucified but whom God raised from the dead. For Jesus is the one referred to in the Scriptures, where it says, 'The stone that you builders rejected has now become the cornerstone.' There is salvation in no one else! God has given no other name under heaven by which we must be saved."
Acts 4:8-12

Peter was emboldened inspite of persecution. Although the apostles were persecuted, Peter continued to act boldly, encouraging all the followers of Christ to do the same. (Acts 5:17-21, 29)

The high priest and his officials, who were Sadducees, were filled with jealousy. They arrested the apostles and put them in the public jail. But an angel of the Lord came at night, opened the gates of the jail, and brought them out. Then he told them, "Go to the Temple and give the people this message of life!" So at daybreak the apostles entered the Temple, as they were told, and immediately began teaching.

Both Peter and John stubbornly and courageously responded with,
"We must obey God rather than human beings"
(Acts 5:29)

Peter spoke up for the Gentiles. Peter became a spokesman at the first church council regarding Gentiles and circumcision and salvation by grace. Peter stood and addressed them as follows:

"Brothers, you all know that God chose me from among you some time ago to preach to
the Gentiles so that they could hear the Good News and believe.
God knows people's hearts, and he confirmed that he accepts
Gentiles by giving them the Holy Spirit,
just as he did to us. He made no distinction between us and them,
for he cleansed their hearts through faith. So why are you now challenging God by
burdening the Gentile believers[b] with a yoke that neither we nor our ancestors were able
to bear? |We believe that we are all saved the same way,
by the undeserved grace of the Lord Jesus."
Acts 15:7-11

REVELATIONS GIVEN TO PETER FROM THE LORD

Peter was an eyewitness to the many miracles of Jesus. This proved to Peter that he could pray for people to be healed as well, since this was the will of God. Peter saw God as a healer and went on to pray for others and see them healed even after Jesus was crucified.

Peter witnessed the Shekinah glory with John and James in the transfiguration. One can only imagine how actually witnessing God's glory would change one's perception of God and of His power. (Matt. 17:1-9, Mark 9:2-13)

Peter had a vision. In Acts 10: 9-23 he envisioned the unclean animals being let down on a sheet before him, and then the command to rise up, kill and eat them even though they were unclean, brought about a huge shift in his thinking about bringing the gospel to the gentiles. Before this, according to Jewish tradition, he would not even enter the house of a gentile and eat with them, but this vision changed his thinking. From that point onward, the gospel message could be preached to everyone, not just to the Hebrew believers.

Peter recognizes Jesus as the Messiah. (Matt. 16:13, Matt. 16:17)

Peter challenged the law of circumcision. Peter explains that Gentile believers do not need to be circumcised because all are saved by grace, and not by the law. Acts 15:7-11

> "Peter responds to Jesus' question "Who do you say I am?" by saying, "You are the Messiah." Jesus' response is, "Blessed are you, Simon son of Jonah, for this was not revealed to you by flesh and blood, but by my Father in heaven."
> *Mark 8:27-30*

PETER'S FAITH/TRUST IN THE LORD

Peter immediately went with Jesus when he was called. Fishing was extremely hard work, but it could be an excellent way to earn a living during Peter's time! Peter was hard at work when Jesus told him to give it all up and follow Him. Peter went immediately! He must have trusted God for his future to make this bold and seemingly reckless step. He would learn to trust this man he chose to follow, Jesus.

> "At once they left their nets and followed him"
> *Mark 1:18*

> "When the angel of the Lord came and rescued Peter and released him from prison, he stated, "Now I know without a doubt that the Lord has sent his angel and rescued me from Herod's clutches and from everything the Jewish people were hoping would happen."
> *Acts 12:11*

When Jesus beckons, from his position on the water, Peter walked out into the deep, even though he has a moment of doubt. Yet, he was the only disciple who stepped out of the safety of the boat to take a risk and trust in Jesus. This step of faith, so to speak, probably set the stage for further bold acts on his part. (Matthew 14)

CHAPTER 25
REVIEW QUESTIONS
Peter

1. What were the political and social conditions during Peter's time?

2. What were the religious conditions?

3. What factors helped Peter in his life's work?

4. What are some lessons we can learn from this worship leader type?

5. What happened in Acts 3, when the crippled man who sat at the Gate of Beautiful, asked Peter and John for money?

6. In Acts Chapter 4, what did Peter and John say when they were told never to speak about Jesus?

7. When the men in the Sanhedrin saw the courage of Peter and John, what was their response?

"Worship is the antidote to worry and anxiety. When we focus our hearts and minds on God through worship, we find peace and rest in His presence."
–Sarah Young

26

John-Disciple of Jesus

Assuming John the Revelator is the same as John the Apostle, we know that he was the son of Zebedee and was the younger brother of James. According to church tradition, their mother was Salome.

John was called "the beloved" and would sit at Jesus' right hand. John 19: 26-27 says, *"The disciple Jesus loved was sitting next to him at the table." At the event of his torture and impending death, Jesus conferred upon John the care of his own beloved mother. 'Then John took Mary into his home and cared for her as his own mother.'*

John was a disciple of Jesus Christ and after Jesus' death, John became an Apostle and was the pastor of the seven churches in Ephesus mentioned in the Book of Revelations. We can see from Revelations 2:1 through 3:22 that he had a strong connection with these seven churches. He states, *"I, John, am your brother and your partner is suffering."* (Revelations 1:9)

John was banished to the Isle of Patmos by the Roman authorities, where he wrote the 'Book of the Revelations of Jesus Christ' as an encouragement to the churches, to all the Christians who were suffering persecution at the hands of Nero.

The author of the book clearly had a strong connection with the seven churches of Asia Minor as evident in Revelation 2:1-3:22. Tradition states that John the Apostle served as the pastor to the churches in Ephesus. The author's circumstances greatly match those of John the apostle. John was also a prisoner on the isle of Patmos. This was during the reign of Domitian, who put pressure on the authorities to persecute the church. John the Apostle's exile matches what we find of the author of Revelation 1:9 -

> "I, John, am your brother and your partner in suffering and in
> God's Kingdom and in the patient endurance to which Jesus calls us.
> I was exiled to the island of Patmos for preaching the word of God and
> for my testimony about Jesus."

WORSHIP LEADER TYPE PROFILE

JOHN

BACKGROUND

- **Political Conditions:**
  - Rome is in power. Christians are being persecuted by the Hebrew people because they believe Jesus is the promised Messiah. They are persecuted by the Romans because they believe in God more than they believe in the divinity of the ruler, the Caesar. They will not bow to Rome or to Roman gods.
- **Social Conditions:**
  - There is a great division between Jew and Gentile.
- **Religious Conditions:**
  - Christianity is exploding; Acts 2:41, 47
  - Christians are being persecuted (imprisoned, killed, exiled); Revelation 1:9

FACTORS IN THE EQUIPPING FOR THE TASK

John walked with Jesus Himself, called to be a disciple/apostle; Matthew 10:1-2, Mark 1:19-20, 3:13-17, Luke 5:10-11, 6:13-14.

> "At daybreak He called together all of His disciples and chose twelve of them to be apostles. Here are their names: Simon (whom He named Peter), James, John, Philip, Bartholomew,"
> *Luke 6:13-14*

John had an intimate relationship with Jesus and strong faith in God - John was considered very close to Christ, and Christ considered John for close to Him, John also keeps the faith even through exile; Matthew 17:1-3, Mark 9:2-4, 14:32-34, Luke 9:28-30, John 13:23, 21:7, Revelation 1:9

> "The disciple Jesus loved was sitting next to Jesus at the table."
> *John 13:23*

John knew the Gospel - John walked with Christ so therefore sat under the teaching of the Gospel and was then sent forth to share both during and after Jesus' life here on earth; Matthew 10:5-8, Mark 6:12, Luke 9:2, Acts 4:33

"So the disciples went, telling everyone they met to repent of their sins and turn to God."
Mark 6:12

John was empowered by Christ to heal diseases and deliver demoniacs - During Christ's ministry, He sent the disciples out two by two, giving them power to heal the sick and cast out demons; Matthew 10:1-2, Mark 3:13-17,6:7, Luke 9:1-2

"One day Jesus called together His twelve disciples and gave them power and authority to cast out all demons and to heal all diseases."
Luke 9:1

He was filled by Holy Spirit - John was a part of Pentecost in the upper room after Jesus had ascended back to heaven; Acts 2:4

"And everyone present was filled with the Holy Spirit and began speaking in other languages, as the Holy Spirit gave them this ability."
Acts 2:4

JOHN'S PERSONALITY

Obedient - John was obedient to everything he was commanded and/or sent to do, which was spreading the Gospel; Luke 9:6, Acts 4:19

"But Peter and John replied, 'Do you think God wants us to obey you rather than Him?"
Acts 4:19

Bold, courageous - John boldly shared the Gospel despite threats and imprisonments; Acts 4:13,19-20

"The members of the council were amazed when they saw the boldness of Peter and John, for they could see that they were ordinary men with no special training in the Scriptures. They also recognized them as men who had been with Jesus."
Acts 4:13

Faithful - John did not waver in his walk with Christ; John 6:67-69, 20:8-9, Acts 4:19-20, Revelation 1:9

"We cannot stop telling about everything we have seen and heard."
Acts 4:20

Fully devoted, dedicated - John remained committed to the Lord from the day he met Him to his death; Acts 4:19-20, Revelation 1:9

> "I, John, am your brother and your partner in suffering and in God's Kingdom and in the patient endurance to which Jesus calls us. I was exiled to the island of Patmos for preaching the Word of God and for my testimony about Jesus."
> *Revelation 1:9*

JOHN'S RELATIONSHIP WITH GOD

Very intimate - John was known as the disciple that Jesus loved, at least according to his account, but it is seen throughout the Gospels how close he was to Jesus and Jesus considered him to be; Matthew 17:1-3, Mark 9:2-4,14:32-34, Luke 9:28-30, John 13:23, 21:7, Revelation 1:9

> "About eight days later Jesus took Peter, John, and James up on a mountain to pray."
> *Luke 9:28*

Trusted by Jesus - Jesus evidently trusted John by how close He kept him to Himself –

Transfiguration, praying in the Garden of Gethsemane - We also see this when He gives His mother to John to care for her the day of the crucifixion; Matthew 17:1-9, Mark 9:1-9,14:33-34, Luke 9:28-36,22:8, John 19:26-27

> "When Jesus saw His mother standing there beside the disciple He loved,
> He said to her, 'Dear woman, here is your son.' And He said to this disciple,
> 'Here is your mother.' And from then on this disciple took her into his home."
> *John 19:26-27*

THE REVELATION OF GOD THAT JOHN RECEIVED AND CARRIED TO THE PEOPLE OF GOD

Jesus is the Son of God; Matthew 17:5-6, Mark 9:7, Luke 9:35, Revelation 2:18

> "Write this letter to the angel of the church in Thyatira. This is the message from the Son of God, whose eye are like flames of fire, whose feet are like polished bronze:"
> *Revelation 2:18*

Jesus is the First and the Last; Revelation 1:17

"When I saw Him, I fell at His feet as if I were dead. But He laid His right hand on me and said, 'Don't be afraid! I am the First and the Last."
Revelation 1:17

Jesus is the Living One; Revelation 1:18

"I am the Living One. I died, but look - I am alive forever and ever! And I hold the keys of death and the grave."
Revelation 1:18

Jesus is holy and true; Revelation 3:7

"Write this letter to the angel of the church in Philadelphia. This is the message from the One who is holy and true, the One who has the key of David. What He opens, no one can close; and what He closes, no one can open."
Revelation 3:7

Jesus is the Amen; Revelation 3:14

"Write this letter to the angel of the church in Laodicea. This is the message from the One who is the Amen the faithful and true Witness, the beginning of God's new creation:"
Revelation 3:14

Jesus is the Lion of the Tribe of Judah, Root of David; Revelation 5:5

"But one of the twenty-four elders said to me, 'Stop weeping! Look, the Lion of the tribe of Judah, the heir to David's throne, has won the victory. He is worthy to open the scroll and its seven seals."
Revelation 5:5

Jesus is the Lamb of God; Revelation 5:6, 12

"And they sang in a mighty chorus: 'Worthy is the Lamb who was slaughtered to receive power and riches and wisdom and strength and honor and glory and blessing.'"
Revelation 5:12

Jesus is the King of the Nations; Revelation 15:3

"And they were singing the song of Moses, the servant of God, and the song of the Lamb: 'Great and marvelous are Your works, O Lord God, the Almighty. Just and true are Your ways, O King of the nations."
Revelation 15:3

Jesus is the Holy One; Revelation 16:5

"And I heard the angel who had authority over all water saying, 'You are just, O Holy One, who is and who always was, because You have sent these judgements."
Revelation 16:5

Jesus is King of kings and Lord of lords; Revelation 17:14

"They will go to war against the Lamb, but the Lamb will defeat them because He is Lord of all lords and King of all kings. And His called and chosen and faithful ones will be with Him."
Revelation 17:14

Jesus is the Word of Life; John 1:1, 1 John 1:1-2, Revelation 19:13

"He wore a robe dipped in blood, and His title was the Word of God."
Revelation 19:13

God is the Alpha and Omega, Beginning and the End; Revelation 21:6

"And He also said, 'It is finished! I am the Alpha and the Omega - the Beginning and the End. To all who are thirsty I will give freely from the springs of the water of life."
Revelation 21:6

Heaven - John received many visions and revelations of heaven, what it will look and sound like; Revelation 4, 7:9-12, 21:10-27.

"So he took me in the Spirit to a great, high mountain, and he showed me the holy city, Jerusalem, descending out of heaven from God. It shone with the glory of God and sparkled like a precious stone like jasper as clear as crystal."
Revelation 21:10-11

Christ's return - John received many revelations of Christ's return, both from Jesus while He was on earth and from Holy Spirit; Matthew 24:30-31, Revelation 1:1-2, 11:15, 21:1-7

> "And then at last, the sign that the Son of Man is coming will appear in the heavens,
> and there will be deep mourning among all the peoples of the earth. And they will see the
> Son of Man coming on the clouds of heaven with power and great glory."
> *Matthew 24:30*

True worship - John received revelations of what worship in heaven will look like, what it is supposed to look like here on earth; Revelation 4, 5:9-14, 7:9-12, 11:15-17, 15:3-4

> "After this I saw a vast crowd, too great to count,
> from every nation and tribe and people and language, standing in front of the
> throne and before the Lamb. They were clothed in white robes and held
> palm branches in their hands. And they were shouting with a great roar,
> 'Salvation comes from our God who sits on the throne and from the Lamb!'"
> *Revelation 7:9-10*

God's love - John greatly stressed the importance of loving the way God loves; 1 John 2:7, 3:11-18, 23, 4:7-12, 16-21, 5:2-3, 2 John 5-6

> "We know what real love is because Jesus gave up His life for us. So we also ought to give
> up our lives for our brothers and sisters."
> *1 John 3:16*

LESSONS LEARNED FROM THIS WORSHIP LEADER TYPE

An intimate relationship with our Savior is imperative to know and do the will of God. John's life demonstrated that we have to spend time with the Lord in prayer and reading His Word to know what His will is; Matthew 10:1-2, 34-36.

> "Jesus called His twelve disciples together and gave them authority to cast out evil spirits
> and to heal every kind of disease and illness."
> *Matthew 10:1*

Holy Spirit is real and He does speak to us. - We must listen and yield to Him; Holy Spirit was speaking and revealing many different things to John; Revelation 4:1-2

> "Then as I looked, I saw a door standing open in heaven, and the same I had heard before
> spoke to me like a trumpet blast. The voice said, 'Come up here, and I will show you what
> must happen after this."
> *Revelation 4:1*

We are not abandoned in times of adversity. - God was very much with John during his time of exile on Patmos, speaking and revealing many different things to him; Revelation 1:9-10

> "It was the Lord's Day, and I was worshiping in the Spirit. Suddenly, I heard behind me a loud voice like a trumpet blast."
> *Revelation 1:10*

It is important to write down the revelations that God gives us. - John was commanded to write down all of these things he heard and saw, just as we should write so that we do not forget; Revelation 1:1-2

> "Who faithfully reported everything he saw. This is his report of the word of God and the testimony of Jesus Christ."
> *Revelation 1:2*

Remain faithful. - John remained faithful, even to death, and we are called to do the same; Revelation 1:9

> "I, John, am your brother and your partner in suffering and in God's Kingdom and in the patient endurance to which Jesus calls us. I was exiled to the island of Patmos for preaching the Word of God and for my testimony about Jesus."
> *Revelation 1:9*

We are to live our lives like Christ is returning. - John lived and encouraged others to live with an awareness that Christ was returning; Matthew 24:42, 1 John 2:28

> "And now, dear children, remain in fellowship with Christ so that when He returns, you will be full of courage and not shrink back from Him in shame."
> *1 John 2:28*

Stay close to the Lord - Again John and Jesus stayed very close during His ministry here on earth; Matthew 17:1, 26:37-38, Mark 9:2, 14:32-34, Luke 9:28-36, John 13:23

> "He took Peter and Zebedee's two sons, James and John, and He became anguished and distressed. He told them, 'My soul is crushed with grief to the point of death. Stay here and keep watch with Me."
> *Matthew 26:37-38*

Be passionate - John's love for Jesus was very enthusiastic and ardent; Mark 1:19-20, Luke 5:10-11, Acts 5:40-42

"And as soon as they landed, they left everything and followed Jesus."
Luke 5:11

Love Christ more than your own life - John made it clear that he was willing to die for the sake of the Lord, and so he did; Matthew 20:22, Mark 10:37-39, Revelation 1:9

"But Jesus answered by saying to them, 'You don't know what you are asking!
Are you able to drink from the bitter cup of suffering I am about to drink?'
'Oh yes', they replied, 'we are able!"
Matthew 20:22

Share the Gospel of Christ relentlessly - Despite threats and imprisonment, John refused to stop sharing the Gospel and expanding the Kingdom of God; Acts 4:19-20, 33, 5:18-21, 40-42

"And every day, in the Temple and from house to house,
they continued to teach and preach this message: Jesus is the Messiah."
Acts 5:42

Heal and deliver people by the power of Christ and His Holy Spirit; Mark 6:12-13

"And they cast out many demons and healed many sick people,
anointing them with olive oil."
Mark 6:13

We should love one another. - John very much emphasized the love of God, loving Him, and loving one another, as Jesus emphasized that these are the two and greatest commandments given to us as believers; 1 John 2:7, 3:11-18, 23, 4:7-12,16-21, 5:2-3, 2 John 5-6

"Dear friends, I am not writing a new commandment for you; rather it is an old one you have had from the very beginning. This old commandment to love one another is the same message you heard before."
1 John 2:7

Share everything you own with all believers. - John, along with the all of the believers at this time practiced sharing all of their possessions with each other, as one body; Acts 2:44-47, 4:32

"All the believers were united in heart and mine. And they felt that what they owned was not their own, so they shared everything they had."
Acts 4:32

WORSHIP LEADER TYPES

Zeal for the Lord

Left everything, immediately, to follow Christ - The day that Jesus called John, he immediately stopped everything he was doing and left to follow Him; Matthew 4:21-22, Mark 1:19-20, Luke 5:10-11

> "He called them at once, and they also followed Him, leaving their father,
> Zebedee, in the boat with the hired men."
> *Mark 1:20*

Refused to stop preaching the Gospel, despite persecution and opposition - Despite being thrown in jail, threatened, beaten, and eventually exiled, John never stopped sharing the Gospel of Christ; Acts 4:19-20, 5:18-21,40-42, Revelation 1:9

> "The apostles left the high council rejoicing that God had counted them worthy to suffer
> disgrace for the name of Jesus. And every day, in the Temple and from house to house,
> they continued to teach and preach this message: Jesus is the Messiah."
> *Acts 5:41-42*

Love of God's Word

Preacher of the Gospel - John passionately and relentlessly preached the Gospel of Christ; Luke 9:6, Acts 4:33

> "So they began their circuit of the villages, preaching the Good News and healing the sick."
> *Luke 9:6*

Writer of a portion of the Bible - wrote the books of John, 1-3 John, and Revelation; 1 John 1:4, 2:12-14, Revelation 1:1-2

> "I am writing to you who are God's children because your sins
> have been forgiven through Jesus."
> *1 John 2:12*

EXAMPLES OF BEING A PRAISE AND WORSHIPPER

John was a praiser. He regularly met with all the believers in the Temple, praising and worshiping God together and enjoying one another; Acts 2:46-47

> "All the while praising God and enjoying the goodwill of the people.
> And each day the Lord added to their fellowship those who were being saved."
> *Acts 2:47*

John rejoiced and praised God when he was beaten because God had counted him worthy to suffer for the cause of Christ; Acts 5:40-41

> "The apostles left the high council rejoicing that God had counted
> them worthy to suffer disgrace for the name of Jesus."
> *Acts 5:40*

John was a worshipper. John met with the believers daily, worshiping, and praising God together faithfully; Acts 2:46-27, 5:12

> "And they worshiped together at the Temple each day, met in homes for the Lord's
> Supper, and shared their meals with great joy and generosity"
> *Acts 2:46*

John was obedient to Christ's Commission to the death - John faithfully obeyed Christ in spreading the Gospel and making disciples until his death; Luke 9:6, Acts 4:19-20, 33, Revelation 1:9

> "The apostles testified powerfully to the resurrection of the Lord Jesus,
> and God's great blessing was upon them all."
> *Acts 4:33*

Constantly in the Spirit - John practiced worshiping in the Spirit and listening and responding to His voice; Revelation 1:10, 4:1-2.

> "It was the Lord's Day, and I was worshiping in the Spirit.
> Suddenly, I heard behind me a loud voice like a trumpet blast."
> *Revelation 1:10*

Prayer
Received revelations of the end times and Christ's return - John was listening and receiving revelations from God concerning what is to come when Christ returns; Revelation 1:1-2

> "This is a revelation from Jesus Christ, which God gave Him to show His servants the events
> that must soon take place. He sent an angel to present this revelation to His servant John"
> *Revelation 1:1*

Doer of the Word
Preacher of the Word - John faithfully shared the Gospel; Luke 9:6, Acts 5:42

> "And every day, in the Temple and from house to house,
> they continued to teach and preach this message: Jesus is the Messiah."
> *Acts 5:42*

ABILITY TO HEAR AND RESPOND TO THE LORD

Clearly received revelations from Holy Spirit - John recognized the voice of the Lord and he responded with readiness to receive what was being said to him and what he was being shown; Revelation 1:1,10, 4:1-2

> "Then as I looked, I saw a door standing open in heaven, and the same voice I had heard before spoke to me like a trumpet blast. The voice said, 'Come up here, and I will show you what must happen after this.' And instantly I was in the Spirit, and I saw a throne in heaven and someone sitting on it."
> *Revelation 4:1-2*

Wrote everything down; Revelation 1:2

> "Who faithfully reported everything he saw. This is his report of the word of God and the testimony of Jesus Christ."
> *Revelation 1:2*

PRESENTER/REPRESENTATIVE OF THE LORD

Relentless - John was determined to let nothing stop him, just as God didn't let even sin or death stop Him from restoring fellowship and relationship with us; Acts 4:19-20,33, 5:18-21,40-42, Revelation 1:9

> "The apostles left the high council rejoicing that God had counted them worthy to suffer disgrace for the name of Jesus. And every day, in the Temple and from house to house, they continued to teach and preach this message: Jesus is the Messiah."
> *Acts 5:41-42*

Love - John very much emphasized the importance and urgency of loving God with all our hearts, and loving others as He has loved us, because He is love; 1 John 2:7, 3:11-18, 23, 4:7-12,16-21, 5:2-3, 2 John 5-6

> "I am writing to remind you, dear friends, that we should love one another.
> This is not a new commandment, but one we have had from the beginning.
> Love means doing what God has commanded us, and He has commanded us to love one another, just as you heard from the beginning."
>
> *2 John 5-6*

JOHN'S FAITH/TRUST IN THE LORD

Kept the faith through banishment and death - John remained faithful through exile to death; Revelation 1:9

> "I, John, am your brother and your partner in suffering and in God's Kingdom and in the patient endurance to which Jesus calls us. I was exiled to the island of Patmos for preaching the Word of God and for my testimony about Jesus."
>
> *Revelation 1:9*

CHAPTER 26
REVIEW QUESTIONS
John, the Disciple of Jesus

1. What roles did John fulfill?

2. What was John called?

3. What does Acts 2:4 indicate about John?

4. Name at least three traits of John.

5. What was John's punishment for being faithful to Jesus and preaching the gospel?

6. What did Jesus do from the cross regarding his mother and John?

7. Name the seven churches John oversaw from Revelations 1:11.

27

John the Baptist

John the Baptist, also called John the Forerunner, was believed to be a second cousin of Jesus. According to Luke 1:36, which states, *"And listen! Your relative Elizabeth in her old age has also conceived a son, and this is now the sixth month with her who was called barren."*

Before John was born, Mary, who was pregnant with the promised Messiah, went to the house of John's father, Zachariah. As she arrived there, Elizabeth met Mary, and both expectant mothers broke out in words of praise and blessings of one another and predictions about the upcoming births of boys who would be instrumental in changing the course of the world.

Luke chapter 3 tells of John preaching to the crowds. His words are prophetic, poetic, stirring, and instructive. John is seen as the fulfillment of the prophecy which says, *"The voice of one crying in the wilderness (shouting in the desert): Prepare the way of the Lord, make his beaten paths straight."* (Luke 3:4) He gives clear instructions to the people of what their part is in preparing for the promised Messiah. He is seen as the fulfillment of Isaiah's prophecy because he preached the same message of repentance and preparation for the coming of Christ.

The book of Malachi ends with these powerful words closing both the book and the Old Testament with the hope of what was still to come.

> "See I will send you the prophet Elijah before that great and dreadful day of the Lord comes. He will turn the hearts of the fathers to their children, and the hearts of the children to their fathers…"
> *Malachi 4:5-6*

"Many years before then, Isaiah had spoken these words about John, who, like himself, would also be a prophet preaching repentance, encouraging people to live for God alone.
"A voice of one calling: In the desert prepare the way for the Lord, make straight in the wilderness a highway for our God"
Isaiah 40:3

John was clothed in camel hair, indicating his allegiance to a group called the Essenes, who led lives of purity in obedience to the Law and lived ascetic lives, apart from the towns and villages, in what is called the wilderness. His diet of locusts and wild honey also indicates his asceticism.

John had his own followers, who became alarmed that there was a competing prophet named Jesus who had a following as well, but John merely told them that his role in the scheme of things was to prepare the way for the coming of the lamb of God. He stated, *"He must become greater, and I must become lesser..."*

Immediately after John was born, his father, a priest who was struck dumb during the time John was in the womb, received his voice again and spoke these words, *"And you my child, will be called a prophet of the Most High, for you will go on before the Lord to prepare the way for him, to give his people the knowledge of salvation through the forgiveness of their sins..."* -Luke 1:76-77

So, John knew he was not in competition with Jesus but that his role was to preach to the people so they would be prepared for the coming Messiah.

"But unto you who revere and worshipfully fear my name, shall the Sun of Righteousness arise with healing in His wings and His beams and you shall go forth and gambol like calves (released) from the stall and leap for joy." -Malachi 4:2 AMPC,

"And the little boy grew and became strong in spirit and
he was in the deserts (wilderness) until the day of his appearing to Israel
(the commencement of his public ministry)"
Luke 1:80 AMP

The story of John speaking truth to power tells us several things:

1) John was fearless about speaking the truth. He knew he was standing against forces over which he had no control. Those in position of rulership had absolute control and could put to death anyone who threatened their position, either by speaking against them or by attempted insurrection.
2) He was zealous for his own people living righteously because he was willing to risk Herod's wrath to rebuke him.
3) John considered Herod one of his own people (a Jew) because only then was he able to speak so plainly and pointedly of his wrongdoing in marrying his brother's wife and divorcing his first wife, Phasaelis, daughter of King Aretas of Nabataea.
4) Herod did not have John beheaded merely because he spoke of his immorality. He feared John might lead those who followed him in an insurrection against him.

The Jewish historian, Flavius Josephus, relates in his *Antiquities of the Jews* that Herod killed John for this reason:

> "When others joined them--for they became highly agitated by his preaching--Herod feared his influence on them to be so great that it might lead to some uprising; for they seemed to be doing everything according to his advice. Therefore, Herod decided that it would be much better to take the initiative to have him killed before he was able to cause some rebellion than to become involved in matters once the revolt had begun, and then be sorry"[47]

So, the rather two-dimensional view of John the Baptist as someone who was put to death because he disapproved of Herod's morals does not take into consideration the political climate of the time nor does it help us to have a complete understanding of the motives of the rich and powerful men who ruled over the poor and powerless.

One reference put the conclusion of John's life very well and I quote:

> "He lived in the desert, took the Nazarite vows and lived his days with specific purpose. His clothing and diet were simple; he wasn't loaded down with the cares and desires of this world. Though his life may seem extreme and most of us may not easily relate to a diet of locusts and honey, the heart of it is this: He chose obedience to God's call. He said "yes" to God's mission, even when it probably was not easy. Even when he could have chosen his own way."[48]

WORSHIP LEADER TYPE PROFILE

JOHN THE BAPTIST

BACKGROUND

- **Political Conditions:**
  - Rome is in power.
- **Social Conditions:**
  - The social dynamic of these days was Jews vs. Gentiles
- **Religious Conditions:**
  - Living according to Law of Moses
  - Jesus has begun His ministry.

---

47 Josephus, Flavius, <u>Antiquities of the Jews</u> 18: 118
48 https://www.crosswalk.com/faith/women/6-powerful-truths-from-the-life-of-john-the-baptist-that-offer-hope-for-today.html (article by Debbie McDaniel)

FACTORS IN THE EQUIPPING FOR THE TASK

Righteous parents - Zechariah and Elizabeth were considered righteous before God, therefore, would raise their son according to the standard of the Lord; Luke 1:6

> "Zechariah and Elizabeth were righteous in God's eyes, careful to obey all
> of the Lord's commandments and regulations."
> *Luke 1:6*

Filled with Holy Spirit before birth - John was filled with the Holy Spirit in Elizabeth's womb; Luke 1:15

> "For he will be great in the eyes of the Lord. He must never touch wine or other alcoholic
> drinks. He will be filled with the Holy Spirit, even before his birth."
> *Luke 1:15*

Spirit and power of Elijah - John was given the prophetic and influential spirit of Elijah; Matthew 17:12-13, Luke 1:17

> "He will be a man with the spirit and power of Elijah. He will prepare the people for the
> coming of the Lord. He will turn the hearts of the fathers to their children, and he will
> cause those who are rebellious to accept the wisdom of the godly."
> *Luke 1:17*

Taught of the Spirit - Isaiah 40:3

> "A voice of one calling: "In the wilderness prepare the way for the Lord[a];
> make straight in the desert a highway for our God."
> *Isaiah 40:3*

JOHN THE BAPTIST'S PERSONALITY

Devoted - Lived his entire life in dedication to preparing for the coming of Christ and His kingdom; Matthew 3:1-7, 11:18, 14:10-11, Mark 1:4-5, 6:27-28, Luke 1:80, 3:3-6, 7:24-28,33, John 1:6-7, 23

> "This messenger was John the Baptist. He was in the wilderness
> and preached that people should be baptized to show that
> they had repented of their sins and turned to God to be forgiven.
> All of Judea, including all the people of Jerusalem, went out to see and hear John.
> And when they confessed their sins, he baptized them in the Jordan River."
> *Mark 1:4-5*

Humble - Lived in humble surroundings and was quick to acknowledge his lowliness, especially when it came to Christ; Matthew 3:4, 11, 13-14, Mark 1:6-7, Luke 3:16, John 1:15, 23, 2, 3:26-30.

> "John announced: 'Someone is coming soon who is greater than I am—so much greater that I'm not even worthy to stoop down like a slave and untie the straps of His sandals."
> *Mark 1:7*

Bold - Spoke and preached with courage and confidence; Matthew 3:7-10, 14:3-4, Mark 6:17-18, Luke 3:7-9, 19-20.

> "But when he saw many Pharisees and Sadducees coming to watch him baptize, he denounced them. 'You brood of snakes!' he exclaimed. 'Who warned you to flee the coming wrath?"
> *Matthew 3:7*

THE REVELATION OF GOD THAT JOHN THE BAPTIST RECEIVED AND CARRIED TO THE PEOPLE OF GOD

The Kingdom of God is near; Matthew 3:1-2,11-12, Mark 1:2-4, Luke 3:3-6, John 1:15, 23

> "In those days John the Baptist came to the Judean wilderness and began preaching. His message was, 'Repent of your sins and turn to God, for the Kingdom of Heaven is near."
> *Matthew 3:1-2*

The coming of Holy Spirit; Matthew 3:11, Mark 1:8, Luke 3:16

> "I baptize with water those who repent of their sins and turn to God. But someone is coming soon who is greater than I am—so much greater that I'm not worthy even to be His slave and carry his sandals. He will baptize you with the Holy Spirit and with fire."
> *Matthew 3:11*

LESSONS LEARNED FROM THIS WORSHIP LEADER TYPE

Preach and speak the truth boldly - John spoke truth, knowing that it would offend, frustrate, and anger those around him; Matthew 3:1-2, 7-10, 14:3-4, Mark 1:2-4, 6:17-18, Luke 3:3-9, 19-20

> "For Herod had sent soldiers to arrest and imprison John as a favor to Herodias.
> She had been his brother Philip's wife, but Herod had married her.
> John had been telling Herod, 'It is against God's law for you
> to marry your brother's wife.'"
> *Mark 6:17-18*

Our treasure is in heaven - Lived in the wilderness, no fancy clothes or shoes, his treasure was seeing the Messiah and the kingdom at hand; Matthew 3:4, 11:7-11, Mark 1:6, Luke 7:24-28

> "John's clothes were woven from coarse camel hair, and he wore a leather
> belt around his waist. For food he ate locusts and wild honey."
> *Matthew 3:4*

Know your place - John knew that his purpose was to go before the One coming after him, he was not his center of attention; Matthew 3:11, Mark 1:7, Luke 3:16, John 1:8,15,23,27, 3:26-30, Acts 13:25

> "He must become greater and greater, and I must become less and less."
> *John 3:30*

Hold to the faith and the truth to the end - John did not compromise his message, even facing death; Matthew 14:10-11, Mark 6:27-28, Luke 9:9

> "So he immediately sent an executioner to the prison to cut off John's head and bring it to
> him. The soldier beheaded John in the prison, brought his head on a tray,
> and gave it to the girl, who took it to her mother."
> *Mark 6:27-28*

Love for the Lord
Speak truth boldly - Refused to say anything that didn't exalt Christ, nor did he back down; Matthew 3:7-10, 14:3-4, Mark 6:17-18, Luke 3:7-9,19-20,

> "Prove by the way you live that you have repented of your sins and turned to God.
> Don't just say to each other, 'We're safe, for we are descendants of Abraham.'
> That means nothing, for I tell you, God can create children of
> Abraham from these very stones."
> *Luke 3:8*

Love for His people
Shared the Gospel - Desperately wanted others to know about Christ and to turn to God wholeheartedly; Matthew 3:1-2, Mark 1:2-5, Luke 3:3-6, Acts 13:24

> "Before He came, John the Baptist preached that all the people of Israel needed to repent of their sins and turn to God and be baptized."
> *Acts 13:24*

Zeal for the Lord
Martyred - Died for his faith and ministry; Matthew 14:8-12, Mark 6:27-28, Luke 9:9

> "'I beheaded John,' Herod said, so who is this man about whom I hear such stories?' And he kept trying to see him."
> *Luke 9:9*

EXAMPLE OF BEING A WORSHIPPER

Forerunner - Lived his entire life as a forerunner of Christ; Isaiah 40:3-5, Malachi 3:1, Matthew 3:1-3, 11:10, Mark 1:1-5, Luke 1:14-17, 76-77, 3:3-6, John 1:6-8, 15, 22-27

> "Listen! It's the voice of someone shouting, 'Clear the way through the wilderness for the Lord! Make a straight highway through the wasteland for our God!'"
> *Isaiah 40:3*

PRESENTER/REPRESENTATIVE OF THE LORD

Telling of the coming of the Heavenly Kingdom - As Jesus came announcing the kingdom, John came just before announcing the coming of Christ; Matthew 3:1-3, 11-12, Mark 1:2-4, Luke 3:3-6

> "Repent of your sins and turn to God, for the Kingdom of Heaven is near."
> *Matthew 3:2*

Martyred - As Christ was killed for truth, John was also killed; Matthew 14:8-12, Mark 6:27-28, Luke 9:9

> "So John was beheaded in the prison, and his head was brought on a tray and given to the girl, who took it to her mother."
> *Matthew 14:10-11*

REVELATIONS GIVEN TO JOHN THE BAPTIST FROM THE LORD

Jesus is the Son of God; Messiah or Chosen One of God; John 1:33-34

"I didn't know He was the One, but when God sent me to baptize with water, He told me, 'The One on whom you see the Spirit descend and rest is the One who will baptize with the Holy Spirit.' I saw this happen to Jesus, so I testify that He is the Chosen One of God."
John 1:33-34

Jesus is the Lamb of God; John 1:35-36

"I didn't know He was the One, but when God sent me to baptize with water, He told me, 'The One on whom you see the Spirit descend and rest is the One who will baptize with the Holy Spirit.' I saw this happen to Jesus, so I testify that He is the Chosen One of God."
John 1:33-34

Jesus as the Light; John 1:19-28

"He came as a witness to testify concerning that light, so that through him all might believe."
John 1:7

JOHN THE BAPTIST'S FAITH/TRUST IN THE LORD

John faithfully devoted his life to the coming of Christ and His kingdom. He lived his entire life preparing for the coming of Messiah; Matthew 3:1-7, 11:18, 14:10-11, Mark 1:4-5, 6:27-28, Luke 1:80, 3:3-6, 7:24-28, 33, John 1:6-7, 23,

"God sent a man, John the Baptist, to tell about the light so that everyone might believe because of his testimony."
John 1:6-7

CHAPTER 27
REVIEW QUESTIONS
John the Baptist

1. What were the political and social conditions of John the Baptist's time?

2. What were the religious conditions?

3. What were the factors that equipped John the Baptist for his task?

4. What are at least three lessons we can learn from John the Baptist?

5. When asked who he was, what did John reply?

6. In John 3:22-26, a debate occurs among John's disciples concerning which baptism is valid, those performed by John or Jesus. What was John's answer?

"Worship is not a performance; it is an intimate encounter with the living God. It is in worship that we experience His love, grace, and transforming power."
–Hillsong United

28

Martha

Martha was a friend of Jesus who, along with Mary, her sister, and Lazarus, her brother, provided hospitality for him and his followers wherever they were in the area. Martha lived in the town of Bethany, which means "house of welcome" or "house of figs." Bethany was a small town located at the foot of the Mt. of Olives, about 3 kilometers (1.7 miles) east of Jerusalem.

Martha, Mary, and their brother Lazarus were some of Jesus' closest friends. John 11:5, NIV, tells us *"Jesus loved Martha and her sister and Lazarus."* This family believed Jesus was the Messiah and saw Him bring their brother back to life. Jesus spent some of his last days on earth in their comfortable home. The story of Mary and Martha gives us amazing insight into their personalities and teaches us some important lessons.

Martha's sister, Mary, instead of helping her with the domestic chores, was found sitting *"at the Lord's feet listening to what he said."* Luke 10:39. Martha, possibly hot and tired from cooking and cleaning, went to Jesus and said, *"Lord, don't you care that my sister has left me to do the work by myself? Tell her to help me!"* Luke 10:40. (NIV)

Apparently, Martha was so comfortable with Jesus that she had no problem venting her frustration. She didn't ask Jesus what His opinion was; she boldly told him what to do. We could kindly call her behavior outspoken, straightforward, and maybe even pushy.

Martha wanted Mary to behave in the traditional woman's role. It was unthinkable for a woman to sit at the feet of a rabbi and listen to him teach. Girls stayed in the home, illiterate, while the boys went to school. Women could only congregate in the Women's Court of the Temple, nowhere near the men. So, for Mary to plop down at the feet of Jesus and listen to his teaching among a group of men was remarkable!

Jesus' answer to Martha was direct but compassionate. We see the familiarity of the two in this exchange. Martha commanded Jesus to tell Mary to get up and help her. Jesus called her name twice, and we can hear the warmth of it. He wanted her to know two things: that her serving was not going unnoticed or unappreciated, but that Mary was doing a valuable thing as well. In that statement, Jesus went against the attitude toward women at the time that women were not sent to school but were expected to wait on men. Jesus gave value to Mary as she sat at his feet soaking up everything He said.

WORSHIP LEADER TYPES

WORSHIP LEADER TYPE PROFILE

MARTHA

BACKGROUND

- **Political Conditions:**
  - Rome is in power and has absolute control.
- **Social Conditions:**
  - Jews and Gentiles are divided. Jews live separate from the Gentiles and do not eat with them or associate with them, believing them to be "unclean."
- **Religious Conditions:**
  - Society functioning under the Law of Moses. The Jews went to the synagogue to hear the law and the prophets being read by the rabbi. Rabbis were held in high esteem and spent their time studying the law and teaching the men, who then went home and taught their children.
  - Jesus has begun His ministry in spreading the Gospel-the Good News.

FACTORS IN THE EQUIPPING FOR THE TASK

MARTHA'S PERSONALITY

Hospitable - Martha was a homemaker with a genuine heart to serve; Luke 10:38, John 12:2

"As Jesus and the disciples continued on their way to Jerusalem, they came to a certain village where a woman named Martha welcomed Him into her home."
Luke 10:38

Practical - Martha was very much about getting things done and doing what was practical; Luke 10:40

"But Martha was distracted by the big dinner she was preparing. She came to Jesus and said, 'Lord, doesn't it seem unfair to you that my sister just sits here while I do all the work? Tell her to come and help me.'"
Luke 10:40

Focused/distracted - Martha was very focused on her tasks and responsibilities, so much that it would distract her from the important things; Luke 10:40

> "But Martha was distracted by the big dinner she was preparing. She came to Jesus and said, 'Lord, doesn't it seem unfair to you that my sister just sits here while I do all the work? Tell her to come and help me.'"
> *Luke 10:40*

"Realist" - Martha was very practical and moved based on what see could see; Luke 10:40, John 11:39

> "'Roll the stone aside,' Jesus told them. But Martha, the dead man's sister, protested, 'Lord, he has been dead for four days. The smell will be terrible.'"
> *John 11:39*

Easily anxious - Martha's anxiety to have the home and dinner prepared was very evident through her frustration with her sister Mary sitting at Christ's feet; Luke 10:41

> "But the Lord said to her, "My dear Martha, you are worried and upset over all these details!"
> *Luke 10:41*

MARTHA'S RELATIONSHIP WITH GOD

Martha had a heart of service for the Lord - Martha very much desired to physically serve the Lord; Luke 10:40, John 12:2

> "A dinner was prepared in Jesus' honor. Martha served, and Lazarus was among those who ate with him."
> *John 12:2*

Jesus loved Martha; John 11:5

> "So although Jesus loved Martha, Mary, and Lazarus"
> *John 11:5*

LESSONS LEARNED FROM THIS WORSHIP LEADER TYPE

Servant's heart - Martha had a genuine heart to serve and to serve the Lord; Luke 10:40, John 12:2

> "A dinner was prepared in Jesus' honor. Martha served, and Lazarus was among those who ate with him."
> *John 12:2*

WORSHIPPER

Works-based - Martha was more focused on what she could do for the Lord rather than spending intimate time with Him; Luke 10:40

> "But Martha was distracted by the big dinner she was preparing. She came to Jesus and said, 'Lord, doesn't it seem unfair to you that my sister just sits here while I do all the work? Tell her to come and help me.'"
> *Luke 10:40*

THE REVELATION OF GOD THAT MARTHA RECEIVED AND CARRIED TO THE PEOPLE OF GOD.

Worship is relationship-oriented, not task-oriented - Jesus tells Martha that her sister Mary knows "the main thing," which is the depth of her relationship with Lord; Luke 10:40-42

> "But Martha was distracted by the big dinner she was preparing. She came to Jesus and said, 'Lord, doesn't it seem unfair to you that my sister just sits here while I do all the work? Tell her to come and help me.' But the Lord said to her, 'My dear Martha, you are worried and upset over all these details! There is only one thing worth being concerned about. Mary has discovered it, and it will not be taken away from her.'"
> *Luke 10:40-42*

MARTHA'S FAITH/TRUST IN THE LORD

Believed that Jesus could raise Lazarus up again; John 11:21-27

> "Martha said to Jesus, 'Lord, if only you had been here, my brother would not have died. But even now I know that God will give you whatever you ask.'"
> *John 11:21-22*

Believed that Jesus was the Messiah; John 11:27

> "'Yes, Lord,' she told him. 'I have always believed you are the Messiah, the Son of God, the one who has come into the world from God.'"
> *John 11:27*

CHAPTER 28
REVIEW QUESTIONS
Martha

1. What were the political conditions of Martha's time?

2. What were the social conditions?

3. What were the religious conditions?

4. What were some characteristics of Martha that made her a prominent character in the story about Jesus?

5. What does Jesus infer when he answers Martha after she requested that Mary should help her in the kitchen?

Whatever we delight in or are attracted to will occupy our thoughts. The Psalmist said, "For I delight in your commands because I love them."
—Psalm 119:47

29

Mary of Bethany

Mary was known as the sister of Martha and Lazarus. She was a friend of Jesus and often played hostess to the disciples when they traveled through. Mary was the woman who "sat at Jesus' feet," listening to his teachings rather than helping her frazzled sister, Martha. "Comparisons and contrasts between the two sisters have already been noticed. Both loved the Master and were loved by Him. Martha sat at His feet, but "her love and piety alike found adequate and satisfying expression at all times in the ordinary kindly offices of hospitality and domestic service." Mary also sat at Jesus' feet and was content to linger there because her disposition and inward, silent brooding made it hard for her to be at home in the world of affairs. Bustling around a house was not native to her deep emotion. In this cameo of her, then, let us try to sketch her as she was, as an individualist.[49]

It has often been posited that Mary Magdalene, who was probably a prostitute, and Mary of Bethany were the same woman. But this seems unlikely.

"But we hold that Mary of Bethany cannot be identified with any other New Testament woman of the same name. Among the women mentioned in the gospels, she occupies a prominent position, for it was she who won the golden commendation from the Lord she dearly loved when He said, "She hath done what she could" (Mark 14:8)."[50]

Mary was a friend of Jesus, who loved to sit and listen to his words. She was close enough to Him that she could rebuke him when her brother, Lazarus, died, saying, "Lord, if you had been here, this would not have happened."

The story of Jesus commending Mary for her choice to sit and listen rather than serve seems to tell us that He was revolutionary in His view of women being capable of attending school and learning as well as men. This story is important in showing us that women have equal value in the eyes of our Creator.

---

49 https://www.biblegateway.com/resources/all-women-bible/Mary-Bethany
50 Ibid

We know Mary was a good listener. This is such an important skill today and almost a lost art. She is a great example of a loyal sister, a good friend, and a woman of great intelligence and spiritual strength. She was thirsty for the truth and seemed unconcerned with the idea that women could not be disciples.

WORSHIP LEADER TYPE PROFILE

MARY

BACKGROUND

- **Political Conditions:**
  - Rome was in power. The power of Rome was absolute.
- **Social Conditions:**
  - Jews and Gentiles are divided.
  - The Jews lived simply, in small one room huts with hard-packed floor and a roof that served as another room, often for sleeping. A woman's day began at sunrise. She would get water from the village well and then return home to bake bread, the main food staple. She might do spinning and weaving, mending and making curds from goat's milk. Along with the staples of bread and wine, they would eat beans, lentils, and cucumbers as well as melons and nuts. In the evening the men would go to the synagogue for the evening meeting.
- **Religious Conditions:**
  - Society functions under the law of Moses.
  - Men went to the temple in the evening. Sabbath was observed.
  - Jesus has begun His ministry in spreading the Gospel.

FACTORS IN THE EQUIPPING FOR THE TASK

MARY OF BETHANY'S PERSONALITY

Childlike faith - Mary simply loved the Lord and just desired to sit in His presence without the worry or anxiety of tasks and responsibilities; Luke 10:39, 42

> "Her sister, Mary, sat at the Lord's feet, listening to what He taught."
> *Luke 10:39*

MARY OF BETHANY'S RELATIONSHIP WITH GOD

Simply loved and adored the Lord - Mary showed genuine affection to the Lord through her "basking" in His presence as well as anointing Him with the most expensive perfume she owned; Matthew 26:7, Mark 14:3, Luke 10:42, John 12:3

> "While He was eating, a woman came in with a beautiful alabaster jar
> of expensive perfume and poured it over His head."
> *Matthew 26:7*

Very intimate - There was a special intimacy between her and Christ that opened emotional transparency; John 11:32-33

> "When Jesus saw her weeping and saw the other people wailing with her, a deep anger
> welled up within Him, and He was deeply troubled."
> *John 11:33*

LESSONS LEARNED FROM THIS WORSHIP LEADER TYPE

Treasure and just dwell in the presence of the Lord; to abide in the Lord, to sit in and enjoy His presence, Luke 10:39

> "Her sister, Mary, sat at the Lord's feet, listening to what He taught."
> *Luke 10:39*

This Christian walk is not task-driven or about what we can physically do for God, but is about loving and abiding in the presence of God and having an intimate relationship with Him. In contrast to her sister Martha who was mostly concerned with household tasks, Mary took time first to draw close to the Lord. (Luke 10:39-42)

> "Her sister, Mary, sat at the Lord's feet, listening to what He taught. But Martha was
> distracted by the big dinner she was preparing. She came to Jesus and said,
> 'Lord, doesn't it seem unfair to You that my sister just sits here while I do all the work?
> Tell her to come and help me.'"
> *Luke 10:39-40*

Never lose sight of the most important thing - Mary did not allow outside tasks and responsibilities to distract her from the one thing that matters most, our relationship with Christ: Luke 10:42

> "There is only one thing worth being concerned about. Mary has discovered it,
> and it will not be taken away from her."
> *Luke 10:42*

Love for the Lord
Treasure Christ - Mary treasured the Lord above all material things, as she anoints Him with her most expensive perfume; Matthew 26:7, Mark 14:3, John 12:3

> "Meanwhile, Jesus was in Bethany at the home of Simon,
> a man who had previously had leprosy. While He was eating, a woman came in with a beautiful alabaster jar of expensive perfume made from essence of nard.
> She broke open the jar and poured the perfume over His head."
> *Mark 14:3*

Love of His Word
Treasured Christ's every word - Mary valued the very words of the Lord above all other tasks and responsibilities; Luke 10:39

> "Her sister, Mary, sat at the Lord's feet, listening to what He taught."
> *Luke 10:39*

EXAMPLE OF BEING A WORSHIPPER

Sitting at Christ's feet - Mary paints a beautiful picture of worship, just abiding and dwelling in His presence; Luke 10:39

> "Her sister, Mary, sat at the Lord's feet, listening to what He taught."
> *Luke 10:39*

Truly treasured and adored the Lord - Mary demonstrated her affection for the Lord by anointing Him with her most valuable perfume; Matthew 26:7, Mark 14:3, John 12:3

> "Then Mary took a twelve-ounce jar of expensive perfume made from essence of nard,
> and she anointed Jesus' feet with it, wiping His feet with her hair.
> The house was filled with the fragrance."
> *John 12:3*

Emotional intimacy with the Lord - There was emotional transparency on both her and Christ's part, demonstrating the closeness of her heart to His; John 11:32-35

> "When Mary arrived and saw Jesus, she fell at His feet and said,
> 'Lord, if only You had been here, my brother would not have died.'
> When Jesus saw her weeping and saw the other people wailing with her, a deep anger
> welled up within Him, and He was deeply troubled."
> *John 11:32-33*

REVELATIONS GIVEN TO MARY OF BETHANY FROM THE LORD

Worship over works - Mary realized and exercised/demonstrated the superiority of taking time with the Lord over daily tasks and responsibilities; Luke 10:39-42

> "But the Lord said to her, 'My dear Martha, you are worried and upset over
> all these details! There is only one thing worth being concerned about.
> Mary has discovered it, and it will not be taken away from her.'"
> *Luke 10:41-42*

MARY'S FAITH/TRUST IN THE LORD

Believed Jesus could raise Lazarus from the dead; John 11:32

> "When Mary arrived and saw Jesus, she fell at His feet and said,
> 'Lord, if only You had been here, my brother would not have died.'"
> *John 11:32*

CHAPTER 29
REVIEW QUESTIONS
Mary of Bethany

1. What were the political conditions of Mary's time?

2. What were the social conditions?

3. What were the religious conditions?

4. What were some characteristics of Mary for the task she was given?

5. What are some lessons we can learn from Mary of Bethany?

30

Paul

Paul was born in Tarsus to Jewish parents of the tribe of Benjamin. Highly educated, he was sent to school at an early age, where he learned both Hebrew and Greek. His parents probably spoke Greek at home, since they were Roman citizens. He was a tent maker by trade.

The personality and character of a man emerge from what he writes, and we are fortunate to have access to Paul's many writings, letters, exhortations, and instructions to the early church. Paul, or Saul, his Hebrew name, was a highly educated man, who studied under the Rabbi Gamaliel. We first see him as the persecutor of the early church, as one who was assigned by the Jewish authorities to seek out those who followed this sect called Christians and throw them into prison with the intention that they would be executed. He seems to have been greatly affected by the stoning of Stephen, which he oversaw, as one who kept the robes of those men who carried out the evil murder of this righteous man. Undoubtedly, he heard Stephen as he cried out to God. Stephen's death surely marked a change in Paul. He watched as the leaders of the Sanhedrin executed Stephen.

"They were furious and cried out against him. But calmly, Stephen gazed up to heaven...

> "'Look,' he said, 'I see heaven open and the Son of Man standing at the right hand of God.' At this they covered their ears and, yelling at the top of their voices, they all rushed at him, dragged him out of the city and began to stone him. Meanwhile, the witnesses laid their coats at the feet of a young man named Saul. While they were stoning him, Stephen prayed, 'Lord Jesus, receive my spirit.' Then he fell on his knees and cried out, 'Lord, do not hold this sin against them.' When he had said this, he fell asleep."
>
> *(Acts 7:56-60)*

This incident preceded Paul's conversion on the road to Damascus. This miraculous change of heart and mind, as he traveled along the road to Damascus with the purpose of persecuting more Christians, is known as a "Pauline conversion." It was swift, definite and very dramatic. Paul was knocked off the donkey he was traveling upon, following a heavenly visitation. A voice called out to him, "Paul, Paul, why do you persecute me?" Jesus identied with the persecuted Christians. This was so traumatic that Paul lost his sight and was then led into a town where the very people he had been persecuting ministered to him. Paul made what is known as a "paradigm shift" when he changed from persecuting rabbi to proselytizing, traveling preacher, and church builder.

Paul is known for his missionary trips, often spoken of as three trips. The first trip is taken from Acts 13 and was from Cyprus and southern Asia Minor. The second was from Acts 19 and was from Asia Minor and Macedonia. Once he left Macedonia, Paul went to Rome, where he was told by the Holy Spirit to travel. (Missionary means "sent.") But, according to Biblestudytools.com, those were not all of Paul's journeys. Here, I would like to quote from biblestudytools.com,

"Paul's journeys began very early after his conversion near Damascus. After being visited by Agabus, Paul immediately began proclaiming the good news of Jesus Christ in the synagogues in Damascus (Acts 9:20). When he was run out of town, Paul went to Jerusalem (Acts 9:26). After staying in Jerusalem for a while, he then went to Caesarea in order to sail to Tarsus, his hometown.

This still is not the end of Paul's journey. He was still in Tarsus when God began to save Gentiles around Antioch. When Barnabas went to Antioch to help the young church there, he went to Tarsus to ask Paul for his help. Once again, Paul found himself traveling, this time going from Tarsus to Antioch (Acts 11:25-26).

By the way, according to Paul in Galatians 1:17, he also traveled to Arabia for three years at some point during the other journeys."[51] It is also concluded from other Bible scholars that Paul traveled to Spain. So, he traveled more than any other disciple, or follower of Christ, to spread the news of salvation and new life through Jesus Christ.

During his travels, Paul was shipwrecked, bitten by a snake, and was even thought to be a god by the people who had rescued him, because he did not die from the snakebite. An angry crowd nearly murdered him, and he was eventually jailed, where he witnessed the Praetorian soldiers while on house arrest. He wrote much of the New Testament (through the help of a scribe) and was very instrumental in defining early Christianity.

Paul went on to become a very effective apostle and teacher of the Gospel of Jesus Christ, writing some of the Epistles to the churches to describe why Jesus had come, as well as what the Christians were to do now that they were His followers.[52] Because of Paul,

---

51 www.biblestudytools.com
52 https://crossexamined.org/paul-write-thirteen-letters-attributed/

we have very extensive teachings on the life of the early Church. He explains, in Romans, the reason Christ died, and what that means to His followers. His teachings dealt with the very practical fundamentals of the Christian life, such as proper behavior of the deacons of the church, (1 Timothy 3:8-13) how to respect one another during the communion meal, (1 Corinthians 11:27-32) how to encourage one another and share transparency, (Colossians 3:16), and many other practical admonitions. These, and many other issues which the early church dealt with, were clearly defined and instructions were given for how to resolve the conflicts which the early church faced. He had a way of putting complex ideas into a very concrete form that the people could understand.

We can view Paul as a worship leader in the sense that he instructed the early Christians regarding their behavior in ministry in the church. "By the time he wrote the letter to the Romans, he could clearly describe his place in God's plan. The Hebrew prophets, he wrote, had predicted that 'in the days to come', God would restore the tribes of Israel and that the Gentiles would then turn to worship the one true God".[53] Paul's leadership brought order to the church and gave instructions that helped to create an atmosphere of awe and respect towards God as well as teaching the people to love and respect one another.

---

53 https://www.britannica.com/biography/Saint-Paul-the-Apostle/Mission

WORSHIP LEADER TYPE PROFILE

PAUL

BACKGROUND

- **Political Conditions:**
  - Rome was at the height of power and had absolute authority over its citizens. Rome allowed people to have their own religion as long as it did not interfere with the might and power of Rome. The early church walked a thin line of being true to their own beliefs and seeking not to offend the Roman government. If, for example, this emerging Christian group decided to revolt against the government, it would be crushed. So, Paul encouraged the church to submit to the governing authorities in his letter to the Romans. If that letter had been intercepted and he was encouraging the church to rebel against the government, it would have meant death to him and his followers.
- **Social Conditions:**
  - The church was not a large building but was a gathering of people in small homes. Since most people lived in two room homes, there could not be more than 20 people in the gathering.
  - Slavery was common. Christian slaves were encouraged to obey their masters. Some forms of slavery were more miserable than others.
  - Travel was made safer and easier because of the roads built by the Romans. Many people traveled by ship since there were many large bodies of water around the Mediterranean area. There were many public inns. But most people stayed with acquaintances. Hospitality was encouraged.
- **Religious Conditions:**
  - Christians were being persecuted. The Hebrew authorities considered them a cult and did not approve of their beliefs that Jesus was the promised Messiah. Christians had to meet in homes but were allowed their own religion unless that religion threatened the might and power of Rome.

FACTORS IN THE EQUIPPING FOR THE TASK

Paul was highly educated for his time. Paul studied under the Rabbi Gamaliel and learned to write in both Greek and Hebrew, being thoroughly versed in the law.

Filled with Holy Spirit - Paul was filled with the Holy Spirit at the start of his ministry; Acts 13:9

> "Saul, also known as Paul, was filled with the Holy Spirit, and he looked the sorcerer in the eye."
> *Acts 13:9*

Empowered by the Lord - Paul was given strength and power from the Lord; Acts 14:3

> "But the apostles stayed there a long time, preaching boldly about the grace of the Lord. And the Lord proved their message was true by giving them power to do miraculous signs and wonders."
> *Acts 14:3*

Chosen - Paul was chosen by God; Acts 22:14-15, Acts 9:15

> "Then he told me, 'The God of our ancestors has chosen you to know his will and to see the Righteous One and hear Him speak.'"
> *Acts 22:14*

PAUL'S PERSONALITY

Relentless and unapologetic preacher of the Gospel; Acts 13:38-41, 14:1,21,25, 16:30-32, 17:3,22-31, 18:11, 19:8, 20:7, 24:24-25, 26:20, 28:23,30-31.

> "Then Paul went to the synagogue and preached boldly for the next three months, arguing persuasively about the Kingdom of God."
> *Acts 19:8*

Bold - Paul was unashamed and unafraid of man or persecution; Acts 13:46, 14:3, 19:8, 20:20, 27, 28:30-31.

> "I never shrank back from telling you what you needed to hear, either publicly or in your homes."
> *Acts 20:20*

Determined - Paul would let nothing or no one stop him; Acts 14:19-22, 20:19

> "I have done the Lord's work humbly and with many tears. I have endured the trials that came to me from the plots of the Jews."
> *Acts 20:19*

Spiritually sensitive - Paul was able to hear, recognize, and respond to Holy Spirit's promptings and direction; Acts 16:6-8, 19:21, 20:22-23.

> "Afterward Paul felt compelled by the Spirit to go over to Macedonia and Achaia before going to Jerusalem. 'And after that,' He said, 'I must go on to Rome!'"
> *Acts 19:21*

Humble - Paul humbly served the Lord, not himself; Acts 20:19

> "I have done the Lord's work humbly and with many tears. I have endured the trials that came to me from the plots of the Jews."
> *Acts 20:19*

Faithful - Paul served the Lord without wavering; Acts 20:26

> "I declare today that I have been faithful. If anyone suffers eternal death, it's not my fault,"
> *Acts 20:26*

PAUL'S RELATIONSHIP WITH GOD

Solely devoted - Paul was fully dedicated to the Lord; Acts 20:24, 21:13-14

> "But my life is worth nothing to me unless I use it for finishing the work assigned me by the Lord Jesus—the work of telling others the Good News about the wonderful grace of God."
> *Acts 20:24*

Continued pursuit of an intimate relationship with the Lord; Philippians 3:5-12

THE REVELATION OF GOD THAT PAUL RECEIVED AND CARRIED TO THE PEOPLE OF GOD

Gospel of the Kingdom; Acts 13:38-41, 14:1, 21, 25, 16:30-32, 17:3, 22-31, 18:11, 19:8, 24:24-25, 26:20-23, 28:23, 30-31

> "Then he brought them out and asked, 'Sirs, what must I do to be saved?' They replied, "Believe in the Lord Jesus and you will be saved, along with everyone in your household.' And they shared the word of the Lord with him and with all who lived in his household."
> *Acts 16:30-32*

Protector; Acts 26:22, 28:3-6.

> "But God has protected me right up to this present time so I can testify to everyone, from the least to the greatest. I teach nothing except what the prophets and Moses said would happen—"
> *Acts 26:22*

He also protected those around him, as God had protected him. When he was in jail and the prison doors were open, he stayed and protected the jailers so they would not be put to death for allowing him to escape. (Acts 16:16-40)

God revealed to Paul that he had to suffer many things; Acts 9:15-16

> "But the Lord said to Ananias, "Go! This man is my chosen instrument to proclaim my name to the Gentiles and their kings and to the people of Israel. I will show him how much he must suffer for my name.""
> *Acts 9:15-16*

Paul was kidnapped; Acts 21:27

He was beaten; Acts 21:30-31; 23:3

Constantly threatened; Acts 22:22; 27:43

Arrested several times; Acts 21:33; 22:24

Shipwrecked; Acts 27:47

LESSONS LEARNED FROM THIS WORSHIP LEADER TYPE

Speak boldly, for others' sake - Others were greatly influenced, encouraged, and even received Christ because of Paul's boldness; Acts 13:10-12, 20:26-27.

> "'Watch now, for the Lord has laid His hand of punishment upon you, and you will be struck blind. You will not see the sunlight for some time.' Instantly mist and darkness came over the man's eyes, and he began groping around begging for someone to take his hand and lead him. When the governor saw what had happened, he became a believer, for he was astonished at the teaching about the Lord."
> *Acts 13:11-12*

WORSHIP LEADER TYPES

Keep going - Paul let nothing and no one stop him, despite suffering and persecution; Acts 14:19-22

> "Then some Jews arrived from Antioch and Iconium and won the crowds to their side.
> They stoned Paul and dragged him out of town, thinking he was dead.
> But as the believers gathered around him, he got up and went back into the town.
> The next day he left with Barnabas for Derbe. After preaching the
> Good News in Derbe and making many disciples,
> Paul and Barnabas returned to Lystra, Iconium, and Antioch of Pisidia,"
> *Acts 14:19-21*

Praise despite circumstances - Paul was able and chose to praise from prison; Acts 16:25

> "Around midnight Paul and Silas were praying and singing hymns to God,
> and the other prisoners were listening."
> *Acts 16:25*

Praise is a spiritual weapon - Paul and Silas' praise set them as well as the other prisoners free; Acts 16:25-26

> "Around midnight Paul and Silas were praying and singing hymns to God,
> and the other prisoners were listening. Suddenly, there was a massive earthquake, and
> the prison was shaken to its foundations. All the doors immediately flew open,
> and the chains of every prisoner fell off!"
> *Acts 16:25-26*

Our influence on others - Our choices to praise and be obedient affect those around us; Acts 16:25-32

> "Around midnight Paul and Silas were praying and singing hymns to God,
> and the other prisoners were listening. Suddenly, there was a massive earthquake,
> and the prison was shaken to its foundations. All the doors immediately flew open,
> and the chains of every prisoner fell off!"
> *Acts 16:25-26*

Lead by example - Paul encouraged others to live for Christ, not just by his words, but by the life he lived; Acts 20:35, 27:33-37.

> "And I have been a constant example of how you can help those in need by working hard. You should remember the words of the Lord Jesus: 'It is more blessed to give than to receive.'"
> *Acts 20:35*

Love for the Lord
His love for the Lord is shown by his obedience to God from the time he was encountered on the road to Damascus. Acts 9:1-9

Love for God's people
Preached the Gospel - Spread the Gospel everywhere he went; His love for God's people is shown by his relentless travel and preaching to all those who were following Christ, even enduring hardships for the sake of the gospel. Acts 13:38-41, 14:1, 21, 25, 16:30-32, 17:3, 22-31, 18:11, 19:8, 24:24-25, 26:20, 28:23, 30-31.

> "So a time was set, and on that day a large number of people came to Paul's lodging. He explained and testified about the Kingdom of God and tried to persuade them about Jesus from the Scriptures. Using the law of Moses and the books of the prophets, he spoke to them from morning until evening."
> *Acts 28:23*

Encourager - Constantly encouraging the body of believers; Acts 14:21-22, 16:40, 18:23, 20:1-2.

> "When the uproar was over, Paul sent for the believers and encouraged them. Then he said good-bye and left for Macedonia. While there, he encouraged the believers in all the towns he passed through. Then he traveled down to Greece,"
> *Acts 20:1-2*

Zeal for the Lord
Suffered for Christ - Willing to be imprisoned, beaten, and even put to death for the Lord; Acts 14:19, 16:23, 20:19, 21:30

> "They were severely beaten, and then they were thrown into prison. The jailer was ordered to make sure they didn't escape."
> *Acts 16:23*

Love of God's Word: He loved to speak what he had learned in revelation of God.

EXAMPLE OF BEING BOTH A PRAISER AND A WORSHIPER

Praiser
Praise in prison - Prayed and sang songs of praise to the Lord from prison; Acts 16:25

> "Around midnight Paul and Silas were praying and singing hymns to God,
> and the other prisoners were listening."
> *Acts 16:25*

Prayer
Sought the Lord - Went to Lord for decision-making; Acts 14:23

> "Paul and Barnabas also appointed elders in every church. With prayer and fasting,
> they turned the elders over to the care of the Lord,
> in whom they had put their trust."
> *Acts 14:23*

Prayer in prison - Prayed to the Lord from prison; Acts 16:25

> "Around midnight Paul and Silas were praying and singing hymns to God,
> and the other prisoners were listening."
> *Acts 16:25*

Intercession - Constantly prayed for other believers; Acts 28:8

> "As it happened, Publius's father was ill with fever and dysentery. Paul went in and prayed
> for him, and laying his hands on him, he healed him."
> *Acts 28:8*

PAUL'S ABILITY TO HEAR AND RESPOND TO THE LORD

Paul was able to hear God from his first Damascus Road encounter, which changed him completely, at least in his purpose. He said he was "sent to Rome" by the Holy Spirit, so he was repeatedly directed in his actions by the spirit of God. He obeyed even knowing it would mean hardship and persecution, so yes, he heard and responded to God.

PRESENTER/REPRESENTATIVE OF THE LORD

God's mouthpiece - Spoke from the heart of God; Acts 13:11

> "'Watch now, for the Lord has laid His hand of punishment upon you, and you will be struck blind. You will not see the sunlight for some time.' Instantly mist and darkness came over the man's eyes, and he began groping around begging for someone to take his hand and lead him."
> *Acts 13:11*

Preached the Gospel - Spread the Good News, as Christ did; Acts 13:38-41, 14:1, 21, 25, 16:30-32, 17:3, 22-31, 18:11, 19:8, 24:24-25, 26:20, 28:23, 30-31.

> "Brothers, listen! We are here to proclaim that through this man Jesus there is forgiveness for your sins. Everyone who believes in Him is made right in God's sight—something the law of Moses could never do."
> *Acts 13:38-39*

Hated by many - Just as Christ, Paul was unapologetically hated by many; Acts 13:50, 14:2,19, 16:22-24, 17:5-6, 18:12, 20:3, 21:35-36, 23:12-14.

> "Then the Jews stirred up the influential religious women and the leaders of the city, and they incited a mob against Paul and Barnabas and ran them out of town."
> *Acts 13:50*

Performed miracles - Performed many different miracles, as Christ did; Acts 14:10, 16:18, 19:11-12, 20:9-12, 28:8-9

> "So Paul called to him in a loud voice, 'Stand up!' And the man jumped to his feet and started walking."
> *Acts 14:10*

Grieved by sin - Brokenhearted over sin, just as God is; Acts 14:12-17, 17:16

> "While Paul was waiting for them in Athens, he was deeply troubled by all the idols he saw everywhere in the city."
> *Acts 17:16*

REVELATIONS GIVEN TO PAUL FROM THE LORD

Jesus with him; Acts 18:9-11

> "One night the Lord spoke to Paul in a vision and told him, 'Don't be afraid! Speak out!
> Don't be silent! For I am with you, and no one will attack and harm you,
> for many people in this city belong to me.'"
> *Acts 18:9-10*

Charged to preach - Acts 23:11

> "That night the Lord appeared to Paul and said, 'Be encouraged, Paul.
> Just as you have been a witness to me here in Jerusalem,
> you must preach the Good News in Rome as well.'"
> *Acts 23:11*

PAUL'S FAITH/TRUST IN THE LORD

Shipwrecked - Believed God in spite of being in peril; Acts 27:25

> "So take courage! For I believe God. It will be just as He said."
> *Acts 27:25*

CHAPTER 30
REVIEW QUESTIONS
Paul

1. What were the political conditions during Paul's time?

2. What were the social conditions?

3. What were the religious conditions?

4. What are at least three things we can learn from Paul?

5. What are some of Paul's characteristics that assisted him in his calling?

6. What was Paul willing to lose that he might "gain something greater?" Philippians 3:5-12

7. What stood out about Paul even as he grew older." Philippians 3:4-7

*It's impossible to know God unless
He reveals Himself. The beauty is that
our God is a self-revealing God.*

31

Jesus

"He was born in a lowly manger so that people of all ages, races, and cultures would have access through Him to the Father. He was heralded by angels and visited by shepherds, representing the angelic and the human—welcomed and acknowledged by both heaven and earth. He was sought by Magi from the East who brought gifts for a king, signifying that all people may seek and find Him to worship the Promised One."

– Dr. John Johnson

Even before He was born, Jesus was the cause of worship. In Luke 1:42–55, we read the account of Mary and Elizabeth, her cousin, who was pregnant with John the Baptist. Mary was greeted with, "You are favored by God above all other women, and your child is destined for God's mightiest praise..." Mary herself responded with praise in what is now called the "Magnificat."

> And Mary said,
> "My soul glorifies the Lord
> and my spirit rejoices in God my Savior,
> for He has been mindful
> of the humble state of His servant.
> From now on all generations will call me blessed,
> for the Mighty One has done great things for me—
> holy is His name.
> His mercy extends to those who fear Him,
> from generation to generation.
> He has performed mighty deeds with His arm;
> He has scattered those who are proud in their inmost thoughts.
> He has brought down rulers from their thrones
> but has lifted up the humble.
> He has filled the hungry with good things

but has sent the rich away empty.
He has helped His servant Israel,
remembering to be merciful
to Abraham and his descendants forever,
just as He promised our ancestors."

At His birth, Jesus was heralded by a host of angels who appeared to the shepherds watching their flocks, all of whom worshiped Him. "Suddenly the angel was joined by a vast host of others—the armies of heaven—praising God." They sang, "Glory to God in the highest heaven, and peace on earth to those with whom God is pleased."

Here we witness heaven and earth worshiping the newborn King. When it came time for Mary's purification offering at the Temple, Mary and Joseph went to Jerusalem to present Him to the Lord. A man named Simeon, "a good man, very devout, filled with the Holy Spirit," took Jesus in his arms and praised God:

"Lord, now I can die content! For I have seen Him as You promised. He is the Light that will shine upon the nations, and He will be the glory of Your people Israel!" (Luke 2:29–31).

At that moment, Anna, a prophetess, who stayed in the temple day and night fasting and praying, began thanking God and telling everyone that the Messiah had finally arrived (Luke 2:36–38).

At age twelve, Jesus went to Jerusalem for the Passover Festival. His parents realized He was missing and searched for Him in distress. They found Him in the Temple, sitting among the teachers, asking questions, and amazing everyone with His understanding. After Mary rebuked Him, Jesus replied, "Didn't you know I had to be in my Father's house?" Yet He returned with them and was obedient, while His mother pondered these things in her heart. Luke 3 tells us about John baptizing Jesus, after which the Holy Spirit descended upon Him and a voice from heaven declared, *"This is my beloved Son; in Him I am well pleased."*

At age thirty, Jesus began His public ministry, filled with the Holy Spirit (Luke 4:1). His ministry was to do the Father's will—to preach salvation freely given by a loving Father, to heal the sick, deliver the oppressed, raise the dead, feed the multitudes, calm storms, and set captives free.

In Luke 10, after the disciples returned from preaching and healing, Jesus, filled with joy through the Holy Spirit, prayed,

"I praise you, Father, Lord of heaven and earth, because you have hidden these things from the wise and learned, and revealed them to little children. Yes, Father, for this is what You were pleased to do."

In Jesus, we find the ultimate worship leader. The Old Testament points to His arrival, and the New Testament illuminates His life and ministry. He is the center of our worship, continuing to lead us by the power of the Holy Spirit. When asked which commandment was greatest, Jesus replied, *"Hear, O Israel, the Lord our God, the Lord is one. Love the Lord your God with all your heart and with all your soul and with all your mind and with all your strength" (Mark 12:30).* When tempted by Satan to worship him, Jesus declared, "Worship the Lord your God, and serve Him only" (Matthew 4:9).

He further taught that "true worshipers will worship the Father in spirit and in truth." Worship in the Spirit is broad, while worship in truth is narrow. We must be grounded in truth as revealed in Scripture, yet free to express worship through the Spirit.

Hebrews 2:12 reveals that the ministry of Jesus was to make the Father known. Jesus Himself declared, *"I and the Father are one."* In the second half of Hebrews 2:12, Jesus speaks to the Father, saying, *"In the midst of the congregation I will sing Your praise."* As our great High Priest, He not only mediates our worship before the Father, but He actively joins in it.

Jesus Christ, who is fully God, both deserves and receives worship (Hebrews 1:6). Yet, as fully man, He also models true worship for us.

> For to which of the angels did God ever say,
> "You are my Son;
> today I have become Your Father"?
> Or again,
> "I will be His Father,
> and He will be My Son"?
> And again, when God brings His firstborn into the world, He says,
> "Let all God's angels worship Him."
> In speaking of the angels He says,
> "He makes His angels spirits,
> and His servants flames of fire."
> But about the Son He says,
> "Your throne, O God, will last for ever and ever;
> a scepter of justice will be the scepter of Your kingdom.
> You have loved righteousness and hated wickedness;
> therefore God, Your God, has set You above Your companions
> by anointing You with the oil of joy."
> *(Hebrews 1:5–9)*

Finally, true worship requires a lifestyle of complete surrender to the Father's will. In the garden of Gethsemane, Jesus prayed, "Not My will, but Yours be done." On the cross, His final words were, "Father, into Your hands I commit My spirit." These closing declarations of His earthly life demonstrate the ultimate example of a surrendered soul.

WORSHIP LEADER TYPES

WORSHIP LEADER TYPE PROFILE

JESUS

BACKGROUND

- Political Conditions
  - The political climate during Jesus' time was volatile and dangerous.
  - The Roman Empire occupied Israel and had established a two-tiered system of government, with Roman overseers and Jewish leaders who ruled in Rome's name. Herod the Great, a "friend and ally" of Rome, ruled Jewish Palestine, and some of his sons ruled other regions as client kingdoms.
  - Many Jewish people hated and were angry with both the Romans and the Herodian family, who they saw as tyrannical and for selling out Jewish heritage.

    https://www.britannica.com/biography/Jesus/Jewish-Palestine-at-the-time-of-Jesus
- Social Conditions:
  - There was a wide gap between the wealthy elite and the impoverished masses. Many peasants struggled with poverty, hunger and disease (Matthew 9:35-36) To all those marginalized groups, (Samaritans, tax collectors and sinners, Jesus reached out with compassion and hope. (Luke 15:1-32)
- Religious climate:
  - The Pharisees, Sadducees and Scribes were preoccupied with strict adherence to the Mosaic law and Jewish traditions (Matthew 15:1-9)
  - Jesus criticized the religious leaders for their hypocrisy and called for a closer walk with God, and more love towards their fellow men and women. (Matthew 23:1-36)

FACTORS IN EQUIPPING HIM FOR THE TASK

Called of God. Jesus was called and sent by God, and He often spoke of this fact.

> "For God did not send His Son into the world to condemn the world, but that the world through Him might be saved.
> John 3:17

Jesus also added in John 3:34.

"For He whom God has sent speaks the words of God."
In speaking about the purpose of being sent, Jesus said,
"My food is to do the will of Him who sent Me and to finish His work."
John 4:34

Blessed by God. God acknowledged and blessed His son as He was being baptized by John the Baptist. God said,

"This is my beloved Son, with whom I am well pleased."
Matthew 3:17 ESV

JESUS' PERSONALITY

Jesus was confident and showed great intelligence.

Even when he was a child at age 12, Jesus sat confidently among the learned men in the temple, "discussing deep questions with them and amazing everyone with his understanding and answers."
Luke 3:46,47

Jesus went to the temple in Nazareth, his boyhood home, and stood up to read the scriptures. After he sat down,

"All who were there spoke well of him and were amazed by the beautiful words that fell from his lips."
Luke 4:16-22

His confidence was manifested in the fact that he did not care if you agreed with him; he was not a people pleaser.

"Your approval means nothing to me, because I know you don't have God's love within you. For I have come to you in my Father's name, and you have rejected me. Yet if others come in their own name, you gladly welcome them. No wonder you can't believe! For you gladly honor each other, but you don't care about the honor that comes from the one who alone is God.
John 5:41-44 NLT

When he was pressed to say which of the disciples would be greatest in the coming

kingdom, (Which they wrongly thought would be a worldly kingdom) Jesus "Stood a little child beside him and said to them, "Anyone who takes care of a little child like this is caring for me! And whoever cares for me is caring for God who sent me. Your care for others is the measure of your greatness."
Luke 10:47-48

He could be bold and confrontational,
especially when challenging the hypocrisy of religious leaders.
Matthew 23:1-36

Jesus entered the temple and overturned tables, and then chased out everyone who was buying and selling, including money changers and those selling doves for sacrifice.
Matthew 21:12-17

Healing the man whose hand was crushed. The religious leaders were waiting to see if Jesus would break the Sabbath law by healing this man. He walked right up to them and asked them.

"Which is lawful to do on the Sabbath: to do good or to do evil? To save a life or to kill?" He was truly angry over their lack of care and their choosing tradition over a human's suffering being relieved. They walked away."

He had keen insight, often confounding his opponents. (Matthew 22:15-22, John 7:45-46) When the Pharisees tried to trap him into saying something for which they could arrest him, they asked him if it was right to pay taxes to the Roman government or not, to which he wisely replied the famous line, "Render unto Caesar what is Caesars and to God what is God's."

JESUS' RELATIONSHIP WITH GOD

Jesus was obedient to His Father: The gospels consistently reveal Jesus as having a great love and devotion to God His Father. Jesus expressed his love for the Father by his unwavering obedience saying,

"I always do what pleases Him."
John 8:29

He said, "I and the Father are one."
John 10:30

Even when it led to suffering and dying on the cross, Jesus said, "My Father, if it is possible, let this cup be taken away from me. But I want your will, not mine." Or in some variations, he said, "Nevertheless, not my will but thine be done."
Matthew 36:29

Jesus' relationship with God was very intimate. In the Gospels, we repeatedly see Jesus in deep, intimate communion with God the Father. He would withdraw from the crowds to pray, even spending entire nights in prayer.
Luke 5:16, Luke 6:12

"Abba", the word Jesus used to refer to God, was an Arabic word meaning "father," a term of endearment.

THE REVELATION OF GOD THAT JESUS CARRIED TO THE PEOPLE

Turn from sin; turn to God.

"From then on, Jesus began to preach, "Turn away from sin and turn to God, for the Kingdom of heaven is near."
Matthew 4:17

Seek ye first the Kingdom of God

"But seek first his kingdom and his righteousness, and all these things will be given to you as well.
Matthew 6:33

God wants compassion and love from us most of all:

When asked which of the laws of Moses was the most important, "Jesus replied, 'Love the Lord your God with all your heart, soul and mind,' This is the first and greatest commandment.'"
Mark 12:30, Matthew 22:37-40

He preached what we call "The Beatitudes", saying that we are blessed when we are persecuted and reviled, that we are blessed when our hearts are pure, for then we will see

God, that we are the world's seasoning, the world's light and that it is not enough to follow Moses' law, but that we must do even better and be pure at heart. We must be full of Agape, or God's love. Do not look for power; look to serve others. If we want to be powerful, then we must give up power. Serve rather than be served. Take the lowest seat. When they go low, we go high. Go the second mile. Give up both your cloaks.

In the Bible, Mark 10:45 says, *"For even the Son of Man did not come to be served, but to serve, and to give his life as a ransom for many."* This verse is a reminder that Jesus came to Earth to serve people and that we should also love and help others.

> "Anyone who wants to be first, must be the very last and must be the servant of all."
> *(Matthew 20:28)*

God is Father: Jesus taught his disciples (and all of us) to call God "Father." He referred to God as Abba, Father" in Mark 14:36. When he taught the disciples how to pray, He began saying,

> "Our Father, who art in heaven…"
> *(Mark 6:9-13)*

LESSONS LEARNED FROM THIS WORSHIP LEADER TYPE

Jesus said:

> "I and the Father are one." (And you are also one with the Father and one with Me)
> *John 10:30*

> "Not my will but thine, O Lord, be done."
> *Luke 22:42*

> "Seek ye first the kingdom of God and His righteousness."
> *Matthew 6:33*

> "And all these things will be added unto you."
> "He who is first will be last. And he who is last will be first."
> *Matthew 20:16*

> 'If you cling to your life, you will lose it; but if you give it up for me, you will save it."
> *Matthew 10:19*

The Sermon on the Mount contains some of the most influential and far-reaching teachings which went counter to the prevailing narrative of pushing oneself ahead regardless of how it affected those around you, of the value of suffering, and the blessings that come to those who are meek and often trampled upon. These teachings today would transform our society if they were followed. But they are so revolutionary, they are often overlooked in favor of laws and edits. Jesus emphasized the inward change, which would affect the outward behavior.

HIS LOVE AND COMPASSION FOR THE PEOPLE OF GOD

The Stoic philosopher Seneca said, "Compassion is the vice of a feeble soul." This was the general attitude of men during the time of Jesus' ministry in and around Jerusalem. Compassion was not considered a virtue. The gods of Greece and Rome were cold, heartless, and indifferent to human suffering. Jesus went against the grain, against the "culture" of his time, when he both preached compassion and showed compassion towards people every day of his life.

Jesus' entire ministry can be summed up in this one word: compassion. This means "to feel suffering with." He felt compassion toward those who suffered physically. Listen to these excerpts from the gospels:

> "Moved with pity he stretched out his hand and touched him"
> *(Speaking of a leper, Mark 1:41).*
>
> "Jesus in pity touched their eyes"
> *(Said about the two blind men outside Jericho, Matthew 20:34).*
>
> "He had compassion on [the crowds]...and he healed their sick"
> *(Matthew 14:14).*

He prayed for Simon's mother to be healed.

> "After leaving the synagogue that day, he went to Simon's home where he found Simon's mother-in-law very sick with a high fever. Standing at her bedside, he spoke to the fever, rebuking it and immediately her temperature returned to normal and she got up and prepared a meal for them.
> Luke 4:38

Jesus also felt compassion for people who were suffering emotional distress. One day, while walking past a little village, Jesus saw a funeral procession in which a widow was going out to bury her only son. *"When the Lord saw her his heart broke"* (Luke 7:13, The Message), and Jesus restored the woman's son to life.

WORSHIP LEADER TYPES

> Most of all, Jesus felt compassion for people who suffered spiritually. "Jesus went through all the towns and villages, teaching in their synagogues, preaching the good news of the kingdom and healing every disease and sickness. When he saw the crowds, he had compassion on them, because they were harassed and helpless, like sheep without a shepherd.
> *Matthew 9:35-36*

Jesus really saw the people even though he was very busy and tired. It is so important to truly be 'seen'. When he saw them he felt sorry, felt compassion for their state. He saw they were harassed and helpless, just like sheep who cannot take care of themselves without the care of a good shepherd.

Examples of Jesus' healing miracles:

- He healed a man with leprosy. (Luke 5:12-13)
- He healed a paralyzed man. (Luke 5:17-25)
- He healed a man whose right hand was deformed. (Luke 6:6-10)
- Healed a centurion's son (Luke 7:6-10)
- Healed the woman with an issue of blood. Matthew 9:20-22, Mark 5:25-34, Luke 8:43-48)
- Healed blind men. (Matthew 9)
- Healed the man born blind. (John 9:1-12)
- Healed Blind Bartimaeus (Luke 18: 35-43)
- Raised three people from the dead: Jairus' daughter, (Mark 5:21-43) the widow's son (Luke 7: 11-17) and Lazarus (John 11:1-44)
- Jesus cared enough to feed a large crowd (more than 5000) and there was more than enough food after he prayed. (Matthew 14:13–21, Mark 6:31–44, Luke 9:12–17, and John 6:1–14.)

When asked to approve of a crowd stoning a woman caught in adultery, Jesus turned the situation around and set the woman free, causing the men to walk away in shame. To her, he showed great compassion when he commanded, *"Go and sin no more."*

Right before his death, Jesus told his disciples,

> "And so I am giving a new commandment to you now –love each other just as much as I love you. Your strong love for each other will prove to the world that you are my disciples."
> *John 13:34, 35*

PRAYER

This was previously stated, but Jesus spent quite a bit of time in prayer, in "communion with the Father." Prayer was an essential aspect of the success of his mission, which was to spread the good news that God loves us so much that He sent His Son to take away the sins of the world. He needed to hear God's encouragement, and he needed to hear God's instructions.

> When John was baptizing him, Jesus was praying.
> "As he was praying, the heavens were opened."
> *Luke 3:21*

We know that after His baptism, Jesus entered the Judean wilderness to be tempted by the devil. There, He prayed and fasted for 40 days and nights (see Matthew 4, Mark 1, Luke 4)

> "On the night before choosing His 12 closest disciples,
> Jesus "spent the night praying to God."
> *Luke 6:12 NIV*

Jesus prayed when he was sad. The Bible mentions that Jesus "often withdrew to lonely places and prayed" (Luke 5:16 NIV)

Luke 9:28 says, "Jesus took Peter, John and James with him and went up to the mountain and prayed."

In John 17, also known as the Farewell Prayer or the High Priestly Prayer, is found the longest prayer of Jesus in the gospels. In this prayer, Jesus asks the Father for unity and protection for his disciples and all believers:

Without including the entire chapter, which is a long prayer, here are a few key scriptures:

> ".....that they might know thee the only true God, and Jesus Christ, whom thou hast sent."
> *John 17:3*

> I pray for them: I pray not for the world, but for them which thou hast given me;
> for they are thine.
> *John 17:9*

> [14] And all mine are thine, and thine are mine; and I am glorified in them.
> I have given them thy word; and the world hath hated them,
> because they are not of the world, even as I am not of the world.
> [15] I pray not that thou shouldest take them out of the world,

but that thou shouldest keep them from the evil one.

¹⁶ They are not of the world, even as I am not of the world.

¹⁷ Sanctify them through thy truth: thy word is truth.

¹⁸ As thou hast sent me into the world,

even so have I also sent them into the world.

Neither pray I for these alone, but for them also

which shall believe on me through their word;

²¹ That they all may be one; as thou, Father, art in me, and I in thee,

that they also may be one in us: that the world may believe that thou hast sent me.

²² And the glory which thou gavest me I have given them;

that they may be one, even as we are one:"

John 17:21-22

Luke 20:40-44 shows us Jesus praying during his most desperate moments at the Garden of Gethsemane when he knew he would be arrested, tortured and killed. He begged that it would not happen, but finally he prayed, "However, not my will but thine, be done."

Finally, Jesus prayed while he was dying on the cross. He cried out in desperation, quoting from a psalm that told the whole tale of His suffering (see Matthew 27:46). He prayed for those who were hurting Him (see Luke 23:34). And He uttered a prayer of surrender of Himself into the Father's hands (see Luke 23:46).

Jesus even taught us how to pray:

'When his disciples came to him, asking how they should pray, Jesus taught them how to pray, in what we call "The Lord's Prayer"

He said to them, 'When you pray, say: Father, hallowed be your name, your kingdom come. Give us each day our daily bread. Forgive us our sins, for we also forgive everyone who sins against us."

Luke 11:1-4)

JESUS AS A SINGER

"I will speak of your name to my brothers;

in the midst of the congregation I will sing your praise."

(Hebrews 2:12)

The Scriptures often exhort believers to sing (Psalm 100:2; Colossians 3:16) and angels also sing (Job 38:7), but this is the only verse where we are told that even God sings. Yet this also is not surprising, for Jesus evidently joined in the hymn at the last supper.

> "They sang a hymn and went out to the Mount of Olives."
> *Mark 14:26*

PRESENTER /REPRESENTATIVE OF THE LORD

Jesus said, "I and the Father are one." (John 10:30)

> "Let not your heart be troubled. You are trusting in God; now trust in Me…I am the way, and the truth, and the Life. No one can get to the Father except by means of Me. "Anyone who has seen me has seen the Father! …Don't you believe that I am in the Father and the Father is in me? The words I say are not my own but are from my Father who lives in me. And he does his work through me."
> *John 14:1-9*

JESUS' FAITH AND TRUST IN THE LORD

Jesus' first act after John baptized him was going into the wilderness to fast and pray. That, in itself, showed faith and trust in God. He would be tempted by the Devil himself, but He was strengthened by his faith in God.

In every miracle he performed, He was trusting God. Every time he stood up to speak, He was trusting God for wisdom and discernment. Raising the dead, healing the sick and infirm, and feeding the five thousand all required faith and trust.

And finally, trusting God, knowing he was to be tortured and killed on the cross, showed faith and trust in His maker. Even while on the cross, he prayed and said, Into thy hands I commend my spirit." He gave up his life willingly. How much more can we show trust and faith?

CHAPTER 31
REVIEW QUESTIONS
Jesus

1. Name an instance of Jesus being worshipped before He was born?

2. What is the name of the man who took Jesus in his arms when His parents took Him to the temple as a baby? What did this man say?

3. Name an instance where Jesus taught the subject of worship.

4. What was the most significant thing Jesus said about worship?

5. When Mary and Joseph realized that Jesus was not with them as they journeyed back home, where did they find Him? What was He doing?

6. Give an instance of Jesus, who is the focus of our worship, also participates with us in worship according to the Hebrews 2:12.

ANSWERS TO CHAPTER QUESTIONS

Answers

CHAPTER 1: ABRAHAM

1. The land Abraham left behind was Ur, in Mesopotamia.
2. Isaac was the "son of promise" and the legitimate heir.
3. God keeps his promises. God is our mighty warrior and will fight for us. God provides (As he did with the ram when Abraham went to sacrifice his son.) God can speak to us as He did to Abraham. When we lead people in worship, we can look to God to speak to us and to provide for us when we do not know the next step. He will fight our battles when we encounter problems we cannot solve.
4. First, Abraham left the only place he had lived to go into a land "he knew not." Then, when he and Lot parted ways, he gave Lot the first choice of where he would go, not choosing the best for himself but believing in the outcome. Then, he proceeded to sacrifice his only son, Isaac, not knowing God would intercept his task and provide him with a ram.
5. Isaac's name means laughter. When the heavenly visitors came to tell Abraham that Sarah would conceive a son in her aged state, she laughed. So he is named "laughter."
6. Abraham fearlessly obeyed God, not knowing the outcome. He had faith that God would take care of him and his whole household. He heard God's voice and obeyed.
7. When Abraham was afraid for his life, he told Sarai to lie and say she was his sister. this happened twice. Later, Abraham takes his wife's servant, Hagar, to have a child through her.

CHAPTER 2: MOSES

1. Egypt was ruled by the Pharaoh, who enslaved many people to build his complex structures, the pyramids, and had absolute power over everyone. He was, in fact, considered a god himself.
2. The Israelites were enslaved people who worked doing back-breaking work. Even in these awful conditions, they had children and prospered as much as possible, so the Pharaoh ordered all the newborn boys to be put to death. It was a sort of population control.
3. The Israelites worshiped one God, and during the Exodus, Moses gave them the ten commandments, which were the foundation of their culture.

4. Moses' name means "drawn out" because he was drawn out of the water by the Egyptian princess and raised in the palace.
5. Aaron was the spokesperson for Moses, who said he was "halting of speech." He also encouraged Moses and strengthened him.
6. Miriam led the women in a song of praise when they were delivered from the Egyptian army. She also spoke against Moses and his wife, then was struck with leprosy.
7. Moses brought the laws of God to the people.
8. That they might worship Him alone. Also, so that Moses could enter the land of promise.

CHAPTER 3: MIRIAM

1. Moses and Aaron.
2. She fashioned a straw boat, placed the baby Moses in it, and watched as it floated in the reeds. Then, when she saw the Pharaoh's sister take the child, she offered to find her a wet nurse who was Moses' mother, Jochebed.
3. Miriam was courageous, resourceful, and quick-witted. She was loyal to her brothers and supported everything they did. She was also jealous, which got her into trouble because she spoke against Moses for marrying the Cushite woman.
4. I will sing unto the Lord, for He has triumphed gloriously, the horse and the rider was thrown into the sea.
5. She sang this when God opened the waters and allowed the Israelites to go through but drowned the Egyptians.

CHAPTER 4: AARON

1. Egypt enslaved the Israelites and made them labor for years until Moses demanded their release. Then they had to form another political system in which Moses was their leader and spokesman for God.
2. The social conditions were the Israelites had to wander in the wilderness for many years and become nomads. Their families were together in groups called tribes.
3. The religious conditions were that Moses came down with the law, which God had given and laid the foundation for an entire new life for the formerly enslaved people. They did not have a temple in which to worship.
4. Aaron was obedient, which helped him in his task. He had to be the mouthpiece for Moses since he had "halting of speech." We do not know what this means, whether he stuttered or was just unsure, but Aaron was his mouthpiece. He had to know God was faithful and merciful for him to do what he was called to do.
5. Trust God. Depend on Him in all circumstances. Obey what He calls you to do, and trust He will equip you.
6. He was afraid of the people, doubted Moses' return, Egypt's idolatry had affected all of them.

CHAPTER 5: HANNAH

1. She was kind, patient, and pious. She did not answer the taunting of Peninnah even though she would have been justified for losing her temper.
2. She was jealous because Elkanah showed Hannah was his favorite.
3. He gave her a double portion.
4. He accused her of drinking early in the day and being drunk.
5. She promised to give Samuel to the temple after he was weaned.
6. Samuel.
7. God blesses Hannah with three more sons and two daughters.

CHAPTER 6: SAMUEL

1. The sons of Eli, who were his apprentices in the service to the temple, were called Sons of Belial, which means worthless. It is used to describe the dissolute, the reprobate and the uncouth. Few stories in the Bible show the shocking degradation of the times than the story of the sons of Eli. Then, Samuel's own sons, despite Samuel's excellent example, took bribes and were known for their perversion of justice.
2. The people wanted a strong king, after seeing the way the sons of Samuel and Eli were not doing well in leadership. Corruption was present in the leadership.
3. There was corruption in the leadership of the priests and the judges.
4. Samuel was upright, righteous and always doing what was right. He was courageous and had great insight.
5. Sometimes we have to say things that are not pleasant and will not be received well. We should obey God even when those around us are obviously not. We must trust God's selection. Worship is our best warfare and defense.
6. As worship facilitators it is important to recognize and properly respond to the Lord. It is an essential aspect of worship.

CHAPTER 7: GIDEON

1. The Israelites were in danger of being captured by the Mideonites. Gideon was appointed a judge in Israel.
2. The Israelites were constantly in danger from the marauding Mideonites who would kidnap them and hold them in captivity or kill them.
3. The Israelites had turned away from God. God raised up Gideon to rescue His people.
4. Gideon was a leader, appointed by God. God sent the Holy Spirit to empower Gideon. He was prudent, humble and obedient to the Lord's commands.
5. We learn that God uses "the least of these." We can ask God for confirmation when we are uncertain. God fights our battles.

6. To destroy his father's altars to Baal, then construct an altar to the Lord in its place. Judges 6:25-27
7. He didn't want them to think they won by their own military might, but by God's power.

CHAPTER 8: DAVID

1. David was a shepherd, a psalmist, a singer, a youngest brother, a mighty warrior, anointed king.
2. Diligent, creative, and intelligent.
3. Be humble, do everything in God's strength, depend on God's timing, ask for wisdom, keep your heart pure, etc.
4. David respected authority. He said, "Do not touch God's anointed." He trusted in God's timing for everything.
5. Returning of the ark. (2 Samuel 6:13, 14). Dedicated his gifts to God. (2 Samuel 8:9-12) When his son died, he acknowledged God and prayed. (2 Samuel 12:19, 20)
6. Funeral song for Saul and Jonathan, Funeral song for Abner, Praise song (Psalm 18) and wrote half the book of Psalms.
7. He wanted Bathsheba to be his own.
8. His first born with Bathsheba died. He suffered from guilt.
9. Psalm 51
10. Because David lived in a place, but the ark of God had no dwelling place. 2 Samuel 7:1-16
11. David couldn't build it because he had "blood on his hands," and he was a man of war.
12. Solomon, David's son.

CHAPTER 9: ELIJAH

1. The kingdoms of Israel and Judah were split. Ahab was king of Israel.
2. There was drought and famine in the land.
3. Ahab led the Israelites to worship of Baal, and the Asherah poles.
4. Elijah had an intimate relationship with God. He was obedient and confident in the Lord for his daily provision and for the protection of his life. This led him to speak with confidence.
5. Elijah told Ahab that a drought was coming and that it would not rain until he (Elijah) spoke it into existence. Ravens fed him beside the brook, and then when he found the widow whom God told him to look for, God provided flour and oil for her and her son as well as Elijah. He raised the widow's son to life. He called down fire from heaven to consume his sacrifice. He told Ahab to, "Go get something to eat and drink for I hear a mighty rainstorm coming."
6. 1 Kings 18:16-40

CHAPTER 10: ASA

1. Judah and Israel were split into the southern and northern kingdoms and were often at odds.
2. Socially, there were 10 years of peace with Asa as King.
3. Asa led the people to faithfully serve and worship God.
4. Asa was King and had a lot of power to change things. He was righteous and "Did what was pleasing to the Lord." He was faithful and had a close relationship with the Lord.
5. God is the Lord, and we trust in Him alone. We must rely fully on God. God is to be reverently worshiped. Don't forget God.
6. He destroys the pagan altars and shrines. He deposed of his own grandmother for her idolatrous practices. He leads the people to follow the Lord.
7. He depended on the King of Aram rather than the Lord.

CHAPTER 11: JEHOSHAPHAT

1. Though the kingdom of Israel was split in two, there was peace during Jehoshaphat's reign. He strengthened Judah's defenses, however, in 722 B.C., the Assyrians attacked the northern kingdom of Israel. The Assyrians were militant and harsh. They didn't want a large number of Jews living in one area to be able to revolt, so they split them up into different parts of their empire.
2. The author of the books of Chronicles generally praises his reign, stating that the Kingdom enjoyed a great measure of peace and prosperity. The blessing of God rested on the people "in their basket and their store."
3. The degeneracy of the kingdom of Judah, as well as Israel, continued because most of the kings and people that followed continued worship only as a matter of formal observance. People do not continue to observe a form of worship that is devoid of power for very long. The real issue in Judah was apostasy - infidelity to Yahweh. Also, Jehoshaphat sent messengers throughout the land to read the Word of God to the people. So the people had become ignorant of the Word of God.
4. Jehoshaphat had a powerful position for change as the King. Also, he was blessed. "God was with Jehoshaphat because he followed the example of his father's early years and did not worship the images of Baal." 2 Chronicles 17:3
   Jehoshaphat was wealthy. He was wise, righteous and discerning and had a strong relationship with God in which he sought after God, His word and His ways. He showed his commitment to God by removing pagan worship in Judah.
5. Discuss
6. What can we learn from Jehoshaphat? Do not join yourselves with haters of God. Don't form alliances with enemies of God. Jehoshaphat knew that the prophets of King Ahab were not speaking for the Lord, and he called for a true prophet. We

learn to trust in God alone. We learn that worship before the battle is necessary and effective. God will fight our battles.
7. He proclaims a public fast. King Jehosphat prays in front of all Judah, in front of the court yard in Jerusalem.
8. The spirit of God comes upon Tahaziel and he prophecies that the Lord will win a great victory for Judah.
9. 2 Chronicles 20:20-30

CHAPTER 12: JOASH/JEHOASH

1. Jehoash was seven. God can use people of all ages.
2. Jehoash's grandmother, Athaliah, killed his father and Jehoash had to be hidden away for seven years.
3. His closest advisor was Jehoida, the priest.
4. He rebuilt the temple.
5. It was financed through taxes and also people promised to give toward the work.
6. His own servants killed Jehoash as revenge for the death of Zechariah.
7. From the story of Jehoash, we can learn many things - the importance of loyalty, how important it is to listen to the right people, etc.

CHAPTER 13: HEZEKIAH

1. The Assyrians were threatening to attack and take everyone into slavery if they were not killed in the battle. The Assyrians were a very cruel people.
2. The Hebrew people had compromised during the previous king, King Ahab's reign. Hezekiah enacted religious reform, calling the people to a purity of worship.
3. The people were under much duress from a threatening army, which had killed many others in their march towards them! So they were very stressed and frightened.
4. Hezekiah was the king, first of all, so he had the power to change things. He had the godly example of his ancestor, King David. He was loyal and devoted, obedient to God, passionate, bold and courageous. He loved and revered the Lord. He received a revelation from God that He is righteous and holy, and He is to be revered, and he communicated that to the people.
5. Refer to #4

CHAPTER 14: JOSIAH

1. Ever since Ahaz, Judah had been a vassal of the Assyrian empire. But after the Assyrian empire fell into chaos; it could no longer assert its authority in Jerusalem. Egypt also was weak, and Judah thus obtained an unusual degree of independence from foreign powers.

2. The people had been accustomed to following the religious practices of a pagan culture and were not used to following the Hebraic law. During Josiah's reign, the people enjoyed 13 years of prosperity and peace.
3. Josiah set in motion a reformation that bears his name and left an indelible mark on Israel's religious traditions (2 Kings 22–23:30).
4. Josiah became king at the age of eight. Fortunately, he was a pious person by nature and not a selfish one who was bent on meeting his own needs for fame and fortune. He was a faithful man, and a man of great integrity who wanted to lead Judah in the path of righteousness. "He did what was pleasing in the Lord's sight..." He obeyed the Word of the Lord. "Never before had there been a king like Josiah who turned to the Lord with all his heart and soul and strength, obeying all the laws of Moses..." 2 Kings 23:25. He feared the lord, and he loved the lord wholeheartedly. He received a revelation of God and from God that he carried to the people.
5. Repentance. He repented immediately (FOR THE PEOPLE) when he discovered from the Word of God that he and the people had sinned. He led by example. He worshiped wholeheartedly. He loved the Lord, and he loved the people of God. He had a zeal for God and for the Word.
6. Josiah launched a major campaign against idol worship and he destroyed pagan altars in Jerusalem, Judah, Manasseh, Ephraim, Simeon, and Naphtali. 2 Chronicles 24:1-7.
7. Josiah ordered repairs to be made to the temple and appointed men to carry out the task. 2 Chronicles 34:8-13

CHAPTER 15: EZRA

1. The Israelites were in and out of captivity under the Babylonians.
2. Ezra was a scribe and a priest during this time. He had a fairly high position in the court for which he toiled.
3. The Israelites had intermingled with foreign nations, many marrying foreign women. This generation didn't know God and the Israelite children grew up not knowing their own native tongue.
4. What equipped Ezra for the task was that he was a scribe, in a high position in the court, and he had favor with the King.
5. Ezra was a man of great zeal for the Lord. He was faithful to God's Word. He was compassionate and just. He was obedient and humble.
6. The power of prayer and fasting. The importance of obedience. The importance of knowing the Word of God.
7. Revelations given to the people were that God is holy, righteous and hates sin.

CHAPTER 16: NEHEMIAH

1. The Israelites were in captivity under the Babylonians.
2. Nehemiah was a cupbearer to the King, a counselor and an advisor. This was during the time of the birth of the Samaritans.
3. The Israelites were intermingling with other foreign nations, violating the Sabbath, and were misusing money.
4. Some factors in the equipping for his task were: He was divinely placed in close proximity to the King, and he found favor with him.
5. He was patient, humble, meek, diligent, a determined leader, compassionate, wise and a man of prayer and faith.
6. He showed his love for the people by weeping for their state, his patriotism, and wisdom and interceding for the people.

CHAPTER 17: JOB

1. Job is said to have lived in the land of Uz, which is thought to be today's Saudi Arabia.
2. He must have lived sometime between the 5th and 7th centuries B.C. Most likely he lived in the 6th Century B.C.
3. Job was a man of integrity, who was faithful, loyal and humble. He feared the Lord (respected Him), yet he was a friend of the Lord.
4. Job's wife told him to "curse God and die!"
5. Job still praised God when he had lost everything. He said, "I came naked from my mother's womb, and I will be naked when I leave. The Lord gave me what I had and the Lord has taken it away. Blessed be the name of the Lord!" Job 1:21. Then he said, "But as for me, I know my Redeemer lives, and He will stand upon the earth at last. After my body has decayed, yet in my body, I will see God! I will see Him for myself. Yes, I will see Him with my own eyes. I am overwhelmed at the thought!" Job 19:25-27
6. Satan, a created being who is not equal with God, has to ask permission to attack Job.
7. Job 1:8, "Have you considered my servant Job?" There is no one on earth like him; he is blameless and upright, a man who fears God and shun evil..." He maintains his integrity even though he is under great attack. (Job 2:3)

CHAPTER 18: EZEKIEL

1. The Israelites went into captivity under the Babylonians.
2. The social conditions were that the people had to re-settle in a new and strange land away from everything that was familiar to them.

3. They were cast out of their community and away from the temple where worship was a major part of their lives.
4. The religious conditions were that God pronounced judgment on the Israelites, but he gave them hope that Israel would be restored.
5. Ezekiel was passionate, faithful, just, obedient, humble, and he hated sin.
6. Obedience is important; Living in sin is unacceptable. God does not desire our destruction but repentance and true worship. We will be accountable for our sin.
7. The people defiled the temple by their "detestable practices." They brought idols into the temple for worship. Ezekiel 43:6-9
8. God allowed some of them to serve in the sanctuary but they were not allowed to come before Him. His presence was denied to the unfaithful priests. The priests who were descendants of Zadok were allowed to come into His presence and serve before Him before they did not go astray. Ezekiel 44:15-31

CHAPTER 19: DANIEL

1. The kingdoms of Judah and Israel have split. Jehoakim is king of Judah. Babylon has taken over Jerusalem.
2. Belshazzar takes over as king of Babylon. Darius the Mede conquers Babylon and becomes king. Cyrus the Persian becomes king.
3. Israel is in captivity. Babylon is a polytheistic pagan nation. Israel worships the God of Abraham, Isaac and Jacob.
4. Daniel was strong and healthy, educated, and was favored and gifted by God.
5. David was faithful, respectful, reliable, responsible, and humble.
6. Daniel refused to eat the food offered by his conquerors, yet they allowed it. He was thrown into the lion's den and came out unhurt. He was able to interpret the King's dream accurately when other wise men failed.
7. Daniel showed courage in the face of great persecution and duress, and he refused to bow to others stronger than him. He showed a strong belief in God rather than fearing man. It is important to determine in our hearts that we will obey God rather than man. Daniel determined he would not bow. "But Daniel was determined not to defile himself by eating the food and wine given to them by the king." He remained faithful no matter what happened. (OTHERS NOT NAMED HERE.)
8. Evil men influenced the King to pass an edict that his subjects must only pray to him, but Daniel continued to pray to God three times a day. Daniel 6:10-15
9. Be steadfast. Obey God and trust Him.
10. In opposition to all the other soothsayers, Daniel not only interprets the King's dream, but he tells him what he dreamed. Even when threatened with death, Daniel remains steadfast. Daniel obeyed God rather than powerful men.

CHAPTER 20: SHADRACH, MESHACH, AND ABEDNEGO

1. Healthy and strong, quick-witted, educated, without defect, handsome.
2. Don't compromise your beliefs. Remain faithful to God and trust God with the outcome.
3. God doesn't abandon us in the fire, or a crisis. We are thrown into the proverbial fire to give glory to God, our worship draws others to Him and others.
4. Obedient, courageous, faithful to God. Not compromising, bold.

CHAPTER 21: HOSEA

1. Hosea represents God's relationship with Israel. The relationship between Hosea, the prophet, and Gomer, his wife - a prostitute, parallels the relationship between God and Israel.
2. Spiritual prostitution and idolatry were going on. People were not following their own traditions and beliefs and were not faithful to the God of Abraham, Isaac, and Jacob.
3. Gomer represents an unfaithful Israel.
4. The factors that equipped Hosea for his task were his obedience to God's Word. He agreed to the unusual command to marry a prostitute and have children with her. He had a relationship with God in which he was fully devoted, evidenced by his willingness to allow his entire life to be used as a prophetic object lesson.
5. The children were named Jezreel, for in the valley of Israel, God will punish King Jehu and put an end to Israel. (Hosea 1:4) Then he had Loruhamah, meaning "no more money." Then Gomer had a son named Lo-Ammi, meaning "not mine." "For Israel is not mine and I am not their God." (Hosea 1:8-9) This sent the message that Israel had really failed and God then rejected the nation.
6. We can learn three lessons from Hosea: 1) Allow God to use you in any aspect of life 2) Say what God says 3) Repentance leads to redemption and healing.

CHAPTER 22: HABAKKUK

1. Nebuchadnezzar was sweeping up entire populations to serve as slave labor to build his projects.
2. Socially, the people were like sitting ducks and were under the control of a despotic ruler who seemed to have complete power over their lives.
3. The religious conditions caused the people to struggle to stay true to their faith because of the hardships imposed by Nebuchadnezzar.
4. Habakkuk loved justice and righteousness. He had a trusting relationship with God. He had a revelation from God for the people.

5. Habakkuk brought every thought of confusion, opinion, question, and concern to the Lord. He waited for the Lord's Word, not the opinion of man. Praise FIRST. He sang a prayer of praise before the situation was resolved.
6. Yet I will rejoice in the Lord! I will be joyful in the God of my salvation. The Sovereign Lord is my strength! He makes me as surefooted as a deer.

CHAPTER 23: ZEPHANIAH

1. There was a feeling of impending doom with the Babylonian empire invading and conquering Judah and taking people into exile. "The prophets lay the blame squarely on the people of Israel, and to a lesser extent Judah, for abandoning the worship of Yahweh in favor of idolatry, and for violating the ethical requirements of the Law. Despite these failings, the people lulled themselves into a false sense of security because of their covenant with Yahweh to be his people."
2. Haggai.
3. He descended from Iddo and from Aaron.
4. Zechariah was both a priest and a prophet.
5. He was the first to mention Satan as a personification of evil in the form of a woman.
6. Four horsemen, four horns, lampstand, and scroll.
7. The meek King, the one sold for thirty shekels, the pierced Savior, and the smitten Shepherd.
8. The Lord your God is with you. Zephaniah 3:17

CHAPTER 24: THE WISE MEN

1. Herod of Judea, was a puppet ruler, but the main ruler was in Rome. Herod still had the power to judge whether a person lived or died or was guilty of a crime.
2. Mary, Joseph, and those around them lived in an oppressive regime where the people had no real power over their lives. They were heavily taxed, paying the wealthy rulers 50-60% of their wealth in crops or livestock. Their taxes did not go for the general welfare of the people as they do in America today, but they went directly into the coffers of the rich rulers who oppressed them.
3. Mary and Joseph were religious Hebrews, who followed the Hebraic tradition of following the law, eating certain foods, and observing religious holidays and festivals. They were all looking for a redeemer, like Moses, who would relieve their suffering and release them from servitude.
4. The Magi were looking for the promised Messiah. They were determined to accomplish that goal. They endured hardship and spent much of their fortune on their trip to find Christ. They also faced danger when the King asked them what they were doing and then commanded them to return and tell him where the child was

whom they sought, knowing he intended to kill the child. They showed an ability to hear and respond to God's voice when Matthew 2:12, says, *"When it was time to leave, they return to their own country by another route, for God had warned them in a dream not to return to Herod."*

5. The worship of the Magi was costly because it involved expensive travel to a foreign land and the risk of angering Herod.
6. Determination, resourcefulness, intelligence, desire for the truth, curiosity about life, etc.
7. Gold represents Kingship. Frankincense represents worship. Myrrh represents mortality, death or mourning.

CHAPTER 25: PETER

1. Politically, there was persecution of the new believers from the Roman emperor Nero. Socially, there was oppression from the ruling Romans. But Peter was self-employed as a fisherman, so he had more independence than some others.
2. There was much persecution of the early Church. There was widespread immorality, and there were many religions.
3. Peter was one of the first disciples to follow Jesus. He was fearless and accustomed to hardship and hard work. He was bold, although this was often not in his favor. He became a humble man later and a great leader of the church.
4. Some of the lessons learned were:
   a. When Jesus calls, we should answer.
   b. God wants a close relationship with us.
   c. We need to be diligent in all that we do.
   d. God does not play favorites.
   e. There is always a second or third chance to change our ways.
   f. We must always be willing to learn and to be willing to change if we are wrong in an area.
5. They answered, "Silver and gold we do not have but such as we have we give unto you. Rise up in the name of the Lord Jesus Christ." The crippled man rose and began to lean and dance because he had been healed.
6. The Apostles respond, "We cannot stop telling the wonderful things we have seen and heard." Acts 4:19-20
7. They realized that they were unschooled, ordinary men. They were astonished and they took note that these men had been with Jesus. Acts 4:13

CHAPTER 26: JOHN DISCIPLE OF JESUS

1. Disciple, Apostle, writer of revelations, and preacher.
2. John the beloved.

3. He was filled with the Holy Spirit and spoke in tongues.
4. Obedient, bold, faithful, fearless, and relentless.
5. Exiled to the Isle of Patmos.
6. Jesus gave over the care of his mother to John.
7. Ephesus, Smyrna, Pergamum, Thyatira, Sardis, Philadelphus, and Laodicea.

CHAPTER 27: JOHN THE BAPTIST

1. Politically, Rome was in power. The Jews had very little say over their lives. Socially, the social conditions were that the Jewish people kept to themselves and tried to keep their own unique religion and lifestyle intact while living in a very pagan world.
2. The Jewish people tried to live according to the Law of Moses. Jesus has begun his ministry.
3. John the Baptist had very righteous parents; Elizabeth and Zechariah, who was also a priest. They raised their son according to God's precepts. John was given a prophecy given that he would not drink strong drinks and that he would be great in the eyes of the Lord. He leaped in his mother's womb when Mary, who was pregnant with Jesus, came to visit and greeted her cousin, Elizabeth. John was devoted; he lived his entire life in dedication to preparing for the coming of Christ and His kingdom. He was bold and fearless.
4. Some lessons are: We should preach the Word fearlessly. Our treasure is in heaven and we must know our purpose. We should hold fast to faith and the truth to the end. We must become lesser so Jesus can become greater.
5. John said, "I am not the Messiah, I am not Elijah. I'm come to prepare the way of the Lord."
6. Jesus is the bridegroom while he (John) is merely a friend of the bridegroom. John 3:27-29. Then John says, "Jesus must become greater while he (John) must decrease."

CHAPTER 28: MARTHA

1. Rome was in power, and the Hebrew people had very little say over their day-to-day lives.
2. The Hebrew people and the Gentiles were divided. The Hebrew people were looking for a Savior to free them from the oppressive rule of Rome.
3. The people observed the Law, performed sacrifices, and attended the temple together.
4. Martha was hospitable and generous. She was hard working, and she was a friend of Jesus along with her sister Mary and her brother Lazarus.
5. The inferences are: Women are not inferior beings meant to only serve men. Women can hear God, sit at the Master's feet, and learn of Him. Before ministering to God, one needs to be ministered to.

CHAPTER 29: MARY OF BETHANY

1. Rome was in power.
2. Jews and Gentiles were divided.
3. Society was functioning under the law of Moses, and Jesus had begun His ministry in spreading the good news, the Gospel.
4. Some of the factors that equipped Mary for the task were her personality, her childlike faith, her relationship with God, and her intimacy with Christ.
5. Some things we can learn from Mary of Bethany are:
   - Learn to abide in the Lord.
   - This Christian walk is not task driven but is about a loving relationship with God.
   - Never lose sight of the most important thing, which is sitting at His feet.

CHAPTER 30: PAUL

1. Rome had absolute power over the people in Jerusalem and the many other countries where Paul traveled.
2. The social conditions were that the people could meet in their homes, but they could not ever rebel against the power of Rome.
3. The Jewish people went to the temple, and the Christians met in their homes. Christians knew they could be thrown in prison at any time if they were a threat to the powers that were in control.
4. Three things we can learn from Paul are that we should speak boldly for the sake of others, we should persevere, and give praise despite circumstances. Additionally, praise is a spiritual weapon. We have a great influence on other people, and that we are to lead by example.
5. Paul was highly educated. He was also filled with the Holy Spirit, empowered by the Lord, chosen by God, and was a relentless and unapologetic preacher of the Gospel; He was bold, and determined, yet spiritually sensitive and humble.
6. Born into a pure-blood, Jewish home, member of a strict Pharisee cult, that demanded obedience to every law and custom. Sincere follower of the Pharisees who persecuted the church.
7. All is worthless compared to knowing Christ, and becoming one with Him. He realized the only thing that really matters is to know Christ.

CHAPTER 31: JESUS

1. Elizabeth expressed her joy and awe that Jesus, the son of God, was inside Mary's womb. The child in her womb, who would become John the Baptizer, leapt for joy at the baby who would become Jesus. [41]"At the sound of Mary's greeting, Elizabeth's child leaped within her and she was filled with the Holy Spirit. [42] She gave a glad cry

and exclaimed to Mary, "You are favored by God above all other women, and your child is destined for God's mightiest praise. ⁴³ What an honor this is, that the mother of my Lord should visit me! ⁴⁴ When you came in and greeted me, the instant I heard your voice, my baby moved in me for joy! ⁴⁵ You believed that God would do what he said; that is why he has given you this wonderful blessing."

2. The man who took the infant Jesus in his arms was Simeon. Luke 2:25 - "Now there was a man in Jerusalem whose name was Simeon and this man was righteous and devout, (cautiously and carefully observing the divine Law) and looking for the Consolation of Israel; and the Holy Spirit was upon him." Luke 2:28 - "Simeon was there and took the child in his arms, praising God." Luke 2:29-31 "Lord," he said, "now I can die content! For I have seen him as you promised me I would. I have seen the Savior you have given to the world. ³² He is the Light that will shine upon the nations, and he will be the glory of your people Israel!"

3. Jesus taught on worship at the well in Samaria when he was questioned by the Samaritan woman about where they should worship. He responded this way: John 4:21-24: Jesus replied, "The time is coming, ma'am, when we will no longer be concerned about whether to worship the Father here or in Jerusalem. For it's not where we worship that counts, but how we worship—is our worship spiritual and real? Do we have the Holy Spirit's help? For God is Spirit, and we must have his help to worship as we should. The Father wants this kind of worship from us. But you Samaritans know so little about him, worshiping blindly, while we Jews know all about him, for salvation comes to the world through the Jews."

4. He made it clear that the place where God is worshipped did not really matter, because it was the manner in which they worshipped that really counted. They were to worship "in Spirit and in truth".

5. Mary and Joseph, after much anxious searching, found Jesus in the temple with the learned men, asking them intelligent questions. Luke 2:46-47 "After three days they found Him (came upon Him) in the court of the temple, sitting among the teachers, listening to them and asking them questions, ⁴⁷ And all who heard Him were astonished and overwhelmed with bewildered wonder at His intelligence and understanding and His replies."

6. How does Jesus participate with us in worship? Hebrews 2:12- "¹² For He says in the book of Psalms, "I will talk to my brothers about God my Father, and together we will sing his praises." This was a prophetic statement that applied to Jesus. He said, "together we will sing his praise."

Sources

Blaiklock, E.M., Today's Handbook of Bible Characters, Bethany House Publishers, Minneapolis, MN. 1979, pp. 106, 109, 125, 127, 209, 237, 249, 254, 265, 280, 491

Harrison, R.K., Old Testament Times, Hendrickson Publishers, Inc., Peabody, Mass., Copyright 1970, Eerdmans Publishing Company, pp 282, 293

Josephus, Flavius, Antiquities of the Jews, Lockyear, Herbert, All the Men of the Bible, Zondervan Publishing House, Grand Rapids, Michigan, 1958, p. 347

Thiele, Edwin, The Mysterious Numbers of the Hebrew Kings, Eerdmans, 3rd Edition, 1965.

The Reader's Digest Association, Great People of the Bible and How They Lived, Pleasantville, NY, 1974, pp. 22, 198

The Editors of Encylopedia, Encyclopedia Britannica, https://www.britannica.com/Magi "The Book of Ezekiel", 20 July, 1998, https://britannica.com/topic/The-Book-of-Ezekiel. Accessed December 2021

The TOW Project (TheologyofWork.org) "Faith and Work During the Exile-Nahum, Habakkuk, Zephaniah" "Jehoshaphat" 23 July, 2010, https://Britannica.com/Biography/Jehoshaphat

Martin, Malachi, "Footsteps of Abraham", New York Times, March 13, 1983 https://www.NYTimes.com/1983/03/13/travel/footsteps-of-abraham-by-mala chi-martin.html

Shosch, Ismar, "The Staff of Moses", Jewish Theologyical Seminary, Torah Online, January 4, 2004

Sperling, SD, Encyclopedia Judaica, Joash, second edition, vol. 11, p. 343 www.libraryloras.edu., http://www.insight.org/resources/bible/the-major-prophets/ezekiel

About the Authors

John Johnson was born and raised in New Mexico. He attended Eastern New Mexico University on a vocal scholarship. Having taught choral music and guitar in the public school system for five years, John then was called into full-time ministry. John began his ministry as a worship leader and was ordained as one of four pastors of New Covenant Church in St Louis Missouri, from 1982-1994.

While there, he co-founded Dayspring School of the Arts, which offers classes and training in all aspects of the arts, such as dance, music, both vocal and instrumental and art, drawing and painting. John enjoys teaching seminars and workshops to train pastors, worship leaders and their teams and especially training and equipping congregations for their ministry of worship to the Lord. John has conducted these trainings in Germany, Jamaica, Scotland, and England.

John has a passion for worship, mentoring and preaching the gospel of the Kingdom dramatically and he will even break into song while preaching to better illustrate a point in the sermon. John seeks to impart the wisdom he has gained through the years to every believer. He believes each person has a unique and wonderful role as a holy priest unto God and an important contributor in corporate worship.

John is the former head of the worship division of Visible Music College and now offers his unique talents and wisdom to churches and ministries across the world. He and his wife, Martha, have been married since 1972 and have four grown children and twelve grandchildren.

EDUCATION:
D.R.E. (Emphasis Sacred Music), Friends International Christian University
M.R.E. (Emphasis Sacred Music), Friends International Christian University
B.M.E. Eastern New Mexico University

For more information about John and what services that he offers to congregations, pastors, and worship leaders please go to his website: www.hisinstrumentsofworship.com or to ask any question that you might have please forward your inquiries to hisinstrumentsofworship@gmail.com.

More from Dr. John H. Johnson

Grace to Praise explores the concept of "wells of praise," the various channels through which God reveals Himself to humanity. Each chapter uncovers these wells and provides insights into how they nourish our intimacy with God, enabling us to declare His excellence for His glory and joy. This book is not just a theoretical exploration of worship; it is a hands-on guide, filled with worksheets at the end of each chapter that provide a practical framework for drawing closer to God through worship. By engaging with these tools, individual readers, small groups, or classes can deepen their understanding of God's nature, strengthen their communion with Him, and express their love and adoration through words and deeds.

Available everywhere books are sold.
ISBN: 978-1-948877-27-5

www.ingramcontent.com/pod-product-compliance
Lightning Source LLC
Chambersburg PA
CBHW081439070526
44586CB00019B/2173